The Mirror and the Road:
Conversations with William Boyd

By Alistair Owen

NON-FICTION
Smoking in Bed: Conversations with Bruce Robinson
Story and Character: Interviews with British Screenwriters
Hampton on Hampton
The Art of Screen Adaptation:
Top Writers Reveal Their Craft

FICTION
The Vetting Officer

The Mirror and the Road

Conversations with William Boyd

EDITED BY ALISTAIR OWEN

PENGUIN BOOKS

PENGUIN BOOKS

UK | USA | Canada | Ireland | Australia
India | New Zealand | South Africa

Penguin Books is part of the Penguin Random House group of companies
whose addresses can be found at global.penguinrandomhouse.com

First published 2023
001

Copyright © 2023 William Boyd & Alistair Owen

The moral right of the copyright holders has been asserted

Set in 12.5/14.75pt Garamond MT Std
Typeset by Jouve (UK), Milton Keynes
Printed and bound in Great Britain by Clays Ltd, Elcograf S.p.A.

The authorized representative in the EEA is Penguin Random House Ireland,
Morrison Chambers, 32 Nassau Street, Dublin D02 YH68

A CIP catalogue record for this book is available from the British Library

ISBN: 978-0-241-98733-9

www.greenpenguin.co.uk

MIX
Paper | Supporting
responsible forestry
FSC® C018179

Penguin Random House is committed to a
sustainable future for our business, our readers
and our planet. This book is made from Forest
Stewardship Council® certified paper.

Un roman est un miroir qui se promène
sur une grande route

Stendhal, *Le Rouge et le Noir*

Contents

Acknowledgements

Credits

Index

Introduction

The final draft manuscript of William Boyd's novel *The Romantic* arrived in my inbox twenty-one years to the day after we sat down to talk for my book *Story and Character: Interviews with British Screenwriters*. When we met for that interview, I was using a microcassette dictaphone and he had recently finished his ninth novel, *Any Human Heart*. By the time I clicked 'record' again, we were videoconferencing and he had just published his sixteenth novel, *Trio*. In between, *Any Human Heart* had become, and remains, one of my favourite novels. I still own the first paperback edition with its striking, multicoloured jacket (which, like all good book covers, became part of the reading experience in some indefinable way) and I revisit the novel at intervals, my reading of it subtly changing with age: the eighty-five-year life of its literary protagonist, Logan Mountstuart, throwing a shifting light on my own life as the decades pass.

We originally planned for this book to coincide with Boyd's seventieth birthday in 2022, but the pandemic intervened. Now it feels fitting that these interviews follow another of his trademark 'whole life' novels, since our conversations ranged across his entire writing career and touched on most of his published and produced work – taking me on imaginative journeys to Europe, Africa and the Americas; across the nineteenth, twentieth and twenty-first centuries; up in the air, down in the trenches and over school playing fields; always returning to the neat, smart streets of his patch of contemporary London, where all our meetings have taken place over the years.

Interview books, on the other hand, occupy a sort of hinterland – an uncategorized space somewhere between biography and autobiography – and editing them can be akin to doing a 1,000-piece jigsaw puzzle without having the box as a guide. In assembling this picture of William Boyd, I've done my best not to leave out any vital pieces, but there are a few deliberate omissions.

The first omission is journalism, which has played a big part in Boyd's writing life. A collection of non-fiction, *Bamboo*, anthologized his essays and criticism from 1978 to 2004, and *More Bamboo*, non-fiction from 2005 to date, is being prepared for publication in 2025. Boyd occasionally refers to these pieces in our interviews, but I've tried, where possible, not to go over the same ground. The chapter titles of *Bamboo* are worth noting, though, since they encompass several of the subjects explored in this book: Life, Literature, Art, Africa, Film, Television and People and Places.

The second omission is Boyd's fake biography *Nat Tate: An American Artist 1928–1960*. Published in 1998 by David Bowie's company 21 Publishing, the book brought together themes and techniques from some of Boyd's previous novels – a whole life, the art world, fiction posing as fact – and combined them into a portrait miniature that prefigured the epic canvas of *Any Human Heart* four years later. The new Penguin edition of *Nat Tate* contains an afterword by Boyd about the celebrated art hoax, and Bowie's role in it, which surrounded the book's publication – so, again, I chose not to discuss it in depth here.

The third omission is unproduced screenplays. Most screenwriting careers are like icebergs, largely underwater, and Boyd's CV is a case in point: forty-nine unproduced and three uncredited screenplays, many of which are listed at the back of the book. I intended to include them all, but in the end there wasn't room. Some of his unproduced plays are covered, and any unmade adaptations of his novels or short stories. A handful of other unproduced screenplays are mentioned in passing, but more detail on, for example, *The Galapagos Affair* (based on the book by John Treherne), can be found in our interview from *Story and Character*, reprinted in *Bamboo* as 'Making Movies'.

We did, however, talk about seventeen novels, five collections of short stories, twelve films, five television series and three stage plays – a total of thirty-three hours of interviews, conducted between November 2020 and April 2022, followed by additional questions and clarifications via email. The resulting Q&A is organized broadly by decade, the chapters alternating between fiction and screenplays – until the penultimate chapter, focusing on Boyd's stage work. Alongside the interviews, he was busy planning and writing *The Romantic*, so I decided to devote the last chapter to that novel, a structure which will hopefully give the reader glimpses of his progress as our conversations unfold.

One further omission is plot synopses of Boyd's fiction, screenplays and stage plays. Firstly because they're readily googled. Secondly because I've tried to indicate the plots in my questions. Thirdly because I've assumed that a fair number of readers will be familiar with a fair amount of his output. And finally because it's an incentive to make the same journey I made through the Boyd oeuvre – one of the pleasures of any book about a writer's work.

Before that journey began, in late February 2020, we met for a pre-interview lunch at our usual venue, the Chelsea Arts Club. After lunch, as I walked back to the Tube and joined the crowds heading underground, I remember thinking, 'I wonder if this Covid thing will amount to anything?' Three weeks later, the country was in lockdown. I'd conducted the interviews for my previous books in person, and had never imagined doing these any other way. But, in the end, I didn't feel that that my conversations with William Boyd suffered for taking place on Zoom. It allowed us to talk when he was at his house in France, sitting in another study, with a different set of bookshelves behind him. And, looking back, one compensation of all the online interactions in that disconnected time was seeing how books of every kind still provide a reassuring backdrop to so many people's lives.

Alistair Owen
January 2023

One

Fiction 1

A Good Man in Africa (1981) – *On the Yankee Station* (1981)
An Ice-Cream War (1982) – *Stars and Bars* (1984)
The New Confessions (1987)

When did you first know that you wanted to be a writer?

That's a good question. When I was seventeen or eighteen, thinking of my life ahead of me as an adult, I thought I wanted to be an artist; that was all I had in my head. I didn't know any artists, but there was a subliminal acknowledgement that I wouldn't be any good at a proper job, that somehow I wanted the freedom of an artistic life – whatever I perceived that to be. I did A-level art a year early and my teacher said I should go to art school. I ran this past my father and got a kind of 'Dream on, mate,' so I abandoned that idea and switched to literature. I was good at English, I ran the Literature Society at school and I thought, 'If I can't be a painter, I'll be a writer.' I'd been at Gordonstoun for nearly ten years by the time I left, and I had a gap year before gap years were invented. After a decade of penal servitude at this boarding school in the north of Scotland, I said to my father, 'I can't go to university right now,' and he said, 'You can have a year off as long as you do something useful.' So I went to the University of Nice because they offered courses for foreigners, and it was in Nice that I started to write; not so much fiction but little vignettes, observations of the life I was leading, and letters home to my parents in Africa. I was eighteen or nineteen, and those were the first stirrings of writerly ambition.

In fact, your first ever short story, 'Reveries of an Early Morning Riser', several stories in your first two collections, and your first unpublished novel, *Is That All There Is?*, all sprang from that year.

My time in Nice was hugely formative. I realized that my education had served me well in one or two areas but in the area of being a human being it was a disaster, so I threw out almost everything that boarding school had instilled in me and became a different person as a result. I had a fascinating circle of non-British, European friends; I had a love affair; I hitch-hiked the length of the Côte d'Azur; I met a guy who was supplying the Rolling Stones with all their drugs; I went to the 1971 Cannes Film Festival and have a memory of seeing John Lennon on the terrace at the Majestic; I went to a talk at Nice university given by Dalton Trumbo, who had come over for the festival, and saw his film *Johnny Got His Gun* and shook his hand. Even though I was callow I was taking notes, and I was able to turn all that into something more concrete in what I later wrote. And the good thing was, I got the autobiographical first novel, *Is That All There Is?*, out of my system.

And into your bottom drawer.

Where it remains to this day.

So, that novel and those stories aside, you wouldn't describe yourself as an autobiographical writer?

I think it's a temperamental thing. There comes a point in a writer's life where this division occurs: you're either a writer who uses your own life as raw material or you're not, and if you're not then you use your imagination – and having used up my own life in those stories and that novel, I realized that I wasn't an autobiographical writer. Evelyn Waugh was a very autobiographical writer – even his most outlandish comedies have close links with his own experiences – but that's not the case with me at all. Of course, there's a lot of you in your fiction, and I can point to bits of my novels or stories that have their starting points in my own life or in characters I know, but I very quickly make them into imaginary people rather than real people. The central character of *Is That All There Is?*, Henry Rush, was a thinly disguised version of me, but the Nice stories feature this character called Edward Scully, and although a lot of the things that happen to him are things that happened to me, he's a much nastier person than I was – or am. He's like my evil twin. So even those first stories I wrote about Nice were a sign of the writer I wanted to become. It's just something in your nature that all writers discover, and I discovered that I'd rather make things up than turn my own life into a sort of, quote unquote, fiction.

'Reveries of an Early Morning Riser' won first prize in a short story competition at the University of Glasgow, where you studied for an MA in English Literature and Philosophy. There were also two writers in residence during your time there, poet George Bruce and novelist William Price Turner. How important was that moment, and that period, for you?

It was very important. When you're a young writer just starting out you have dreams and fantasies about your talent, and winning a prize or seeing your name in print somehow means you've passed the test and you're not fooling yourself. More than anything else, winning that prize gave me the confidence to continue. I wrote that first novel, I wrote a play, I wrote other short stories, I wrote journalism. And for somebody who didn't know a single writer or publisher or editor or agent, meeting two real writers inadvertently opened a door for me. So, although my time in Oxford, where I next moved to do my DPhil, seems more significant to my writing career, what I did at Glasgow was very important in my development as a writer, particularly the journalism. I became arts editor for the university newspaper, I appointed myself theatre and film critic, I reviewed every play that appeared and went to see all the new movies – and I met the stars who came up to Scotland to promote them. I also met my wife, Susan, at Glasgow, so my personal life was very settled and secure. We'd been together for two years by the time we moved to Oxford, and we got married in order to get a student flat, and being a married man in my early twenties changed everything – in an extremely good way. I had a grant from the Scottish Education Department to pay for my DPhil studies and Susan had a good job with the Oxford University Press, so there was a benign and reassuring sense that the domestic foundations of my life were already well established and settled.

You've dedicated every book you've written to Susan. Is she your first reader?

Absolutely. She has been from day one. We have very similar tastes, we have the same sense of humour; the things we notice in life, we notice together. She's also a very honest person: she's not going to flatter me or let me off the hook easily, and if she thinks something is amiss she doesn't hesitate to tell me. So she's the ideal first reader. It's important for any writer to have a touchstone who will be honest with you and say, 'This bit isn't funny,' or, 'The ending is really boring.' I know writers, contemporaries of mine, who have nobody telling them these things any more, and it's not good for the finished article. But fortunately for me I still have that stringent, gimlet-eyed first reader at my shoulder. I'm an incredibly lucky man – and novelist.

You wrote your second unpublished novel, *Against the Day*, after you moved to Oxford. What was the inspiration for that?

Against the Day was set against the background of the Biafran War, which I'd lived through in Nigeria and had a profound effect on me. Again, I was a callow youth and I took things on board without really thinking about them, but when I look back I see how extraordinary these experiences were. Watching hideous pictures of people being shot and chopped down with machetes on the news every night. Seeing fighter jets parked alongside civilian airliners, and tanks and armoured cars everywhere you went. Being stopped at a roadblock in the middle of the bush and ordered out of the car by six drunken troops with AK-47s. Getting strip-searched at Lagos airport by two soldiers who thought I was running drugs or currency. Now I think, 'How could I have been so calm?' but at the time you don't see the bigger picture, you just do as you're told. My experiences in Nigeria in 1968–70 were as important as my experiences in Nice in 1971. They had a massive effect on my thinking and a knock-on effect in my fiction.

In your introduction to *The Dream Lover* you describe *Against the Day* as 'self-consciously experimental'. Is that why it was never published?

It was a comprehensible novel, it wasn't completely baffling, but I probably was going through a short-lived pretentious phase. That was at the time of my doctoral thesis, so maybe I'd been infected by literary theory. My memory of the novel is of a modernistic collage – letters, journals, first-person testimony, fictitious newspaper reports – and it might have worked better as an orthodox novel. But it was quite an exciting story, and some people who read it enjoyed it, so that was the one I started sending out.

And one of those people was your first mentor, Alan Ross.

That's right. By that time I'd had a short story published in *London Magazine*, which was edited by Alan, and he became a crucial figure in my literary development. I felt I'd arrived, in a modest way: published in a highly regarded literary magazine, having lunch with the editor, being given free hardbacks and getting paid to review them. It seemed like the literary life to me. I told him I'd written this novel and he asked to see it, because he was a reader for various publishers, and he couldn't understand why it wasn't picked up. I used his recommendation to get a literary agent, Anthea Morton-Saner, but she couldn't get the novel published either, and we parted ways amicably. I started getting a bit desperate, so I wrote a novel called *Truelove at 29*, about a poet who inadvertently gets involved with a drug cartel. He wins a prize in Mexico and goes over to collect the award but in the plinth of the cup are two kilos of cocaine. Then he realizes that all traces of him are being erased: his books being removed from libraries and never returned, photographs of him being taken down off walls, until he becomes a non-person. It was a sort of thriller about an innocent being sucked into this perilous narco-plot.

Your second and third novels, although unpublished, carry echoes of the ones that followed: *Against the Day* a story of conflict in the mould of *An Ice-Cream War*, *Truelove at 29* a fish-out-of-water story like *Stars and Bars*.

It's true that I've pillaged those novels to a certain extent, particularly *Against the Day*. A lot of that novel went into *An Ice-Cream War*, and, in fact, the moment in *Solo* where Bond is awoken by the muzzle of a rifle against his forehead and sees six heavily armed mercenaries in the room came straight from *Against the Day*, as well. Nothing is wasted. Everything can be recycled. And you're right that a lot of your apprentice work foreshadows the kind of writer you're going to be. I'm sure that's true of a painter or a composer as well. Your first stab at a string quartet may manifest itself in the symphony you write twenty years later. I never actually sent *Truelove at 29* to anybody, because I suddenly thought I could do better by getting a short story collection published. By now – 1979 – I'd had eight stories published or broadcast, and in those days collections of short stories were still a good route to having your first book published.

Which it was in your case, albeit a circuitous route.

Yes. The short story that Alan Ross took off the slush pile was my first story about this dissolute character Morgan Leafy – a minor British diplomat in a fictitious West African country – which I called 'Patience at Spinoza's', Patience being the name of a prostitute and Spinoza's being the name of a brothel. Alan said, 'I'm sorry, you can't have that title, nobody will know what you're talking about.' So I called it 'Next Boat from Douala' and that was the first story of mine that was properly published. There was a second Morgan Leafy story, 'The Coup', in the collection I sent simultaneously to Jonathan Cape and

Hamish Hamilton, and something made me put a PS in my letter to both of them: 'By the way, I've written a novel featuring this character, Morgan Leafy.' And Christopher Sinclair-Stevenson at Hamish Hamilton replied – a great day, I remember it vividly – saying, 'I want to publish your short story collection, but I want to publish the novel first.' The problem was, I actually hadn't written the novel; it was a white lie. So I told another white lie and said, 'The manuscript's in a shocking condition and I need to retype it. Give me a few weeks and I'll get it back to you.' I got a grant from the Arts Council, I borrowed some money from my mother, I gave up the teaching I was doing to make ends meet and I wrote *A Good Man in Africa* in about three months flat. Christopher received it, and accepted it, in September 1979 and said he wasn't going to publish it until January 1981, so I had a long wait for my first novel to appear. But he really liked it, so I was off and running.

Since you wrote the stories first, I'd like to talk about them first. In the introduction to *The Dream Lover* you say that 'different mental gears are engaged, different pleasures experienced' writing a short story than when writing a novel. How different *are* those mental gears, those pleasures?

Angus Wilson, who made his name as a short story writer, was asked to define the short story, and he said it's something you can write over a weekend. He was working at the British Museum as a curator, and on Saturday and Sunday, when he wasn't at work, he could write a short story. That's partly what appeals to me, that it's something you can do very quickly. There's another good definition, it might be Edgar Allan Poe's, that a short story is a work of fiction that can be read at one sitting. There's something contained about a short story, so its effect is different from a novel, more akin to a lyric poem as opposed to an epic poem. You don't read *Paradise Lost* in the same way as you read 'The Whitsun Weddings', for example. A short story is a very different thing to write as well. In those ten or twenty pages you can distil something that can stand on its own and deliver an aesthetic charge that's different from the aesthetic charge that a novel delivers. So I do think that the two forms are quite distinct. I also think – because I have this slightly nerdy tendency to classify things – that there are basically seven types of short story.

Which you identify in an article that was reprinted in *Bamboo*: Event-Plot, Chekhovian, 'Modernist', Cryptic/Ludic, Mini-Novel, Poetic/Mythic and Biographical. Do you consider the category of story you're writing as you're writing it, or does that only reveal itself when you've finished?

There's always the wisdom of hindsight, but usually if I have an idea for a short story I very quickly realize what kind it's going to be. As we speak, I've got a short story being broadcast on Radio 4, 'The McFeggan Offensive' – read by my friend John Sessions, who tragically died only last week. It's only about 2,000 words, but I can see it's a mini-novel short story: very realistic, with a distinct setting. I still don't think there's another variation of the short story that I'd add to that list. It encompasses virtually every story that's ever been written.

In that article you also wrote, 'The Chekhovian point of view is to look at life in all its banality and all its tragicomedy and refuse to make a judgement,' and the same could be said of your own fiction.

That's probably true of all modern fiction. Victorian novelists judged all the time, and pointed out good behaviour and bad behaviour and what was admirable and what was reprehensible. But Chekhov made a virtue of not condemning his sinful characters, because he was a shrewd and worldly enough man to realize that wasn't the fiction writer's place or mandate. Serious fiction, literary fiction, doesn't judge or condemn, or its condemnation is implicit rather than moralistic. And I think that's Chekhov's abiding influence, particularly on twentieth-century English literature, because his point of view is very amenable to the British psyche: everything is inherently funny or stupid, and people's behaviour is odd and absurd. His short stories were revolutionary, with a tone of voice so modern that they're timeless, and it's hard to write a literary novel today without being influenced by his example, even unconsciously.

What other short story writers inspired you, then and now?

I started reading F. Scott Fitzgerald's short stories at school, and that may have stirred a literary ambition in me. I have this theory that as an adolescent your best introduction to literature is through empathy, reading something that somehow chimes with your own life, and Fitzgerald's series of autobiographical short stories about a young boy called Basil Duke Lee were the very first time I clicked like that with a great writer. Then, in Nice, I remember reading Ernest Hemingway's short story collection, *In Our Time*. A lot of them are war stories or post-war stories, but there are little italicized interstices between them which were an influence on the vignettes I was writing in Nice. I was bowled over by his stories, and now I'd cite him along with Chekhov as one of the one of the greats in short fiction. I can't get on with his novels, but his early stories had a huge influence on my writing.

The first story in *On the Yankee Station*, 'Killing Lizards', prefigures the second story in *Fascination*, 'Varengeville': the setting is completely different, but they're both about a boy's first glimpse of the adult world via his observations of his mother's affair. Had that ever struck you?

I think that's true, although the impulse to write from the point of view of the child was different in each case. In 'Varengeville' I wanted to write about the artist Georges Braque, who makes a brief appearance in *Nat Tate*, and I thought I'd do it through the eyes of a child. It's an old device: the innocent who can't see the significance of events but the reader can. But I wasn't thinking of 'Killing Lizards' when I wrote that. 'Killing Lizards' is a very early story, and a far more sinister one than 'Varengeville'.

It also prefigures some of the elements you'd use in your first novel: not just the African setting but the university campus. So, again, there's an autobiographical element.

It's the university campus in Ibadan, Western Nigeria, where my family lived, and I'm deeply ashamed today to say that I and my two friends must have killed hundreds of these lizards with our catapults without a qualm. It was a blood sport. So that was drawing on my own background, but the boy's need to get his mother's love, exclusively, and dreaming of his father and sister dying in a car crash, is all invented.

Sex features to one degree or another in almost all of the stories – and its connection to death and violence and even insanity. Presumably you were aware of that?

A short story collection is slightly misleading because the stories could have been written years apart, and it's only when they're collected that you can see the same themes keep cropping up, as if I'd been sitting there thinking about them all the time. Also, I later expanded that collection: there were more stories in the paperback edition. Sex and death are the great themes of art, so it's hardly unlikely that as a young writer I'd be exploring those concepts – and as the motor-drive for a narrative you can't beat them – but no, it wasn't something I was aware of. Failure is more of a theme in them, it seems to me. An early reviewer of my stories said that I seemed to be 'preoccupied with human unsuccess', and I do feel that disappointment and unrequited love are interesting areas to explore. But there's no doubt that there are facets of the human condition that interest you more than others, and you inevitably find yourself returning to them even if you told yourself not to. At the same time, I think it's important as a writer not to be too self-analytical; to have a degree of ignorance about why you write about certain things, and an area of instinct where your unconscious mind can operate.

Thinking about the two strands of 'Killing Lizards' – the boy engaged in this wholesale slaughter and trying to get the love of his mother – is it important for a short story to reach a thematic conclusion?

You have to have a sense of closure or catharsis, however mild. Going back to the lyric poem analogy, when you read a six-line poem there's a satisfaction about that form. The event-plot story, with all the knots neatly tied, was the dominant story form before Chekhov, but he showed that the open-ended story is truer to life, and I often leave the endings of my stories and novels open because life is not all neat and tidy. What you need for a short story is a distillation of experience, and somehow the satisfaction, the sense of closure, is provided in that distillation, even though the story may end with you not knowing what happened. That feeling of catharsis is very important in novels as well as stories, but you haven't got as much time to generate it in a story, so your last line is often very important to establish the tone and mood. You're looking for a poetic conclusion rather than a narrative one.

Can you get away with more, in terms of form, in a short story than in a novel?

I think so. Again, Chekhov could write a deeply satisfying short story where nothing seemed resolved – and Hemingway, Raymond Carver, Katherine Mansfield, for example, all learned from what he did and took it a step further. Hemingway's 'Hills Like White Elephants' – a very short short story – is utterly baffling until you decode it. The text is almost banal – two people at a railway station and one of them is waiting to leave – but once you analyse the subtext you realize that the woman has had an abortion and their relationship is falling apart. It's all implicit and doesn't end with a narrative thud, but it's very cleverly done and shows you the freedoms you have in a short story that you wouldn't have in a novel. There's a very weird story in *On the Yankee Station* called 'Extracts from the Journal of Flying Officer J.' that I wrote for an anthology. All the stories had to have some bearing on a Shakespeare play, and mine was an elaborate rewriting of *As You Like It* in the tone of W. H. Auden's long poem *The Orators*, and Flying Officer J. was Jacques. I stuck illustrations in it as well, Rorschach blot images – a device that prefigured some of my later fiction, incidentally. I'd never attempt something so oblique and arcane at novel length, but with a short story you do have more licence. I've also learned lessons from writing short stories that have been fantastically useful when I've come to write novels. A lot of the structural stuff in *Brazzaville Beach* I'd explored in short story form. Another story in *Yankee Station*, 'Love Hurts', is written in the form of a diary, so I was trying that out as a narrative device decades before

I wrote *Any Human Heart*. And splitting the narrative between different voices, seeing how they interact and interconnect, as I did in *Ordinary Thunderstorms*, I'd already done in short stories. Short stories are like a laboratory for me. You wouldn't want to spend three years writing a novel and finding out that something didn't work. So I'd say it is inherently a more experimental form.

Several of the stories in *On the Yankee Station* are set in California, which you also wrote about in later collections, and in your novels *The New Confessions* and *The Blue Afternoon*. It rarely seems to be a happy place in your fiction: a neo-noir landscape of sex, violence, obsession and self-deception.

I've often written about places I've never been to, and there are three cities in particular – Los Angeles, Berlin and Lisbon – that I wrote about before I ever went to them. The Los Angeles stories were inspired by my love of movies; by an English writer I really like, Gavin Lambert, who wrote a series of short stories set in Los Angeles called *The Slide Area*; and also by the Pat Hobby stories of F. Scott Fitzgerald. I was fascinated by the myths of Los Angeles, and I wanted to see if I could inhabit the place vicariously through my imagination.

Well, if you're preoccupied with human unsuccess, what better place to explore that preoccupation than the home of Hollywood?

Exactly. The film industry is fertile ground for that kind of story. I read a lot of American fiction when I was a young writer, and the American imagination was more congenial to me than the British imagination. It was a long time before I set a novel in Britain, because it didn't seem that interesting. My African life was so vivid and colourful, and British life didn't provide the same charge.

I hadn't noticed that until you pointed it out. Even the stories in *On the Yankee Station* reflect that. Only one of them takes place in Britain. The rest are set in Africa, America, France and Scotland.

And on a US aircraft carrier off the coast of Vietnam.

The Yankee Station of the title, and the longest story in the collection. Did the collection coalesce around it, or did you make it the title story because it stood out in terms of its setting and scope?

I just liked the title. Titles are hugely important to me. I was very interested in the Vietnam War – which also features in *Sweet Caress* – and in my reading about it I learned there was this area in the South China Sea called the Yankee Station where all the US aircraft were based on aircraft carriers, and I thought Yankee Station had a great ring to it. It's the same with my other short story collections: *Fascination*, *The Destiny of Nathalie 'X'*, *The Dreams of Bethany Mellmoth*. They seemed like good titles to me. You want people who don't know your name to be drawn to your book in a bookshop or library, so it's very important to have an intriguing or arresting title, it seems to me. That's true of everything I've written, from short stories to novels to screenplays: I take a lot of care over the title, and I won't publish it or send it out until I've got a title that's bang on.

The story reminded me of Graham Greene's Vietnam novel *The Quiet American*, another story of male and colonial oppression in their various forms.

I think you're right. It's also about bullying and persecution, about being a dweeb, as they'd say, among these horrible macho fighter pilots. My first film, *Good and Bad at Games*, is very similar, about a boy being savagely bullied at school and the consequences of that – and the story that's being broadcast today, 'The McFeggan Offensive', is also about bullying, so it's gone full circle. It's quite a funny story, but at its heart is a boy whose life is utterly miserable. I wasn't bullied at all at school, and neither was I a bully, but I saw shockingly bad bullying going on, and it's obvious from what I've written that it had an effect on me.

Were there any other influences on this particular story?

I'm trying to remember what films or stories might have influenced me. I've read a lot of literature about the Vietnam War, and Michael Herr's *Dispatches* had recently come out when I wrote it. And I've always loved planes and aviation – because I've been flying all my life, from the age of six months, from Africa to Europe and back again – which is why I thought of an aircraft carrier. I have this definition of a novel, that it's the sum of all the things the novelist was interested in at the time of writing. That's certainly true of my novels. Because the novel form is so generous and capacious – 'large, loose, baggy monsters' as Henry James described them – you can factor in stuff you're intrigued by that might seem inimical to your narrative, like primatology, or anaesthesia, or early powered flight, or the philosophy of insurance. And it's the same with the short stories. If something intrigued me, I could write a story about it. There's an annual funfair in Oxford, the St Giles' Fair, and one year there was a stall called 'Bat-Girl!' which, of course, was irresistible: I had to go in and see what the hell that was all about. And it was exactly as described in the story: a very bored girl and a semi-comatose bat – that was your twenty-pence worth. It was funny and absurd, and I thought, 'There's a short story there,' and off I went.

'Bat-Girl!' is the only story in the collection written from a first person female point of view. Was it also the first piece of fiction you wrote from a woman's viewpoint?

Yes, it was. And I didn't do it again until *Brazzaville Beach* – although I did write third person female point of view for Liesl and Charis in *An Ice-Cream War*. I've now done it many times, and I think I know how to do it well, and women readers have confirmed that. But it's a risk. And it's a risk the other way around, too: for women to write from the point of view of men. When I came to write *Brazzaville Beach*, I was far more conscious of the pitfalls ahead. When I wrote 'Bat-Girl!', I didn't think twice about it. I just did it unreflectingly, with the brash confidence of the young writer. It seemed the obvious way to tell the story, from the point of view of the girl in the cage. Also, one of the pleasures of writing from the point of view of a woman is that you get to look at male behaviour from that angle and see the frustrations, stupidities and irritations of it.

On the Yankee Station also includes your first treatment of a subject you would later return to in fiction, non-fiction and on film: boarding school. You originally planned to devote an entire collection to the subject, didn't you, of which the story 'Hardly Ever' is the only one you wrote?

That's right. Of all British institutions, the one that has been most ignored in film and literature is the boarding school. Every other institution – the law, the Church, the army, you name it – has been analysed with gritty realism, but most depictions of boarding school life are utter fantasy. Where are the great novels about boarding school? Where are the great movies? You can almost count them on the fingers of one hand. There's a novel by David Benedictus, *The Fourth of June*, which is about Eton. There's a TV film by Frederic Raphael called *School Play*, where the boys are played by adults, that is absolutely on-the-nail real. Otherwise you're in Harry Potter land. Without doubt the best book I've ever read on the boarding school experience is non-fiction: *The Hothouse Society* by Royston Lambert, which came out in the late '60s and I read when I was still at school. Lambert was a trained sociologist who went to lots of schools and spoke to both boys and girls on the condition of anonymity, and the accounts that these adolescents gave of boarding school life rang 100 per cent true to me, much more than any fiction I'd read. These institutions have a massively disproportionate influence on British society, but it's as if there's some code of *omertà*, that once you leave you're not allowed to tell anybody what it was really like. I was going to attempt to rectify that by writing a series of stories set in boarding school that would be as uncompromising as Lambert's book; but having written that one story I was then commissioned to write two TV films – *Good and Bad at Games* and *Dutch Girls* – and, when they were made, I realized that my anthropological ambition to expose this little-known tribe and their strange customs had been achieved.

Would all the short stories have featured the same characters?

I can't remember, to be honest. The collection was so embryonic that I hadn't really figured it out. One of the characters in 'Hardly Ever', Quentin Niles, is the main character in *Good and Bad at Games*, so he was probably going to be my running alter ego figure – although he's evolved a bit in the film; he's less of a sportsman in the story.

And more of a storyteller: he discovers a talent for fiction by inventing tales of his sexual exploits.

Which was also true: the most brazen lying went on about people's sex lives. We were all satyrs in our imaginations. When I wrote that story I must have been in my late twenties, so my memories of school were still very vivid. I actually found an old play I wrote in my first year at university, which, again, was about public school. It was the first play I'd ever written and I entered it into a playwriting competition at the Citizens Theatre, Glasgow. It got nowhere, but it shows you what was on my mind. Ten years in a boarding school was half my life, so that was the raw material that I wanted to put out there. I was obviously thinking, 'I've got all this experience, and I have to tell it like it is.'

What was it about the character of Morgan Leafy in the stories 'Next Boat from Douala' and 'The Coup' that made you want to devote an entire novel to him?

In fact, it was Susan's idea that I could write a novel about Morgan. It was also partly to do with what we talked about earlier: the thing that most interests me is using my imagination, and inhabiting somebody who's absolutely unlike me is more attractive than writing some thinly disguised autobiography. It was also partly to do with the premature death of my father, who died in 1979 at the age of fifty-eight. I started writing the novel shortly thereafter, so he was a very dominant presence in my mind. He was a doctor on this huge university campus in Nigeria and he looked after 40,000 souls: about 5,000 students, a few senior staff – as the professors and lecturers and their families were known – and thousands of what were called junior staff, the Nigerians and Ghanaians who ran the place. The campus was the size of a town, so he had to supervise seven clinics and a small hospital. He was very good at his job and much loved and admired, but he was a classic Scot of his generation who didn't wear his emotions on his sleeve, and I remember observing a curious relationship he had with this dissolute English lecturer at the university. They seemed to get on extremely well, which was very odd because he was the kind of person my father would normally have dismissed – shambolic and unshaven, with his shirt always hanging out – and I never got to the bottom of why my father enjoyed the company of this shady character. So I dreamed up this drunken British diplomat, Morgan Leafy, who was equally overweight and sweaty and licentious, and opposed him with this dour Scottish doctor, Dr Murray, who was a two-dimensional portrait of my father. The idea of somebody whose moral compass is very shaky coming up against somebody whose moral compass is rock solid was the dynamic I wanted to explore. I often do that in my novels: pit my protagonist against somebody who has an absolutely sure and certain view of life and how it should be conducted – not necessarily in a good way. It's the same with Lorimer Black and George Hogg in *Armadillo*, for example. To a degree, it reflects my relationship with my father, because I realized that he tried to brainwash me from the age of fourteen: 'Save one sixth of your income,' 'Don't study art, study sciences,' 'Don't get married until you're over thirty.' All this advice was pumped my way, and all of it I completely ignored. I got on perfectly well with my father, but I was a totally different type of person and still a student when he died. In a way, in *A Good Man in Africa*, I was exploring what that relationship might have been had he lived longer and I'd had the chance to get to know him more as an adult.

Was the novel ever intended to dovetail with the two short stories?

No, it wasn't. In fact, there's a third, unpublished story about Morgan Leafy, which I also wrote before the novel. I don't even remember if I offered it to anybody, but it's certainly somewhere in my archive. So there were three short stories, but they don't dovetail with the novel at all. The novel stands apart.

The novel is reminiscent of Kingsley Amis's *Lucky Jim*. I also wondered whether Evelyn Waugh was an influence?

I'm sure the serious comic novelists I admired were subliminally in my mind: Amis, Waugh, J. G. Farrell – who had a similar deadpan sense of humour. But I wasn't consciously aware of writing like anybody else, or trying to. I absolutely loved *Lucky Jim*, but it wasn't an attempt to write a *Lucky Jim*-type novel.

In the autobiographical non-fiction piece, 'Memories of the Sausage Fly', you describe yourself and the other white children in Nigeria as 'colonial brats: lazy, self-regarding, pleasure-seeking and utterly incurious about the country we were living in', which could equally apply to the British diplomats in your fictional country of Kinjanja.

I was being a bit harsh on my younger self by saying that, but it's true – although if I'd been born and raised in Edinburgh or Cheltenham, I might not have been very curious about my surroundings either. I did end up travelling quite widely in West Africa, but I wasn't a tourist, I wasn't looking for experience – and when I look back at my African childhood and youth and early adulthood, the thing that makes it different from other visits to foreign countries is that it wasn't foreign to me, however exotic it seems in hindsight. My parents were a young, middle-class Scottish couple and they were living like nineteenth-century aristocrats, with servants to cook and clean the house and wash the car and mow the lawn, whereas if they'd been living in Scotland my father would have been out with the lawnmower himself. The privileges of that post-colonial life were remarkable, but at the time you didn't think anything about it.

Why did you set the novel in a fictional country rather than a real one?

It's a common fictional trope – and it was a very thin disguise. The book blurb probably said that I grew up in Ghana and Nigeria, so it wouldn't have been difficult to make the connection. But if you want to embellish and invent, a thin disguise is better than the reality. Whereas if you make it more precise, you have to be more authentic. I also did it in later African novels, *Brazzaville Beach* and *Solo*. By not specifying the setting, I could create the country's history and tensions. I do it in screenplays as well: as soon as you fictionalize something the shackles come off. When the novel was published, my mother was terribly worried that people would be offended or sue me or something like that, but I reassured her that it wasn't based on anybody we knew and the only real character was Dr Murray.

Did your mother enjoy the novel?

Once she read it for a second time and her anxieties were reduced, I think she did enjoy it. It's a very accurate portrait of the lives we led, in terms of the texture and the detail. But it's an odd experience, that. And when you're a young writer you must banish your family from your mind, because you know they'll recoil at the sex scenes or the profanities.

It's thought of as a comic novel, and it certainly has some farcical scenes, but the humour is often very dark – and it turns almost tragic towards the end. What tone were you aiming for overall?

It's the same tone I always aim for. I see myself as a comic novelist: my vision of the world is that it's absurd and stupid and makes no sense, and attempts to make it make sense are doomed to failure. But comedy can also be very serious, and all my comedies have a dark edge to them, because that's life. There are two writers I often quote. One is Vladimir Nabokov: 'A good laugh is the best pesticide.' The other is Henry de Montherlant: 'Happiness writes white on the page.' I'd never sit down to write a deeply serious, tragic novel, because I tend to go for the laugh rather than weeping and wailing and tearing my hair out. At the same time, I don't want to write a wholly sunny, happy novel, because it just doesn't work. However comic the ambience is, to make the novel realistic you need tension, you need conflict, you need complex characters. That's true of all the novels I've written. They may be funny, but there's also a recognition of life's random cruelty. *A Good Man in Africa* was exactly in that tradition. You're right, it is very dark: from the dead body of the woman struck by lightning that Morgan has to get rid of, to the tragedy at the end when the actual good man in Africa is killed. So there is a moral lesson buried within the novel, and you do wonder if, as a result of Dr Murray's death, Morgan will become a better, more serious person. He doesn't jump into bed with the wife of the High Commissioner at the end of the book, which he would have done at the beginning, because he's got the example of Dr Murray hovering at his shoulder. The urge to make a moral point in my comedies is perhaps some vague trace of F. R. Leavis, because if you studied English Literature at university in the '70s the Leavisite tradition was still being absolutely drummed into you: the only great fiction is moral fiction, and books that don't have a moral message aren't going to enter the pantheon.

Would you describe the novel as satirical in any way?

Not really. My portrayal of post-colonial society, and political life in an African country, is mild compared to what Nigerian writers were doing at the time. It's got a very vibrant literary tradition, Nigeria, and its writers have constantly excoriated the powers that be, but I wasn't trying to do that. I just wrote it as realistically as possible based on what I knew. I'd lived through upheavals in both Ghana and Nigeria, particularly the military coups and civil war in Nigeria, so I knew what those countries were like and what their problems were.

It's very much a portrayal of white life in a Black country, and the Black characters are mainly either exploiting or being exploited by the white characters. Would you approach the novel differently if you were writing it now?

One treads more cautiously today, with good reason – and I entirely approve of that kind of watchfulness and care in what you write and say – but I don't think I have anything to apologize for in *A Good Man in Africa*. It has been criticized by some African critics as a post-colonial view of African life; but everything is seen through the eyes of Morgan Leafy, that's the point of view of the novel, and when I look back at it I don't see anything that isn't real or true. If you're writing a comedy, people behave badly, and with the exception of Dr Murray and Morgan's cook, Friday, nobody emerges from the novel very well. Morgan's relationship with Friday is quite affecting, I think, and he's called Friday for a very good reason: the Crusoe echo is meant to be picked up. So it isn't crass, it seems to me, and it isn't insensitive. The same is true of *Stars and Bars*, where I take my characters to the Deep South and they encounter types down there who might raise hackles in Louisiana or Alabama, but if it's done in good faith I don't think the author has anything to worry about.

The structure is quite intricate for a comic novel: Part One takes place in the present, Part Two in the past, Part Three in the present again. Did you plan that in advance, or did it emerge in the writing?

I planned it in advance, as I plan all my novels. In fact, my then-agent suggested I make it chronological, and had I not already placed the book with a publisher I might have taken her advice. But I'd been at university for ten years by then, studying and teaching English Literature, and I knew my way around the novel – I could strip it down to its component parts and reassemble it and explain how it worked – so I very deliberately structured *A Good Man in Africa* that way. My working maxim is, 'All intelligent suggestions gratefully received', but if a suggestion isn't particularly intelligent I'll ignore it, and that was just change for the sake of change. She didn't advance any coherent reason why I should make it chronological. I wanted it to start with a bang, *in medias res*, and that's why I structured it with the big flashback in the middle. You'd be drawn into this awful problem, then you'd get the backstory. It's not revolutionary but nobody complained – and, on the whole, it got fantastic reviews. As a debut, it couldn't have gone better.

Not least because it won the Whitbread First Novel Award and the Somerset Maugham Award. Did winning those have any effect on your estimation of yourself as a writer?

It's always nice to win a prize, but even back then I wasn't that bothered. It helped me secure a paperback publisher, because in those days your hardback publisher didn't publish you in paperback. *A Good Man in Africa* was turned down by Pan before it was picked up by Penguin – which actually made me happier, because it's every undergraduate's dream to join that rank of orange-spined books on your rickety bookshelf. The recognition also helped me get an American publisher, which happened fairly swiftly. So there's a pragmatic, career reason why prizes are good – and, if you're a first-time novelist, it announces you've arrived. But because the novel was accepted in September 1979 and not published until January 1981, I'd written most of my second novel, *An Ice-Cream War*, during the fourteen months in between; then six months after *A Good Man in Africa* was published, in July 1981, *On the Yankee Station* came out, so I had two books out in one year; then the next year, September 1982, my second novel came out, so I had three books published in twenty months. By then I was also TV critic of the *New Statesman* and my first film had been commissioned by Channel 4, so I was already well under way and brimming with confidence.

And twelve years later, the film of *A Good Man in Africa* came out, directed by Bruce Beresford – which was structured chronologically.

As you well know, Alistair, any film adaptation of a novel involves at least 50 per cent of the novel being thrown out, because the two art forms are so different. This is true of every single novel I've adapted. Long form television may be something of a saving grace, but you still have the problem of the relentless objectivity of the lens: everything is seen through the camera, and subjectivity is extremely hard to achieve in a subtle way. Even though they're both narrative art forms, film-making is a world of parameters and impossibilities, whereas the novel is a world of liberation and infinite possibility. Things you can do effortlessly in a novel can be hugely problematic when you move into the medium of film, and it was immediately apparent that it would take a lot of effort *not* to make the film of *A Good Man in Africa* chronological. I wrote a script that I thought was very filmable, and Bruce and I had worked extremely well together on another African movie, *Mister Johnson*, so we set about negotiating the many minefields you face in getting any film off the ground.

The casting is interesting. Colin Friels as Morgan Leafy, for starters: a slim, handsome Australian actor playing a sweaty, overweight British diplomat.

That was one of the minefields. There were two superb actors I knew very well who would have killed to be Morgan Leafy: one was the late great Mel Smith, and the other was the wonderful Timothy Spall. Tim did the radio version of *A Good Man in Africa*, he loved the book and he was born to play Morgan, but there was no way that a Hollywood studio was going to accept him or Mel in the role for various absurd and perverse reasons. So what do you do? Do you say, 'Right, we won't make it, then'? No. You say, 'Okay.' It was hard to find an actor who would satisfy the paymasters, and it was Bruce who found Colin – and of course he's clean-cut and good-looking, but he's also a talented comic actor. It was one of those situations where art and commerce collide.

Do you think it made a difference? That commercial casting can sometimes compromise what you had in mind when you wrote the book?

That doesn't bother me, actually. The book is always there. The film is entirely separate. When you're making the film you shouldn't be thinking about how faithful it is to the book; your focus as a writer or a director should be on simply trying to make the best film you can. You can't replicate everything that's in the novel on screen; the art form, and the industrial process of film-making, doesn't allow it. So I never worry unduly about that book–film comparison, and with *A Good Man in Africa* I don't think it made any difference at all. What did make a difference is that the comedy vacillated between broad and deadpan, between something over the top and something quite dark and deadpan, and you can't do that on film otherwise you confuse the audience: is it a belly laugh or is it a knowing chuckle? I'm as much to blame for that as anybody, in the sense that it was only after we'd edited the film that we realized there was this flaw in it. That's often the problem with film-making: when you watch it piecemeal you think, 'We're onto a winner here,' but when you see it whole your heart can sink to your boots. When we watched the rushes of *A Good Man in Africa* we were all falling around laughing, but when we saw it cut together we realized it had this tonal dichotomy – which is why we added the voiceover, in an attempt to rectify it.

The voiceover did feel slightly tacked on.

Voiceover is a great device but it has to be integral to the film, it has to be there in the script. If you add it later, it's usually a sticking plaster to staunch the flow of blood. In the case of *A Good Man in Africa*, it didn't quite work. In hindsight, we should have made the film deadpan through-out, then perhaps the comedy would have emerged naturally. It took me a while to learn that lesson: if you're making a comic film you need to pick a tone and stick to it. We didn't entirely nail it in the film version of *Stars and Bars*, either, which was made before *A Good Man in Africa*. But in the TV version of *Armadillo*, which was made after-wards, I think we nailed it completely. There were other aspects of *A Good Man* that came off brilliantly well, though: Sean Connery is perfect as Dr Murray.

Sean Connery was a much bigger star than Colin Friels, but was playing a supporting part, not the lead. Was there a risk that his presence would unbalance the film?

Possibly, but it was a way of helping the budget and boosting the profile of the film, and Sean was very insistent that it shouldn't be 'Starring Sean Connery'; he didn't want that at all, and I didn't tailor the script for him. It's really an ensemble piece: if you look at the poster you've got Colin, Sean, Joanne Whalley-Kilmer, John Lithgow, Lou Gossett Jr. and Diana Rigg. The Morgan Leafy–Dr Murray conflict is at the narrative heart of the film, but there's a sense in which everybody was equal in it. Also, getting a big star made the money men relax, and if Sean hadn't said yes I don't think the film would have happened.

In a strange way, the uneven tone of the film of *A Good Man in Africa* reflects the chaos inherent in the novel, summed up in its final line: 'The thunder passed on towards the coast and, somewhere, Shango, that mysterious and incomprehensible god, flashed and capered happily above the silent dripping jungle.'

The novel is definitely an early instance of a theme I've often returned to: life's unpredictability. Shango, the lightning god, is like the lord of misrule, and if we managed to get a sense of that in the film, that's a bonus. But that's exactly the kind of point you can easily make in a novel. It's much harder to do it on film and make the subtext resonate.

An *Ice-Cream War* represents a step up in scale from *A Good Man in Africa*. Were you conscious of the novel being that much more ambitious?

It does have more of a sweep than *A Good Man in Africa* — it was set in the past, it was told from several points of view, it was my first full-length attempt at writing from the point of view of women — but that was never a conscious thing. It's one of my longer novels, that's for sure, but I wasn't thinking, 'I must do something bigger.' I've never plotted my way forward like that: 'What would be a good thing to write now?' It's always just been, 'What do I want to write next?' Having lived through the Biafran War and then written *Against the Day*, I wanted to write a novel about war and warfare that emphasized the absurdity of human planning in the face of these chaotic forces. That was my ambition: to reflect my new thinking about war, and how it confounds every expectation. I'd also come to the conclusion that life is like that too, and one of the reasons for writing about war is because it's life writ large: nobody knows what's going to happen. I might fall down the front steps at home and sprain my ankle, but in a war zone I might get shot through the head by a sniper; the random good luck/bad luck aspects of life are enhanced a thousandfold on a battlefield, which allows you to reflect more on the nature of your boring diurnal existence. So that was another ambition. But it all stemmed from what I witnessed in Nigeria in my late teens. I remember talking to our cook, whose name was Israel. His village was over-run and his house was knocked down; he was conscripted into the Biafran army and deployed in the bush; and I said to him, 'What did you do?' And he said, 'I threw away my gun, took off my uniform and ran away.' That seemed to me more true of one man's experience of war than storming a machine-gun nest, and that informed my thinking when I wrote the novel.

Again, Evelyn Waugh seemed to me to be an influence – particularly *Sword of Honour*, which you later adapted for TV – and perhaps Joseph Heller's *Catch-22* as well. Were there others?

I recently tried to reread *Catch-22* and stopped at page 10, because it was ruining my youthful memory of it; but when I first read it at the age of nineteen, I thought it was one of the greatest novels ever written. I'd probably read *Sword of Honour* by the time I wrote *An Ice-Cream War*, and Waugh's take on the 1941 debacle of the Battle of Crete, as a sort of crazy comedy, struck me as a way of writing about war that was truer to its nature than 'The third battalion moved up on the right wing' approach. I'd also read a book by the military historian John Keegan, *The Face of Battle*, where he looked at Agincourt, Waterloo and the Somme from the point of view of the individual soldier rather than as massive historical events. I remember reading the chapter on Waterloo, and he said that whole regiments were ordered to sit down and never fought in the battle because they weren't actually needed. Having witnessed those incongruous aspects of warfare in Nigeria, I simply took them and plonked them down in World War I. Because I was living in Oxford and had the Bodleian Library at my disposal I could access all the books that dealt with the First World War in East Africa, from regimental histories of the West African field force to novels written by South Africans who had been in the war, so I read my way through the literature of the war and I knew that the novel would cover the four years of that conflict.

The First World War is one of several elements of *An Ice-Cream War* which recur in later novels. Why do you find that particular subject so fascinating?

I've written about this a lot. I don't think it's just me, I think it's a national obsession, and one reason is that almost every child in the land has been taught about the

First World War – probably since the First World War. I don't know to what extent war poetry is children's introduction to First World War history today, but when I was at prep school we were reading Wilfred Owen and Robert Graves and it embedded itself in our young minds. In my case, family legend also had a bearing. My grandfather was wounded at the Second Battle of Ypres, and my great-uncle was wounded at the Battle of the Somme, and the question that comes instantly to mind is: 'How the hell did anybody get through it – let alone survive it?' There's a level of incomprehension about the First World War that makes you want to understand it, and that's what I've been trying to do as a novelist – and as a film-maker, with *The Trench*. I've been asked to write a film about the Battle of Arnhem, looking at one particular aspect of that catastrophe, and it comes down to the same question. It's quite extraordinary what those paratroopers went through in that eight-day period, but how do you show that on film? How do you make it real and authentic, and give people some understanding of what it was really like?

Another recurring theme in your fiction is that the lead characters – Felix Cobb, in this case – have close relationships with their mothers and absent, remote or martinet fathers.

Interesting. Yes. I mean, if you look at *The New Confessions*, the opening line is: 'My first act on entering this world was to kill my mother.' And it's true, I do seem to have certain types of father figure in mind. Another thing I often write about is brothers. I don't have a brother, I have two sisters, but brothers pop up in my fiction quite a lot. In the case of Felix and Gabriel that's a warm relationship which is betrayed, but more often than not it's an antagonistic relationship. This is where you shouldn't go looking for answers, and just trust your instincts and your imagination. Where do these things come from? I don't know. And it's not that I don't want to know, it's that I don't think knowing would be helpful.

As it happens, betrayal also crops up repeatedly, and adultery – here, Felix's affair with Gabriel's wife, Charis. Why do you find that such fertile ground for your fiction, and do you think it ties into your fascination with spying, in the sense that duplicity is at the heart of both?

Well, again, 'Happiness writes white on the page.' You need betrayal, you need duplicity, you need bad faith and bad behaviour to give you the material for a narrative. Having an affair with your brother's wife and impregnating her is adultery plus plus, as it were, it makes the level of betrayal even worse and gives me great stuff to work with. I also wanted to demythologize war and soldiers and Edwardian types, so Gabriel is this golden-boy warrior who isn't what he appears to be; whose obsession with Liesl is almost Oedipal and who can only have sex with Charis if he infantilizes it – which Felix doesn't know but we, the readers, do. But I do think there's a very strong connection between spying and human behaviour, because in the spy genre you get everything that's in human relationships but with the volume turned up. We've all lied, we've all betrayed people, we've all pretended to be somebody we're not, and that's stock-in-trade for a spy. When you take these emotions or situations and move them into the arena of the spy novel, you see aspects of every human life but with far more jeopardy, far more at stake, far more serious consequences. So I think that's a very good point: the war novel and the spy novel allow me to explore aspects of our lives in a way that's more dramatic and powerful than if I was writing, say, a Hampstead adultery novel. That's what attracts me to those genres: they're very relevant. Whereas the detective or science fiction or fantasy genres don't seem to me to have quite the same bearing on, or relevance to, people's everyday lives.

An Ice-Cream War is the first of your novels where real people appear alongside fictional characters. What do you think that mixture of fact and fiction brings to the book?

This is something I've since refined. I know why I do it now, but at the time it may have been less thought-through. As I said, I'm a realistic novelist: I want the world of the novel to seem real, I want the characters in the novel to seem real. If you like, I want to colonize the world of the real – the world of journalism, of history, of documentary – to make my fiction more powerful. For example, the Battle of Tanga in *An Ice-Cream War* is almost exactly how that episode played out in reality. It's gone down in military history as the most unsuccessful battle British forces have ever fought, a series of catastrophic miscalculations and wrong assumptions and sheer bad luck. The Germans were massively outnumbered but contrived to exploit the British and colonial forces' manifest inadequacies. I wanted to explain that battle to people who had never heard of it, so I drew on actual sources and put in real people, like the German commander Paul von Lettow-Vorbeck. Quite a few of the fictional characters are based on real people as well: Von Bishop is based on a real person, Bilderbeck is based on a man called Richard Henry Meinertzhagen who was at the battle and kept a diary. He used to execute soldiers on the battlefield, and must have killed forty or fifty people in cold blood during his military career. A more diplomatic writer wouldn't have written about that, but Meinertzhagen was clearly slightly mad and didn't care, which made it more convincing. When I wrote *An Ice-Cream War* all this was just in the interests of making the fiction more real, but I now see it as part of a longer-term project to make fiction more powerful than fact. Maybe the two ambitions are conjoined: two sides of the same coin.

How do you decide which characters to depict under their real names and which to fictionalize?

It depends on the story I want to tell. Meinertzhagen left the East African campaign in around 1915 and ended up in Palestine – he went to join the Arab Revolt alongside Lawrence of Arabia and wrote about that as well – but as I wanted my character to be in East Africa throughout the war it was a simple move to change his name. That decision was purely pragmatic. But when a real person interacts with a fictional character you get a very interesting dynamic. In *Trio*, Virginia Woolf's husband, Leonard, appears for a few pages and interacts with a fictional character, Elfrida, which makes her story more believable, I feel. The novel I'm going to write next will do the same thing. It allows you to write about real people to suit your fictional purposes and try to pin down their motivations in a way that a biographer can't. I do a similar thing in my scripts: when I'm writing about historical figures, like Hitler or Lawrence of Arabia, I often stick a fictional character in their midst, which takes the narrative out of documentary and into drama – and also makes exposition much easier. In *African Fever*, the TV series I wrote about the nineteenth-century explorers Burton, Speke, Stanley and Livingstone – never made, by the way – I created a character who's the librarian of the Royal Geographical Society and knows all four men and acts as the link between them, and, for example, I could cut back to her as she plotted Stanley's attempt to find and rescue Livingstone on a map hanging on the wall of the society. Having a fictional character in the historical mix is a very useful device for crucial exposition and also gives you the freedom to invent, which is what drama is about. You're writing a fiction, so you might as well use all the fictional tools available to you.

In a multi-character story like *An Ice-Cream War*, what determines when you change point of view?

My feeling is that it's just narrative instinct: it's time to stop telling this story and move on to that story. It's like when you end a chapter: what's happened between the end of this chapter and the start of the next? These are very important decisions in novels, and if you get them wrong the novel will suffer. When to shift point of view is all to do with your sense of the story's rhythms and cadences. I don't think you can say that each section should be ten pages long or thirty pages long. Of course, when you finish the novel you may look back and think, 'I need a bit more of this,' but that's just fine-tuning. In the actual process of writing these decisions are taken on the hoof, and something in you says, 'Time to move away from Felix and go to Erich von Bishop.' But if you asked me, 'Why Erich? Why not Charis?' my answer would be, 'Because I felt it was right.' I couldn't give you anything more cogent or reasoned than that. It's all about how you tell a story, whether it's a novel or an anecdote in the pub. Some people are terrible at anecdotes: 'Oh, I forgot to tell you about . . .' The story begins to break down. It's a narrative skill or gift that you have, like an ear for dialogue. Some people have a tin ear for dialogue, other people have a great ear for it.

Although set, once again, in Africa, there are fewer African characters in the book than in *A Good Man*. Did you consider exploring the impact of the war on the indigenous population?

No, because the story is told from the point of view of Felix and Gabriel and the Von Bishops, who are soldiers and colonialists. It's true that the war, particularly as it advanced, was fought largely by African soldiers with white officers – and the supply chain for all these roving troops were thousands of African bearers, who were unwritten about and unspoken about. Again, though, the novel was written in 1981. If I was writing it now, I'd probably make the point more forcefully that without this massive army of African soldiers and bearers, the war simply couldn't have been fought. But, in the end, the book isn't about that subject, it's about these two brothers.

Do you ever write biographies of your characters?

Occasionally, for the longer novels, to remind myself how tall they are and what their favourite food is and whether their parents are still alive, but nothing more than that. I made notes on filing cards for *An Ice-Cream War*, because there are so many characters in it and it stopped me having to flick back all the time. But I've answered a lot of questions I need to ask before I start writing, so I'm not making it up as I go along.

An Ice-Cream War won the John Llewellyn Rhys Prize. It was also nominated for the Booker Prize, which must have had some effect on your career.

I'm extremely grateful to the Booker Prize. It wasn't as big an event in 1982 as it became in the '90s and noughties, but I was interviewed by the *Guardian* and I was on telly. Thomas Keneally won for *Schindler's Ark*, which isn't really a novel at all, it's a true story – and Keneally, who's a delightful man, has gone on the record saying *An Ice-Cream War* should have won that year. But it was great to be nominated. I was just thirty years old when the prize was awarded, and maybe it would have been a bad thing for me to have won so young, but it was a massive boost to my profile and the book did fantastically well. The thing that really changed my fortunes was that *An Ice-Cream War* became a huge bestseller in France, and its success in France meant that it was then published all over the place. So my second novel did have a huge impact on my career, and the Booker Prize was definitely part of that.

You've written three screenplays based on *An Ice-Cream War*: a feature script in the 1980s, a TV script in two feature-length parts in 2011 and, more recently, another TV script, this time in six parts. The earlier versions combine certain strands of the novel but the latest adaptation separates them out again, which is more faithful both to the letter of the book and to its theme of lives and events randomly intersecting. Which version do you feel works best?

The six-hour version is probably the best, because it's got more of the novel in it and you can investigate the characters at greater length. I haven't read the feature script for donkey's years, but I suspect that 70 per cent of the novel isn't in it. That version was actually semi-cast at one stage: we had Colin Firth playing Felix, Marthe Keller playing Liesl von Bishop and Helmut Griem playing Erich von Bishop, and it was going to be directed by Gavin Millar.

We did two recces in East Africa and then it collapsed because the production company, Working Title, was acquired by Polygram, who threw out all these interesting British films and said, 'We're going to make American movies.' I then wrote the miniseries version, which was twice as long, for my long-time producing partner, Sue Birtwistle, who I'd worked with on *Dutch Girls*, *Scoop* and *Armadillo*. And I revisited it again for the six-hour version. But it was a hard one to pull off. It's period. It's war. Between 2014 and 2018 was the perfect moment to make it, because of the 100-year anniversary, but even that wasn't sufficient to get it beyond first base. We had a director attached – Michael Samuels, who directed *Any Human Heart* – but we hadn't cast it and we couldn't get anybody interested in it. But it still belongs to me – I never sold the film rights to the book, and I was never paid to write the script – so one of these days it might get made.

One notable change from the novel in the TV versions of the script is the scene where Felix first set eyes on Charis at her wedding. In the novel, he looks down at the ground and initially dislikes her. In the scripts, their eyes meet and she is oddly unsettled by it. Then at the wedding reception there's an edgy moment between them, and as she drives off with Gabriel she's craning back to see Felix and he's left alone deep in thought. In other words, you're emphasizing the forbidden love angle right from the start.

That's a very good instance of film language as opposed to novel language. In the novel, Felix loves Gabriel and is jealous of Charis. She's really nice to him because he's Gabriel's brother and she wants him to like her, but he's cold towards her because she's stealing away the big brother he idolizes. Now how do you film that? How many scenes would it take to make that clear? Quite a lot, I think, because it's a complex chain of emotions. So what's the answer? Their eyes meet across the room and they fancy each other. It's a very simple fix and it gives you an obvious frisson. Similarly, in the novel of *Stars and Bars*, Henderson Dores is having an edgy affair with his ex-wife; but trying to get that backstory into a film is difficult, so I changed it to the boss's daughter, and it suddenly became a very clear-cut relationship. Sometimes the demands of an adaptation will necessarily throw up a more graceful, simpler solution.

Have you made any changes in the course of writing the three adaptations, either to the story or the characters, which you wish you had thought of when you were originally writing the novel?

If I was to look again at the six-hour version I would make Felix's sergeant an African soldier – which, going back to your earlier question, would acknowledge the role that the askaris, as they were called, played in the conflict. In the novel the sergeant is a Scot, but it would be more interesting for him to be African. I don't think I'd change any other aspects of it.

Stars and Bars **is as different from** ***An Ice-Cream War*** **as that novel was from** ***A Good Man in Africa.*** **Again,**

was that simply the answer to the question, 'What do I want to write next?'

I think so. I wanted to write another comic novel after *A Good Man in Africa*; I'd started going to America in the '80s; and I suddenly had this idea of writing an American novel. My first trip was to New York in 1980, and it's like your first encounter with Venice: it does live up to its billing. On our very first day there, Susan and I checked into the Algonquin – for its literary associations – and then we went for a walk, and as we were heading up Park Avenue who should be walking towards us but Woody Allen and Diane Keaton, as if laid on by the New York Tourist Board. New York would come to play a much larger part in our life because Susan ended up working as Editor at Large for *Harper's Bazaar*, but at the time I wrote *Stars and Bars* I'd been there maybe four or five times and I just loved the place. There was a great buzz about Manhattan, and all that stuff about the 'city that never sleeps' and 'so good they named it twice' really hit home for me – although, by then, I'd also realized that Manhattan wasn't a guide to the rest of the country.

I can remember the genesis of the novel vividly. I was on a book tour for *A Good Man in Africa* and I'd been put up in a hotel in lower Park Avenue. Unlike all the other north–south streets in New York, Park Avenue has a dividing line of grass and flower beds, and I was looking out of the hotel window one afternoon when this cycle messenger in spandex pulled up, parked his bike in the central reservation, unzipped his flies and had a piss as the traffic moved to and fro. He made no attempt to shield himself or conceal what he was up to, and I was amazed by his unconcern for potential embarrassment because it was something I personally could never do. I started thinking, 'What would be the most embarrassing thing that could happen to you in New York?' and I thought it would be to wake up naked in a back alley in downtown Manhattan and then think of how to somehow get yourself out of this hellish predicament. And that was the beginning of *Stars and Bars*.

How did the plot evolve from that starting point?

I went through my usual question-and-answer process – who is this person, why is he here? – and the plot evolved from there. Some friends of mine worked for Christie's, and I was buying quite a lot of art at the bottom end of the market, so I knew that world and was very interested in it – and I thought of a middle-class Englishman sent to the New York office of this auction house and being swallowed up and spat out by the monster that is the USA. I still hadn't seen anything of the real America, though, so after my next book tour, for *An Ice-Cream War*, Susan and I flew to Atlanta and rented a car and went on an epic trip through the Deep South. I don't drive but, luckily for me, Susan does, so we drove from Atlanta to North Carolina, then back into Georgia, through Alabama, and ended up in Louisiana in New Orleans. I wanted to go to the secessionist South rather than Texas or Arizona or the West Coast, and it was like going back to the 1930s: you'd pull up in some little town and there'd be a diner and a courthouse and clapboard houses and a Baptist church – with a memorial to the glorious Confederate dead. It took us a couple of weeks and was a great experience, and provided me with exactly the material I needed. I looked around and took notes and listened to local radio stations, and it all went into the novel.

Once again, Evelyn Waugh came to mind – *The Loved One*, this time.

That's a good comparison, although Waugh hated America. He only went there to make money, and had a certain contempt for it. But rather like me seeing that messenger pissing into the bushes on Park Avenue, he went to Forest Lawn Memorial Park in California and just thought, 'I've got a novel here.'

Would you say your novel is somewhat less satirical than his, though?

Well, like all my novels, nobody gets away without some sort of indictment. And the redneck household is, to some degree, parodic. But Loomis Gage, the paterfamilias, has made a fortune and amassed an incredible art collection, so he's no fool. The comedy is more directed against the Englishman, who's utterly adrift. It's my *Scoop*, if you like, which is also about an innocent abroad, and Henderson Dores is more of a William Boot figure than the protagonist of *The Loved One*. Of the comic novels I've written, I think it's the most purely comic. The darker undercurrents aren't as present.

Like Morgan Leafy, Henderson Dores is a basically decent man who struggles to curb his more self-destructive impulses. Is there a sense in which both books are comic morality tales?

Both of the protagonists come up against value systems that challenge them, but in Henderson's case it's a simple matter of survival. He isn't facing a moral dilemma, it's more a sense of meeting an immovable, alien force and either learning from it or finding a way to deal with it. The old adage that Britain and America are two countries divided by a common language is absolutely true and ripe with comic potential. There are moments where Henderson can't understand what members of the Gage family are saying and they take offence at entirely innocent things he says, thereby exacerbating the cultural differences between them. They simply can't communicate. I often take my characters and put them down in a hostile environment to see how they cope, and Henderson is thrown back on his reserves of guile and integrity and just about makes it. But the anarchic forces that he thinks he's escaped are still there on the last page, as he runs down the street pursued by a lunatic with a gun.

In fact, that ending is foreshadowed at the start, where the opening passage of narration concludes with the line, 'Up ahead the lunatic is waiting' – although it's not actually the same lunatic.

That was written after I finished the novel. I wanted the set-up of an Englishman in New York but I realized I needed a different way into it, so I went back and wrote a new opening with this omniscient authorial presence who introduces you to the story. It was going to start in an orthodox way but the new opening is more meta, almost an address by me to the reader – 'Look at Henderson Dores walking up Park Avenue' – then quite quickly it shifts point of view, moving from this first-person injunction into the third person. I spend a long time planning my novels; I don't start until I know what the ending is. But once I have started I write from the beginning to the end; I don't stop and go back and rewrite. So I've sometimes found when I've got to the end that the beginning isn't quite right, and I've gone back and rewritten the opening page or a few pages, or even just the opening paragraph, to give that kind of welcome to the reader and make it more narratively satisfying. I did it again in *Armadillo*, and in *Ordinary Thunderstorms* – as if the novelist and the reader are in cahoots and are about to watch the story unfold – then it stops, there's a break and the orthodox narrative starts.

Why did you feel you needed a different way into the novel?

I've always felt that the first page of a novel is vitally important. You have your reader there for maybe just the duration of that page and you have to make it alluring, you have to make them wonder what's going to happen next, and something about that direct address – 'Hey, look' – is slightly surprising. I may have been influenced by Anthony Burgess; I read his 'Enderby' novels at university – which are amazing, and in some ways his greatest work – and the first one, *Inside Mr Enderby*, starts like that: with the novelist, or an authorial presence, addressing a group of readers. They're time-travelling school kids who come back from the twenty-second century to look at this dishevelled poet in his horrible flat, and they gather in a ghostly way at his bedside and watch him tossing and turning and coughing and farting. It's a brilliantly inventive, postmodern opening to a comic novel. Also, fresh from all those years of English Lit., I was hugely aware of the literary antecedents and literary possibilities of a novel, and perhaps wanted to allude to the fact that I knew more than I was giving away: pay attention, don't just dismiss this as a comic novel, it's more sophisticated than that. Of course, these things are all said with the wisdom of hindsight. At the time I probably just felt that the novel needed a better set-up, and that this initial shift of point of view did the trick.

How many drafts of your novels do you write?

It's hard to say, because I have what I call the period of invention and the period of composition, and the period of invention is longer than the period of composition. Typically it was two years and one year, but as I'm getting older I'm speeding up, so now it's more like one year and nine months. In the period of invention I do all my plotting and planning, and go up blind alleys and come back down again, and fill notebook after notebook as the novel evolves and takes shape. Then I write a draft from start to finish. But that draft is endlessly reworked, because I always write longhand – on the right-hand page, with the left-hand page blank. And if you look at the manuscripts of my novels, you'll sometimes see that the whole left-hand page is filled up with notes and sentences and arrows to the right-hand page and so on. Then I transfer that to the computer and rework it again. So I suppose you could say that there are two distinct drafts and every single word of the novel is written at least twice, but one page might be written nine times and another page might just have a few incisions and erasures.

I was struck by another line in the opening narration, which could apply to several of your leading characters who go to foreign countries to reinvent themselves, including Logan in *Any Human Heart*: 'He wants to change – he wants to be different from what he is. And that, really, is why he is here.'

That's what Henderson is hoping will happen to him in America. He's fed up of being diffident and well behaved and wants to be confident and unafraid. He wants some of that American swagger. But it all goes hideously wrong because he can't connect to the country and the culture. It's true, though, that you can reinvent yourself in America. I know quite a few British people who have gone to live there and never come back. There's something about the US that encourages the feeling you can change yourself for the better. It's somehow stitched into the DNA of the country that anybody can become famous or become a millionaire – or become President. That old cliché of the 'land of possibility' is very alluring, and people who are unhappy with their status quo feel they might flourish there. Film directors in particular feel that Los Angeles is the promised land, and once they've entered paradise they can't leave in case they aren't readmitted. I've been to restaurants in Hollywood with British film directors and it's as if they're minor royalty: 'How are you today, sir? Your usual table, sir? Come this way, sir.' If you buy into all that you're lost, but sure enough they do buy into it and it's often been disastrous for their careers. When you're doing well, the country flatters you. As soon as you're not, you're dropped. There's a line in *Any Human Heart* where somebody screams at Logan, 'You English loser,' and he realizes that's the biggest insult anybody can offer in America. It's like a different planet. I've loved going to America over many years and I've got many close American friends, but, funnily enough, I have no urgent desire to go there at the moment. I feel I've been there and done that. Old Europe seems far more interesting to me now.

There are a lot of larger than life characters in *Stars and Bars*, as there were in *A Good Man in Africa*. How do you avoid slipping into stereotype when telling that kind of story?

There's an element of exaggeration in all comedy; it's almost the defining comic trope. Everything is slightly larger than life, and the disasters are slightly larger than your average disaster. There is a risk of it becoming a bit panto, but you instinctively know where to draw the line. The minute you feel it losing connection with real life is when alarm bells should go off. But then real life is so weird anyway that you can go pretty far. I went to a hotel in Atlanta where there was a huge pond in the atrium and you had to skip across stepping stones to get your room key, so it was no great stretch to go one step further in the novel and make Henderson have to take a canoe to paddle to the reception desk. People are weird, too. I think it was Muriel Spark who said, people are much more odd than you realize, which is a good piece of advice for novelists. The odder you make your characters, the more real they seem – and the fewer stereotypes there are, the better the book will be. The Gage family, however outlandish, had to be more idiosyncratic than just Central Casting rednecks. So that's the short answer: idiosyncrasy is the enemy of stereotype.

You said earlier that you didn't entirely nail the tone of the film version. Was it *too* idiosyncratic?

I don't think so. The film suffers slightly from the same problem that we identified in *A Good Man in Africa*: there's an occasional change in tone from deadpan comedy to broad comedy. If it had been played consistently straight, it would have been even funnier, I now think. It's sort of Southern Gothic, weird and full of grotesques, and the way that you do Southern Gothic is to pretend it's completely normal. Again, I'm as much to blame as anybody. I went out to the set and watched it being shot and was delighted with what I saw, but when everybody's having a good time it's easy for the performances to get slightly overblown, and then it's very hard to bring things back down. Nobody spots it on the day, and it's only when you're back in the cutting room that you realize it feels like a scene from another movie. Daniel Day-Lewis is obviously a highly accomplished actor and can do comedy extremely well, but some of the situations he encounters veer into being broader, and you can destabilize an entire film with a couple of scenes that just feel wrong. When you're shooting it you think, 'This scene is meant to be funny, let's turn up the volume a bit,' which is exactly what you shouldn't do, and there are moments in *Stars and Bars* where you can see that happened. Having said that, I think the film should have done much better than it did, but it fell victim to a regime change at Columbia.

Which, for a brief period, was run by David Puttnam.

That's right. David optioned the book for his company, Enigma, then he got the job running Columbia and *Stars and Bars* suddenly became a Hollywood studio picture instead of a British independent film. It was thanks to David that the film got made. The producer, Sandy Lieberson, was an old partner of his, and David chose the director, Pat O'Connor, who became a very good friend of mine. Pat was coming off the back of *Cal*, which had been in competition at Cannes, so he was a very hot director, and he put together an amazing cast, led by Daniel Day-Lewis and Harry Dean Stanton. Daniel had done *My Beautiful Laundrette* and *A Room with a View* – and *The Unbearable Lightness of Being*, which hadn't been released when we were shooting – but he was still pretty much unknown. People kept saying, 'Why Daniel Day-Lewis?' and Pat stuck to his guns. We had a great experience making the film, and they were very confident of it at

Columbia. Then David left, and his successor, Dawn Steel, dumped all the films Puttnam had on his slate. *Stars and Bars* eventually opened in two cinemas in America, one in New York and one in Los Angeles, and its poster was black and white. Sabotaged deliberately. I mean, who doesn't have a colour poster in this day and age? So it was a very harsh introduction to the brutal reality of Hollywood politics. The film wasn't a success because there was absolutely no interest in making it a success. The same thing happened to me on *Mister Johnson*, which received incredible critical plaudits but was sunk by 20th Century Fox's purblind need to flush what it perceived to be a foreign body out of the studio.

Do you think *Stars and Bars* might have fared better as a British independent film?

I think it would, actually – although, of course, it was set in America, so that might have prevented it being a British film because it would have cost too much. It was a seven- or eight-million-dollar movie, which doesn't sound very much but was quite a lot for the 1980s. It was probably ahead of its time, just before that British comedy revolution of Richard Curtis and *Four Weddings and a Funeral*. Pat and I still talk about the film when we meet up; it bugs us that it wasn't given a fair chance. But we got it made and it's still out there – and the novel has never been out of print, so I've always seen the film as a bonus.

Film-making is at the heart of your next book, *The New Confessions*, which was also the first of your

'whole life' novels, starting in 1899 and ending in 1972. Why did you focus on that particular period as the backdrop for the life of your fictional film director, John James Todd?

John James Todd's life parallels the history of cinema, and I felt that film-making had reached its apotheosis by the 1970s and there wouldn't be anything more of interest to say had we followed him into the 1980s. It just seemed like a good time span – and lifespan. I was able to deal with all the aspects of twentieth-century history that intrigued me, and to draw out the parallels with Jean-Jacques Rousseau's life. Also, I didn't want to bring it up to being exactly contemporary with when I was writing it, in the mid-'80s. I do think setting a novel in the recent past saves it from built-in obsolescence. *Vanity Fair* is set thirty years before Thackeray wrote it. Same with George Eliot and *Middlemarch*. Same with Joyce and *Ulysses*. That passage of time is very helpful for a novelist, because everything is fixed and certain. If you set something in the past you know what happened in the news on a particular day, whereas if you set something today you don't know what will have happened by the time the novel is published and you might be scrambling to make changes. The early '70s was a world I knew well, but it was still fifteen years earlier than when the novel was written. Even when I've written contemporary novels, like *Armadillo* or *Ordinary Thunderstorms*, you won't find anything in them, any cultural or political or historical reference, that dates them to a particular year.

Which came first, the ambition to write something sweeping about the twentieth century, or the idea to attempt a modern version of Jean-Jacques Rousseau's *Confessions*?

It was definitely the Rousseau connection. At Oxford I was writing my doctoral thesis on the philosophical background to Shelley's poetry, and I thought that Wordsworth had pinched a lot of his ideas from Rousseau – unacknowledged, because Rousseau was reviled in England in the early nineteenth century. The *Confessions* was the book everybody objected to and you can hardly believe it was written in the mid-eighteenth century. It's so self-serving and at the same time so honest and unsparing that it has an incredibly modern ring to it. I was reading this, thinking what an extraordinary man Rousseau was, and I thought, 'What would he be if he was alive today?' Light bulb goes on above head: a film director. Ego, power, disaster, paranoia: everything that was in Rousseau's life would be easily replicated in the life of a film director. I'd written a few films by then, but I didn't write the novel until five or six years later, when I finished *Stars and Bars*. I wanted to write about a Rousseauesque figure, and I had this idea of using cinema as a backdrop, then slowly but surely I realized that the form was autobiography. So that's what I wrote, a fake autobiography, and as I took my character through the twentieth century, a lot of stuff that's in Rousseau's *Confessions* found its way into the novel. John James Todd knows incredible highs and incredible lows, he feels persecuted and neglected and betrayed – and he's trying to make a movie of the

Confessions, which is an unfilmable book, for most of his adult life.

So you didn't necessarily know it was going to be such a long novel?

I had no sense when I started that I was going to write a 500-page book; I just wanted to tell this story. But as I wrote it, it became more and more elaborate. And when I finished it, I realized it was far and away my longest novel – and it set me off on a road that I'm still following. It got a very good review in *The Times* from Bernard Levin who said – and I'm paraphrasing – that he was so convinced by the autobiographical form that he found himself leafing through the pages for the photographs. I thought, 'Ah-ha!' It really did show me something that maybe I was only unconsciously aware of: that you could make fiction seem so real that readers began to forget it *was* fiction.

Was Todd modelled on any actual directors?

Abel Gance was the main model, because his *Napoleon* had been restored and re-released before I started writing the book. That was an immense silent movie, and extremely advanced film-making for almost the beginning of the art form. But there are quite a few examples of that type of maverick film-maker. Stanley Kubrick wanted to make a film about Napoleon for ages and never quite got it together. *Chimes at Midnight* was a long-term obsession for Orson Welles. It was tremendous fun researching the novel, and a real education – and I also had my own considerable experiences in the film world, so I was equipped to write about it from a position of some knowledge.

You were similarly equipped to write about Todd's childhood in Edinburgh, and you do seem to be exploring your Scottishness for the first time in this novel.

A lot of Scottish critics don't like to call me a Scottish novelist because I wasn't born in Scotland, so I'm seen as a sort of exile and I'm quite happy with that. I'm a novelist who just happens to be Scottish. But it's definitely part of my life experience, so it inevitably finds its way into my fiction. There's the Scottish character in *An Ice-Cream War* who nobody can understand – I got a bit of a kicking for that from another Scottish writer who said I was making fun of the Scots – but I did begin to investigate it properly in *The New Confessions*. Edinburgh is the city I got to know first as I grew up because our family home was only a half-hour drive away, near Peebles in the Scottish Borders, and I did a lot of research to get the portrait of the place in the early twentieth century absolutely right. Then the story moves on and John James Todd becomes an exile from Scotland, a bit like me – and a bit like Rousseau, who came from Geneva and had a very ambivalent relationship with his native city. It's probably true that all exiled Scots have a complicated relationship with Scotland, but I'm reluctant to analyse it too much and see if there's anything quintessentially Scottish about my world view.

John James Todd is a less flamboyant name than many of your other lead characters: Morgan Leafy and Henderson Dores, for example. Do you give a lot of thought to naming your characters?

Henderson Dores actually came to me by chance. We were in a garage renting a car and the plate-glass frontage of the showroom was being replaced, and the workmen had 'Henderson Doors' on the back of their overalls. I thought, 'What a great name! Just change it to Dores and we're off and running.' But I usually give names a massive amount of thought. Just as human beings are much odder than you think, people's names are much odder than you think. You only need to open a telephone directory and scan a couple of pages to see the strangest names, names I wouldn't dare put in a novel. You don't need to go the full Dickensian route, but naming characters well is very important, I believe, and if the name is slightly out of left field, then that character is almost living and breathing without you having written a word. I've always done that, even for minor characters, so they stand out but not to a degree that they become risible. John Todd is a solid, boring name, but he calls himself John James Todd, which is more interesting and memorable. Another trick is that if you give your central character a Christian name that sounds like a surname, it creates a distance from that character. In *Lucky Jim*, the central character is called Jim Dixon, but Kingsley Amis refers to him as 'Dixon' throughout, which is a shrewd move on his part because if he said, 'Jim got out of bed,' or, 'Jim had a terrible hangover,' it's more intimate and suggests that the author is on the character's side. If you choose a name like Morgan or Henderson, it implies a certain distance between the author and his creation. I've also done that with my female characters: Amory Clay in *Sweet Caress*, Hope Clearwater in *Brazzaville Beach*. Hope is an abstract noun, and I'm sure that makes a subliminal difference to the way you read that novel.

Todd is a much harder character to like than Logan in *Any Human Heart*, your next 'whole life' novel. How important do you think a sympathetic lead is in a novel, particularly a novel of this scale?

Absolutely unimportant. When I'm giving a talk and somebody says, 'I thought Logan Mountstuart was a bit of a shit,' I'll say to the audience, 'Put your hand up if you think you're a completely nice person,' and of course nobody puts their hand up. People do behave badly. People do betray others. People do let themselves down. Everyone is complicated and there are many facets to a character. John James Todd, like Rousseau, is an egomaniac who behaves appallingly badly. And sometimes he also behaves well. He has love in his life, which is important even though it's unrequited. If he'd married Doon Bogan maybe he would have turned into a happier, more contented soul. But he's a living, breathing person and I genuinely don't think any serious novelist should ever ask, 'Will people like this character?' That's for beach-blanket bestsellers. Who do you like in *Macbeth*? Who do you like in *A Streetcar Named Desire*? The reason those things work is because the characters in them are fascinatingly difficult and flawed, and that's true of all great fictions. Reviews of novels that say, 'I didn't love the characters,' make me want to scream. I don't want you to love them, just acknowledge that they're well portrayed. It's a Hollywood idea that's trickled down, that you have to like the central character. You go to a script meeting and an executive will inevitably say, 'Who are we rooting for in this movie?' It's a constant battle, and one we're always destined to lose.

The concept of the 'character arc' has also trickled down: the change that a character goes through in the course of a story, which is a staple of Hollywood screenplay structure. But it seems to me that Todd lives his entire life without changing. He always thinks that everybody is against him and never sees that he can be his own worst enemy.

I think that's true, and that's very like Rousseau: his self-belief is what kept him going. John James Todd is the hero of his own life, and his pigheadedness when he's down on his luck is his greatest armour. When nobody will hire him and he's on his uppers, it's his absolute conviction that the world is wrong and he's right that keeps him getting out of bed in the morning. It's quite admirable, really. But you're right, there's no sense in which he has a Damascene moment and realizes that he has to change his ways. He's driven by this obsession and can't see beyond that. Sometimes the way he behaves leads him down the wrong track. Other times it's a great buttress against the slings and arrows of outrageous fortune. He achieves a kind of serenity on this Mediterranean island – which is actually Ibiza, where we went on holiday four years running; the house he's staying in is the house we rented – but he's still paranoid about his past catching up with him. He's probably one of those people who'd find it impossible to settle.

There's a diary extract at the end of each chapter, written by Todd on Ibiza in 1972. Why did you choose to tell those sections in that way, when the novel as a whole isn't presented in that form?

There's a simple technical reason for that. The problem for you, the novelist, is the passage of time. I've encountered this in the other 'whole life' novels I've written. You can't really write a novel about a whole life because it would be 3,000 pages long, so you have to find a way of eliding certain periods. Fracturing the narrative with these reflections, or interjections, allows you to move things along in an elegant, apparently seamless way, summarizing what you're not going to tell the reader in the main narrative. I've done that in shorter novels, too. I did it in *Brazzaville Beach*. I did it in *Armadillo*. That shift of point of view is quite interesting, and also allows you to see somebody from both the inside and the outside. So there are lots of reasons for doing it. Whether it was something that I knew I was going to do from the outset, or was a solution that presented itself to me in the writing of the book, I can't remember, but I obviously wanted to find a way of getting from one place to another without having to say, 'And then he got the boat at Southampton and fourteen days later . . .' It's what they call 'shoe leather' in the movie business: leave the house, walk down the path, get into the car, start the car, drive off. Sometimes you need that in a narrative, and other times you just want to cut to the next thing.

It's the first of your novels with chapter titles. What do you think those bring to a book?

That's a very good question. The way any novelist indicates the chapters, or divisions, of their novels is interesting. It's a decision I make quite early on, but I don't have a rule of thumb as to why I do it. For a long novel it's quite good to have chapter titles because 'Part Two, Chapter Eleven' becomes too chronologically blurry, whereas if you give a chapter a title it focuses the attention and encapsulates what that chunk of the book is going to be about. In *Trio*, which is a shorter novel, I titled the three parts with single abstract nouns, but within each part the chapters are simply numbered. It's entirely how the mood takes me, I suppose, or whether it's technically useful to me.

It's also your first novel told in the first person. How important is point of view in a novel?

Another very good question. The choice of pronoun that a writer makes is crucial to the way a novel works, and how it works on you – and if you want to unlock or strip down any novel the first question you should ask is, what's the point of view? When you ask yourself that, the mechanics or architecture of the novel will become clear – and it will also be clear when the point of view goes awry, because the structure will be ruptured or won't function. Within that question, there are other minor decisions, also: will you have an omniscient narrator, will you have a restricted point of view, will you change point of view from paragraph to paragraph or have some sort of break or division to show it? My previous novels were all written in the third person restricted point of view, but with *The New Confessions*, because I was aping Rousseau, I felt I had to write it in the first person. The tense is also a key decision. It determines how the novel is written, and has a major effect on how the novel is read. John Updike wrote the 'Rabbit' novels in the historic present, which is a very interesting decision given that they're all set in the past. Hilary Mantel has had an enormous influence on people writing historical novels: every other historical novel I pick up these days is written in the historic present, as if somehow the past is made more alive by being in the present tense. I decided not to write my next novel in the historic present, precisely because it's almost a cliché now. Flashing back in historic present is also tricky, and you can be very easily caught out and get your tenses in a muddle. So it has an immediacy, and works really well in a short story – for example, all my stories about Bethany Mellmoth are written in the historic present – but it works less well at novel length, I feel.

The diary sections are a mixture of past and historic present. The rest of the novel is past tense, except for one scene in Chapter One where the young Todd is sitting in a seaside café with the man he believes is his real father: the narrative slips into the present tense, presumably because in that moment, possibly

for the first time in his life, he experiences a feeling of happiness and belonging.

I'm pretty sure that's exactly what I was doing there. In a movie you might mute the ambient noise and enhance the dialogue to register its significance, and in a third person past tense novel you can slip into the present tense to heighten the moment. What I find hard in novels is when the writer shifts point of view within a paragraph. A casual reader might not notice it, but as a fellow practitioner you think, 'How did you suddenly jump into somebody else's mind?' Ian Fleming does it all the time, jumping from Bond's point of view to M's point of view and back again, and it's very disconcerting. If you're going to do it, you have to be consistent. If you aren't, then I believe you've broken the technical laws of storytelling. I stuck scrupulously to point of view in *An Ice-Cream War* – and even in *Ordinary Thunderstorms*, where there are several voices, every time I change point of view I change chapter, so you only get that character's point of view in that chapter.

How concerned are you with setting up a reason for a first person narrator to be telling the story, assuming that the diary form doesn't do it for you automatically?

I don't worry about it, actually. I don't think you need to set it up. Some people only write first person singular novels, so it's an entirely acceptable device. Thinking about the novel I'm going to write next, I am going to set up the structure because it will help me write the novel in the way I want to and allow me to do things that an orthodox past tense third person novel wouldn't allow me to do. There will be a ghostly editorial presence, a bit like *Any Human Heart*. *Lolita* is written like that as well: it's edited by Vivian Darkbloom, which is an anagram of Vladimir Nabokov. All these things are available to you as a novelist, to guide the reader to the type of reading you want – which is never guaranteed, but at least you can signpost the road ahead.

You return to the world of the boarding school in *The New Confessions*, when Todd is packed off to a Scottish academy reminiscent of Gordonstoun. Were you drawing on your own experiences?

Well, it's set before World War I, when boarding schools were pretty grim places, but even in my era, the 1960s, it was pretty revolting: twenty people in a dormitory, beds eighteen inches apart, no heating to speak of, horrible food – and all the secret pressures of the hothouse society: cruelty and bullying and crudity and racism. W. H. Auden famously described living in a boarding school as like living in a fascist state. It's another of those challenging environments where my characters have to fall back on their own resources in order to survive; John James Todd is forced to find a way of being himself while coexisting with the various powers that control the school. He runs away, doesn't he? That isn't something I contemplated, but it's the ultimate answer if you find yourself in a society you're in revolt against. The story which was broadcast on the radio last week is also about a boy who decides to run away from boarding school because he just can't take it any more – and even though I changed the names I've already had a letter from a housemaster at Gordonstoun claiming to recognize one of the characters. All my portrayals of boarding school are very much based on my own experiences, but in the interests of telling it as it actually was, not making it out to be some soft-focus *Tom Brown's School Days* or *Goodbye, Mr. Chips* fantasy.

Chapter Three is entitled 'L'homme de l'extrême gauche' – the man on the far left-hand side – as Todd becomes the first soldier at the Belgian end of the Western Front in the summer of 1916. It's a striking idea and a slightly comic image, and emblematic of his marginal status throughout his life.

That's true. There was a French expression, *'L'homme de l'extrême droite'*, for where the Western Front trench line ended at the Swiss border, so I thought, 'There must have been somebody at the other end.' In fact, I've seen photographs of the other end of the line, in the dunes on the Belgian coast. It wasn't quite as abrupt as a frontier, but I still thought it was a nice concept – and, again, evidence of my enduring fascination with the First World War. I spent many hours in the Imperial War Museum and watched many hours of newsreel footage, much of which I'd never seen. They keep using the same three or four clips when Remembrance Day comes around, and they're all faked. The footage which isn't faked is quite shocking. There's one film of a burial party, and you can see that the young soldiers bringing the dead back from the battlefield are absolutely trauma-tized, but they never showed that in the cinemas on the home front. There's very little footage of soldiers actually going over the top which wasn't shot at base camp, so I deal with all that in that chapter. It's a dominant impulse in my work – and this may be true of all serious writers of fiction – that I'm trying to arrive at a truth about the human experience through the medium of – in Julian Barnes's phrase – 'beautiful lies'. It's a paradox. You often get as close to whatever the truth may be by inventing the truth as you imagine it, rather than by going out with a camera and a notebook and trying to record it and write it down.

Just as Todd ends up as a solitary POW in *The New Confessions*, so does Logan in *Any Human Heart*. Just as Todd becomes a war reporter, so does Amory in *Sweet Caress*. There seem to be these echoes in your work, particularly the 'whole life' novels, certain themes which you come back to.

You're probably more familiar with these echoes than I am, but I can look back myself and see themes that I return to again and again: betrayal, duplicity, true love, unrequited love, the importance – and absence – of trust. In any novelist's work you'll see the same interests and obsessions explored in constructs or characters that echo other constructs and characters in their other novels. Solitary confinement is a very good place to test a character's resolve, for example. And, in the end, there are only so many themes out there.

Revisiting *The New Confessions*, I found the ending more moving than I remembered from previous reads. Todd's stubbornness had stuck in my mind, but not necessarily the poignancy of his journey – and there is something poignant about following a character from youth to old age, regardless of how sympathetic that character is.

That's the great thing about this sub-genre, the 'whole life' novel, as I call it. When you've read the story of a person's whole life, with its ups and downs, its successes and failures, its boring bits and exciting bits, you come to know that character the way you might know a close friend or a member of your own family – which isn't always the case when you read an orthodox novel, however detailed or well written, because most novels don't give you all that stuff, all that information. I particularly noticed that in the response to *Any Human Heart*: the book seemed to affect young readers and elderly readers in the same way. I was in the Chelsea Arts Club one day and this old gent, who I didn't recognize, tapped me on the shoulder and said, 'I am Logan Mountstuart' – which I thought was a very nice compliment. Yet the first letter I got about the book was from a sixteen-year-old girl in Amsterdam who said, 'Now I know what it's like to be old.' So I think you're right: there's something about these 'whole life' novels which can be very affecting. The last chapter of *The New Confessions* is called 'John James Todd on the Beach', and the last line is that he's 'in tune with the universe'. There is a catharsis in the ending, even though I probably could have written another chapter or two. A few of my novels end on beaches. *Sweet Caress* does as well – and *Brazzaville Beach*, of course.

There's also an ambiguity in the ending: he – and we – can only guess at what the universe still has in store for him.

That's right. What fate is coming down that trail? Is it a goat? Is it a stray dog? Or is it the hitman from LA? I like that kind of ending, because that's how life is: you don't get neat conclusions. I often leave my endings open, in the way that Chekhov does, and let the reader ponder what the future might hold for that character.

Two
Screenplays 1

Good and Bad at Games (1983)
Dutch Girls (1985) – *Scoop* (1987)

Your first two screenplays, *Good and Bad at Games* and *Dutch Girls*, were published together as *School Ties* in 1985. How did you come to write two films about boarding school life back to back?

I was approached in 1982 by Channel 4 and a company called Quintet Films, which comprised the film director Jack Gold, the theatre director Mike Ockrent, the screenwriter Jack Rosenthal, the playwright Willy Russell – and Victor Glynn, the young whizz-kid producer for this very interesting troupe. Channel 4 had this idea for their new Film on Four strand: let's not ask the usual suspects to write films for us, let's ask some novelists instead, and the brief was that it had to be contemporary and it had to be British. I had all these ideas in my head for my putative short story collection set in boarding school, including a revenge story about bullying, so I suggested that as the plot of *Good and Bad at Games* and was commissioned to write it. It went into production very quickly, had its premiere at the London Film Festival in 1983 and was shown several times on Channel 4. Not long after that I was approached by the producer

78

Sue Birtwistle, who asked me to write a comedy about schooldays, so I wrote *Dutch Girls*, based on a hockey tour to Amsterdam which I went on in 1969. And if anybody wants to know what it's like to be at a single sex boarding school, those two films will give them a pretty good idea.

Along with your introduction to the published screenplays, which was reprinted in *Bamboo* under the title 'The Hothouse', in reference to Royston Lambert's non-fiction book.

That's right. That was my attempt to write non-fiction about the boarding school experience and not pull any punches.

It certainly doesn't pull any punches. You wrote that when you and your contemporaries left school you were snobbish, racist, sexist, elitist, intellectually philistine, squirearchical Tories. You were looking back to 1970, yet it explains so much about this country and its leaders today.

I don't recant that, it's absolutely true, certainly of my generation of public school boys. Boris Johnson and David Cameron are a generation behind me, but I bet you they left school with attitudes not a lot different – and their value systems haven't changed that much, no matter what they might say in public. It's stitched deep into the psyche of that class, and this country is steeped in class. Something like 6 per cent of the population is educated at private schools, yet the power and influence of that tiny elite is enormous. When we did the film of *Stars and Bars*,

I wanted Daniel Day-Lewis to see the British Establishment up close, so a friend of mine got us into White's, the gentlemen's club in St James's. It was like time travel: we could have bumped into Evelyn Waugh, who was once a member there, and you heard the kind of English upper-class voices that you imagine baying for blood. I often put clubs in my novels and films because they're such extraordinary places. Going inside one you realize that the British Establishment is still utterly secure; it's just hidden behind these stuccoed facades.

'Baying for blood' is a good description of bullying at its most extreme. What effect did the bullying at your school have on you?

I emerged pretty much unscathed but I know many people who didn't, and I wonder what scars some of those people are still carrying. When I was researching *Good and Bad at Games*, I asked a friend of mine about his schooldays, and he opened up about being hideously bullied at Eton. He said, 'There are still people in London who I want to do serious harm to.' If you looked at him, you saw a handsome, successful, self-confident, upper-middle-class Englishman, but dig a little deeper and you found all this boiling resentment. For the first couple of years of my school career, the house I was in was near anarchy – people stole your property, trashed your room, inflicted corporal punishment on you – and when you're thirteen or fourteen and you're being routinely terrorized by seventeen- and eighteen-year-olds, the survival instinct becomes second nature: feral and tribal. The bullying and mockery were constant, yet there were masters in their flats fifty yards away. Things did eventually get better, and the school began to reform in the late '60s and '70s, but it's the nature of that educational system. All schools have it to a certain extent, but if you're at a day school you go home at night to somewhere you're theoretically welcomed, whereas in a boarding school we were shut up together for three months at a time. The private life of a boarding school is something that teachers and parents really don't have much idea of and it can be very savage, even if publicly everything seems normal and sunny. It's like *Lord of the Flies*: the kids create their own society – and it can be benign or malign, depending on the personalities and the freedoms they have.

The film tackles bullying in various forms: suffering it, inflicting it, witnessing it but not stopping it, and experiencing it without realizing it. To put it another way, it's about the things people will do to fit in and the things which might happen to them if they don't.

Exactly. It's also about how a certain talent can gain you access to an elite, but once that talent isn't needed any more the class system reapplies itself. As an adult, Niles isn't somebody they want to hang out with but he's very good in the cricket team: 'Difficult match on Saturday. Better get Quentin along.' The title gives it away: at these schools, if you're good at games, it's a passport to all sorts of rewards – and if you're bad at games, it's almost like the mark of Cain. It wasn't quite like that at Gordonstoun when I was there; it was the '60s so it was cool not to like playing rugby. But there's no doubt that if you were good at games you became a sort of sporting hero, with a mythic status that only a rock star would achieve in the real world. That's often the problem with schooldays: if they were the best days of your life, what do you do with the rest of it? I knew these paragons at school, and when you meet them ten years later you wonder what on earth you were thinking.

Martyn Stanbridge, who played Niles, was in his late twenties. Anton Lesser, who played Cox, the bullied schoolboy who seeks revenge as an adult, was in his early thirties. Do you think the age of the actors affects the realism of the piece?

It never bothered me, actually. There were guys at school who were eighteen and looked thirty-five. And in film you nearly always cast older people because you can't find enough good actors who are the right age. That was very much an issue when I made *The Trench*. With both *Good and Bad at Games* and *Dutch Girls* we went for actors in their twenties if we could. It wasn't such an issue with *Dutch Girls* because there wasn't the ten-year time shift, but I think Colin Firth and Tim Spall were both in their mid-twenties when the film was made. In *Good and Bad at Games*, Anton was clean-shaven in the early part of the story and bearded in the later part, which was an attempt to address that. It's easier to age an actor up than age them down, in my experience.

Dutch Girls shares some of the themes of fitting in and misplaced loyalty that you explored in *Good and Bad at Games*, particularly in the way that the lead character's best friend betrays him. Did you see that film purely as a comedy, or did you want it to have a serious undertone?

It is primarily a comedy, but it's also an attempt – again, with my anthropological zeal – to show what it's like to be in that intense, testosterone-rich, adolescent world. There's a thesis I advance in *Trio* that the big emotions in your life – love, hate, betrayal, depression – are at their most acute in your adolescence. You feel them more intensely because you're experiencing them for the first time, and they become the template for your understanding of yourself as you grow older. If I'm writing and I want to imagine what it's like to feel abjectly embarrassed, I don't think of something that happened to me last year, I think of something that happened to me when I was seventeen, because I can recall those emotions so vividly. In *Trio*, Talbot Kidd rejects this theory because he's been suppressing his sexuality all his life and it's only as a mature man that he feels liberated. But I think it holds true, and I wanted to investigate the nature of that in *Dutch Girls*.

So how autobiographical is your second film?

Some scenes are absolutely autobiographical, from our trip to the ferry at Harwich, with everybody crammed into the train and smoking away, to our coach inadvertently leading us through the red-light district of Amsterdam – which was an extraordinary experience for a bunch of seventeen- and eighteen-year-olds. I just developed that and exaggerated it for the film; nobody bunked off to try and buy themselves a prostitute in real life. We had a reunion in 2009, and of the thirteen boys in the team we managed to get eleven. Even the coach came, who was in his late eighties. There was a screening of the film, then we all went for dinner, and it was uncanny: I hadn't seen some of these people for forty years and it was as if I'd seen them last week. That's another thing about the boarding school experience: you have this weird shared history, like being an ex-con or an ex-soldier. So we were reminiscing about what was true and what was invented, and the goal-keeper, who came all the way from Australia for this weekend, was very offended at my portrait of him. His character wasn't really exaggerated – I was billeted with him on the tour, in the village where we were staying – but I could tell he was upset. He became quite proud of it because people would say, 'Timothy Spall played you in that movie,' but on the night it was pretty tense. Don't have reunions with your school mates, is the moral there.

At least, not if you've written about them.

Exactly. But it was very interesting to see how the raw experience that I had was transformed into the film that was made. What was also interesting was that once we got into something approximating real life, the cool guys at school were suddenly diminished. The schools we were playing were co-educational, so we met lots of Dutch girls; and they were very curious about these English boys and moved in on us, in the way teenagers do; and, of course, they were much more sophisticated than we were. I was one of the youngest boys on the tour, and I remember having the veils stripped from my eyes as the older boys were exposed as having serious feet of clay. You saw that they weren't being hit on, and saw through their pathetic attempts to explain it away. And that's what happened with Colin Firth's character – what's he called?

Neil Truelove – recycled from your unpublished novel *Truelove at 29*.

That's right. It was also the actual name of a boy I knew. Anyway, Neil Truelove experiences a similar Damascene moment when he realizes that his so-called best friend is actually shallow and envious and resentful. And that's something I wanted to expose: that people aren't necessarily what they seem to be, and you shouldn't put your faith in heroic figures because they're likely to let you down.

***Dutch Girls* also deals with sexual conditioning: how these boys view girls, how the girls in turn see the boys, the difficulty of striving for something more than just lust at that age and in that world. I was reminded of a line in your boarding school story, 'Hardly Ever' – 'He felt that his sexual nature, whatever it might be, was irretrievably corrupted' – and I wondered whether that conditioning had any impact on your early writing, particularly of female characters?**

It's certainly true that there was what you might call a sexualization of our adolescent minds at school. In my introduction to the screenplays I talk about the vile abuse that was directed at the young women who worked in the kitchens. God knows what it was like for these sixteen- or seventeen-year-old girls as 400 horny boys filed through for lunch. Did they think, 'You disgusting, privileged little wankers'? I suspect the answer is yes. It was unremittingly crude, but it doesn't take long in the outside world to realize that these attitudes just won't do. When I spent that January to August of 1971 in Nice, the female friends I made were all French, Swedish, German – and, again, were much more sophisticated than I was. If you say something that you think is unremarkable and everybody in your peer group swivels their heads and looks at you in astonishment, you learn fast that this is obviously *not* the thing to say. The early '70s was also a very radical time – the Vietnam War was going on, there were demonstrations and strikes at the university – and after ten years of indoctrination as one of these ghastly, unreflecting, squirearchical Tories, I swiftly became extremely left wing, because the radical ideas in the zeitgeist were more congenial to me once I was removed from the boarding school hothouse. Glasgow also had a radical student body, much more left wing than Oxford, which seemed a sleepy, complacent place in comparison. So I don't detect anything in my early writing that would have conformed to the kind of person I was at school. Maybe I'm not the person to make that judgement, but I think I'd done a massive U-turn and was on what I perceived to be the right road, having been travelling down the wrong road. I re-educated myself by spending that time in France and becoming a European – and realizing that all those attributes I listed in that introduction had to go.

Then you must be thrilled with the direction in which Brexit has taken Britain.

Brexit is deeply dispiriting and thoroughly mendacious, and everything that could possibly be wrong about it, is wrong. But my friends in America can't understand how Donald Trump ever got elected President, so shit happens. I try to look at it through the long lens of history: maybe in thirty years' time we'll be back in the EU and this act of self-harm will be seen as an aberration. It's all to do with myth and chauvinism and misplaced patriotism, a post-imperial clinging on to a time when half the globe was part of the British Empire. There are also class elements in it. I've been researching the Battle of Arnhem for this film I've been asked to write, and it's up there with Waterloo and Trafalgar as one of the great battles in our history, despite being a total disaster. There was a lot of heroism, but it was a completely botched military campaign, and tens of thousands of soldiers and civilians died because nobody would say 'boo' to these posh generals. We seem to have this capacity to take a shameful defeat – like Arnhem, or Dunkirk – and see it as our finest hour. I don't know of any other European country that does it.

You'd never written a screenplay before _Good and Bad at Games_. How did you set about teaching yourself this new form?

I did write a couple of trial screenplays, or trial scenes from screenplays, to acquaint myself with the grammar and vocabulary of this new language I was employing. My way of teaching myself was to watch a film I liked with the screenplay on my lap – which was quite hard to do in those days, because there weren't that many published screenplays. Also, the Quintet people were hugely experienced film-makers, and the notes they gave me were very useful. I quickly realized that I couldn't do in a film what I could do in a novel, and both films benefit from being written directly for the medium.

You included a fair number of camera directions in the scripts, which screenwriters are generally advised to avoid these days.

I completely disregard that rule. I stick in camera directions all over the place, on the principle that if it isn't in the script, it won't be on the screen. If you write, 'Huge close-up on Truelove's face. Camera dollies back to reveal that he's walking along a corridor,' then ninety-nine times out of a hundred that's exactly how it will be shot. But if you just write, 'Truelove walks along the corridor,' then it's up to the director and the cinematographer to figure out how they want to shoot it – and it might not be the way I imagined it. If you think being close on the face of the person being spoken to delivers more dramatic heft then you should put it in, otherwise you might find in the cut that you're close on the person speaking when actually the reaction was more important than the words. Another rule is not to tell the actors what they're feeling.

You're not meant to write, 'Truelove (with heavy irony)'. But I disregard that as well because I think you need that stuff, not just for the actors but for everybody else reading the script, to give them a sense of the film in your head. I also put in quite detailed analysis of what's going through the characters' heads, which you won't be able to see on screen but avoids interpretations that are against the spirit of piece. It's all a pre-emptive strike for the finished film.

In your novels you give very detailed physical descriptions of your characters – much more detail than you include in your screenplays.

When I was starting out as a novelist I described more than I do now, because I realized that there are ways other than simple description of conveying the look or the nature of a character. But I do it because I want the reader to see in their mind's eye everything about that moment: the people, the setting, the weather, whatever's important. If you're Samuel Beckett or Albert Camus, maybe you don't need to do that. If you're writing a realistic, richly textured novel, I think you do. With screenplays, your writing style has to be punchier and pithier. I've never counted the number of words in the average screenplay but it's probably about 10,000, whereas the average novel is 100,000. You only have a few words, so you deal in broad strokes. You visualize the scene as you see it in your mind, you indicate the type of person you want that character to be, but a precise physical description is redundant because that will depend on the casting. Even specifying a character's age is a bad idea sometimes: it's better to put 'thirties' than 'thirty-three', because they may cast somebody older or younger. In fact, in screenplays these days, they don't like you to describe a person's looks, particularly in American scripts. I was always taught that the lead female role had to be written as 'beautiful' and the lead male role had to be written as 'handsome', because the actor or actress reading the script would think, 'Yes, that's me, exactly.' It was a pragmatic thing, a lure for actors, but now it's frowned upon. 'An incredibly beautiful woman with long blonde hair walks into the room' seems rather sexist, so now you just say, 'A woman walks confidently into the room'. That's part of the changing times, and you realize that the male gaze often determined how you approached writing female parts.

Perhaps film itself is a medium of broad strokes.

It is a much simpler art form, and I don't mean that in a derogatory way. As a film-maker, the tools you have at your disposal are in some ways very sophisticated. Something like *mise en scène*: in a novel it might take you five pages to describe a house; in a movie or on television you can do it in seconds. My education in film has been almost as long as my education in writing novels, and as I move from one to the other and back again, I'm more and more aware of the fact that film is photography, that you're always on the outside looking in. And if that's the dominant feature of film, then you should always play to that strength. If you attempt to subvert it, you're swimming against the current. Understanding the nature of the art form you're working in seems to me to be absolutely crucial, and increasingly I think the best films are made from original screenplays, they're not adaptations; you're writing something that's intended to be filmed, not taking something that already exists and trying to reshape it for this medium, like banging a square peg into a round hole.

Good and Bad at Games and _Dutch Girls_ marked your introduction to working with directors. Were there any differences between your creative partnerships with Jack Gold and Giles Foster?

Jack was a very nice man and very happy to have me hanging around, so I went to the set of _Good and Bad at Games_ almost every day. That was really my introduction to filmmaking; I saw the film being made from start to finish. I got on equally well with Giles, and was present for a lot of _Dutch Girls_. The main difference was budget. We had a very small budget for _Good and Bad at Games_; it was shot in something like sixteen days and every penny was counted. Whereas _Dutch Girls_ was a London Weekend Television movie and had quite a lavish budget; we recreated the red-light district of Amsterdam in Brick Lane at some expense. We had a bigger cast as well, and a brilliant cinematographer: Roger Pratt, who also photographed _Scoop_. There's no doubt that _Dutch Girls_ is better lit, probably purely because of budget. Wolfgang Suschitzky was the cinematographer on _Good and Bad at Games_, and he's a legend, but he didn't have as many lights to work with. So it was a very interesting learning curve.

Did you learn anything in writing those scripts which you brought to bear when adapting *Scoop*?

It's hard to say. I'd probably written other, unproduced screenplays by the time I wrote *Scoop*, so I had more screenwriting experience. I think in my early films I just wrote blithely away. Latterly I have become more conscious of how I write scripts. I've learned a lot from reading other people's screenplays, and often what you learn is that you can break all the rules – which is quite reassuring.

We talked about the influence of Evelyn Waugh on your first three novels, and you've adapted two of his works for television: *Scoop* and *Sword of Honour*. What is it about Waugh that strikes a chord?

Fundamentally, it's his sense of humour. His more serious novels have their moments, but I find them imperfect because he's striving to be serious, to put it very simply. For me, the comedies that he wrote at the beginning of his career – *Decline and Fall*, *Vile Bodies*, *Scoop* – are his greatest work, and I remember finding them fantastically bracing when I first read them. What made his comedy so striking, and so enduring, is its utter ruthlessness. *Scoop* has a sunnier dimension to it, but its comic potential is pushed to the absolute wince-making limit, and that's something I savour. I've maybe got a dark streak in my comedy, but he probably saw the world like that. He got it from other writers, too: he got it from Chekhov and he got it from William Gerhardie, an English writer who's sadly little-known now. Waugh actually said to him, 'I have talent, but you have genius,' and he stole a lot from Gerhardie, particularly in *Vile Bodies* and *Scoop*. But if you read other comic novels of the time, nobody pushes the envelope as far as Waugh. He's also a very economical writer – his style and vocabulary are self-consciously unmodern – and his dialogue is usually superb. So I've taken lots of things from him in a writerly sense, but I also find him fascinating as a case study, because he seems to me typical of a certain type of English writer – maybe a certain type of English man. I think he was consumed with self-loathing and constructed a persona of utter unconcern for the opinions of others, much like Ian Fleming. They didn't like each other, but they were very similar in that way, and that character trait informs *Scoop*. In some ways it's a classic comedy, in that the ordered world of William Boot is massively disrupted then order returns at the end, which is a shape you find in Shakespeare's comedies, like *Love's Labour's Lost*. The novel follows the demands of that form, but within it there's a lot of this unsparing black humour, and for me that's what was really original about him.

If you think *Scoop* is one of his greatest novels, were you daunted by the prospect of adapting it?

I *was* slightly daunted by it. No novel is perfect but it's as close to a perfect comic novel as you can get, and I think it has the funniest chapter in all of English literature, when Mr Salter goes to Boot Magna to try and persuade William to return to the newspaper. It's also a novel that people know less well than they think they do. They remember the Fleet Street stuff with Lord Copper, but they forget the stuff in Africa with Boot as a foreign correspondent, and the strange journalists he meets and the love affair he has. The novel could be subtitled, 'How William Boot Loses His Virginity'. But I was trying to make a good film, not a faithful reproduction of the book, and I was really pleased with the adaptation. I still am. We had an amazing cast and got a massive audience, but boy did we get slagged off in the reviews. The TV critics were sharpening their pens, waiting to take us down a peg or three. One of the things I was taken to task for was that I left out the classic joke about William Boot's sister changing 'great-crested grebe' to 'badger' in his nature column. I didn't put that in because the only way it would work on film was if you read it. You'd have to see him write 'great-crested grebe', then you'd have to see his sister cross it out and write 'badger', and that seemed to me to fly in the face of what film was all about. I was sufficiently au fait with screenwriting by then to realize that there are things you can do in a novel that you can't do in a film, and reaching for the techniques of fiction in order to reproduce a literary joke on screen was obviously going to be counterproductive.

There's another joke in the novel which you do reproduce in the film: Mr Salter, the foreign editor, often says, 'Up to a point, Lord Copper,' when he means, 'No.' But the nuances of saying one thing and meaning another are harder to land on screen than on the page.

You're absolutely right. In the novel you can describe Salter's panic, but it's not as nuanced in the film. Denholm Elliott acts 'sweaty' better than anybody, so you tick that box, but it doesn't resonate in the same way as the novel. At the same time, Donald Pleasence is a wonderful Lord Copper. He's creepy and grotesque, and the director, Gavin Millar, shot him with some sort of fisheye lens to make him seem even more surreal. So that's a strength of the film. Boot Magna is brilliantly recreated on screen because that's *mise en scène*, whereas one of the most famous jokes in the novel is effectively unfilmable. They're two distinct art forms, and they both have their own strengths and weaknesses. Many more weaknesses, in the case of film.

On the other hand, some of Waugh's techniques lend themselves to adaptation: the sections of uninterrupted dialogue, for example.

He's a master of that kind of dialogue, and in some cases I just lifted it straight from the page and put it in the screenplay. As a young man he was a great cinema-goer and actually made a silent film himself, so he was thoroughly familiar with film and maybe that was where his terse dialogue came from.

We talked about tone in relation to your adaptations of *A Good Man in Africa* and *Stars and Bars*. Did you need to tone down *Scoop* in translating Waugh's world to a more recognizably real world?

My critique of *A Good Man in Africa* and *Stars and Bars* doesn't apply to *Scoop*, because I think we got the tone

95

right and sustained it – and that tone is very faithful to Waugh's. The opening scene, when the war correspondent William Boot goes to visit Mrs Stitch, is obviously high comedy, and the film stays in that heightened world of upper-class eccentricity throughout. It's all slightly preposterous, but it's never deadpan. It has a unifying comic voice, and you're confident in the world you're inhabiting.

The novel is rich in incident but relatively short on plot. Were you concerned about sustaining the story in dramatized form?

I don't think so, because the boiling-down aspect of adaptation meant that even the sparseness of the plot of *Scoop* was more than enough to fill the length of the film. There was always enough stuff going on to move the scenes forward, so I never had a problem with narrative sag.

Similarly, William Boot doesn't have a character arc as such: he goes through all these experiences, only to end up doing exactly what he did before, which is quite unusual for a dramatic character.

Again, it's the classic comic form: order, disorder, order. At the end, things are back to square one and all's well with the world. It's not about emerging as a different person. He's an innocent, William Boot, a kind of Candide character. He's gone out and had all these experiences, and he realizes that what he wants is to be back at Boot Magna writing his nature column. He's seen the world and said, 'Not for me, thank you.' So you're right: the things that happen to him barely seem to have an effect on him.

What should we make of the racial attitudes in the novel? And what account did you take of them in your adaptation?

Well, there's no doubt that it's racist, but you can't avoid the fact that those were the attitudes that pertained at the time. I think you have to tread very carefully when you're adapting anything fifty-odd years after it was written: things that were considered irrelevant at the time are often deeply offensive to modern sensibilities – Ian Fleming again being a classic example. The early Bond novels are beyond offensive to virtually everybody you can think of, but times change, attitudes change. You just have to be sensible about the context. A book like *Black Mischief* would be much harder to adapt than *Scoop. Black Mischief* is almost parodically racist, whereas in *Scoop* you're seeing everything through the eyes of this innocent, and he's not sneering or condemning, he's just experiencing.

How closely did the final film match what you saw in your head when you read the novel and wrote the script?

Pretty closely. There was one scene I wrote where we see Boot Magna nestling in its valley in deepest, darkest England, and for some reason they never got that shot, so we don't get as clear a sense of the remoteness of the place as we should. But it's such a fickle business, making a film: a lot of it is wing-and-a-prayer, on-the-day stuff. Maybe it was pissing with rain that day, or they couldn't get the trucks up the hill to shoot the long shot. Whatever the reason, it was probably purely pragmatic. But broadly speaking the film turned out exactly as I wanted, and I thought the cast was superb. Michael Maloney was great as William Boot. It was my second film with Sue Birtwistle as producer, so she and I were a tight-knit team, and Gavin Millar was also delightful. I didn't go out to Morocco with them, but I saw them a lot while they were filming in this country. The Jacobean house we used for Boot Magna is in a place called Chastleton, between Oxford and Moreton-in-Marsh, and I later used that as the model for the village in *Restless*. Nothing is wasted, you see.

Three

Fiction 2

Brazzaville Beach (1990) – *The Blue Afternoon* (1993)
The Destiny of Nathalie 'X' (1995) – *Armadillo* (1998)

Brazzaville Beach starts where The New Confessions ends: with a narrator on a beach looking back at their life. Was that a conscious echo, or just a coincidence?

I'd like to say it's a thematic link, but I think it's just a coincidence. It's another example of me rewriting the opening of a novel once I'd finished it. I was looking for a really good title, and for various reasons I couldn't think of one. For ages I was going to call it *The Chimpanzee War*, but then I thought that would be off-putting. I often find the right title at the last minute, and that's what happened with *Brazzaville Beach*. The beach features in the novel anyway, so I went back and wrote that preface chapter to tie it in – although it's not actually in Brazzaville.

In fact, you don't specify where it's set.

No, I deliberately kept it vague. I don't even specify which ocean it's on, the Atlantic or the Indian, so it could be Guinea-Bissau or Angola or Mozambique. I did a lot of research into those Portuguese colonies and their civil wars, but I decided it would be more interesting not to root it in any particular place. The minute you root something in a place or time, you're constrained by dates and facts. I'd just finished the book when Richard Attenborough asked me to write the script for *Chaplin*, and one day on the set the cinematographer, Sven Nykvist, said to me, 'I was born in Brazzaville and there's a beach there, on the Congo River. Was that what inspired you?' And I had to say, 'No, I'm afraid it came out of the blue.'

Did the idea for the novel also come out of the blue?

I can absolutely trace how that novel came about. One of my philosophy lecturers at Glasgow University was Stephen Clark, whose speciality was animal rights. He subsequently wrote a book called *The Moral Status of Animals*, and because I'd been taught by him I read this, and in it he referred to an event known as the Chimpanzee War of Gombe. I thought, 'That's a great title,' so I looked up the footnotes and the bibliography and read about what had happened. One of the first observational primatologists, Jane Goodall, had set up this camp in the Gombe Stream National Park in Tanzania where she familiarized herself with a chimpanzee tribe: she named them, she could identify them, she would walk around with them. The knowledge about chimpanzee society that was coming out of Gombe was extraordinary, a revolutionary kind of science; then suddenly this tribe split into two, and one side began systematically eradicating the other in a very human genocide. And this was what

Stephen Clark was referring to in his book: that chimps, whose society we always thought was altruistic and prelapsarian, turned out to be as vicious and malicious as humans – which isn't surprising given that there's only a 1½ per cent difference between their DNA and ours. The metaphor was so rich that I thought, 'This is the background to a novel,' and that led me into researching primatology. I used to go to London Zoo and spend hours in front of the chimp house watching them interact, which was completely fascinating. I also realized as I did my research that the four leading primatologists in the world were women – Jane Goodall; Dian Fossey, who studied gorillas; Shirley Strum, who studied baboons; and Birutė Galdikas, who studied orangutans – and that was when the light bulb went on above my head that I should write this book from the point of view of a woman. I'd flexed those muscles before, in 'Bat-Girl!' and sections of *An Ice-Cream War*, but *Brazzaville Beach* was my first novel-length attempt to write from one woman's point of view. I covered my tracks a bit by shifting pronouns from 'I' to 'she' so I could get a multifaceted view of Hope Clearwater, but it was the thing I was most worried about. Susan read it and said, 'Relax, she's a real person,' but you never know what the critics will say, so I was more apprehensive than usual when the book came out. In fact, it got very warmly reviewed – particularly by women, who complimented me on creating a living, breathing character, not a male version of what a woman is like – and after *Any Human Heart* it's probably the one book of mine that stays with people. I still get letters about it, even though it's thirty years old.

Did you draw on your research into Jane Goodall and the female primatologists when creating Hope or was she entirely a creation of your imagination?

She's entirely a creation. There's no doubt that the set-up at Gombe was a model for the Grosso Arvore camp in the book – and I have been in contact with Jane Goodall and support her foundation – but there's no sense that Hope is anything like Jane Goodall.

Regardless of whether *The Chimpanzee War* would have been an off-putting title, it would have been a misleading one, given that the book covers a lot more ground than that.

Well, the other thing I was really interested in at the time was pure mathematics. I barely scraped through O-Level maths at school, but because I did philosophy at university the philosophical ideas behind things like Heisenberg's Uncertainty Principle and Gödel's Incompleteness Theorem were very intriguing to me. Hope's marriage to this crazed mathematician is what drives her to go to Africa and explains the kind of person she is out there, because she's been hardened by the trauma of what happened to her husband. Her work on hedgerow dating is also part of her story, and another thing I got obscurely interested in. My academic experience went into the mix as well, because there's all the stuff about internecine academic rivalry. I also took a lot of my Biafran War experience and put it into *Brazzaville Beach*; I really liked the scenes at the end when she's captured by the freedom fighter, Amilcar, and his Atomique Boom volleyball team. So there is a lot more in that book than the Gombe Chimpanzee War. From that original catalyst it became something much wider.

Todd's best friend in *The New Confessions* is also a mathematician, and the last chapter of that book references both Heisenberg and Gödel, so your interest in that area clearly lasted several years.

That's right. I always have this image of the fiction writer as a blue whale with mouth agape, ingesting vast amounts of krill: the krill of everyday life goes into your creative stomach, then emerges as a novel later on. But every novel is different, and the ideas that come together to fire it up are often only recognizable with hindsight.

The African sections are written in the first person. The English sections are written in the third person. And separating them are italicized sections, each with its own title, alternating between first and third person. Or, as Hope explains in the prologue, 'I am Hope Clearwater. She is Hope Clearwater. Everything is me, really.' How did you arrive at that structure?

I wanted to have Hope look back on her married life but do it in the third person, so you could see her from the outside as well as from the inside, and the italicized sections allow that elision between her past life and her present life. That was the idea behind it. But in one or two cases the voice in the italicized sections is not necessarily Hope's; they sometimes work as an editorial commentary on what comes before or after. So that's another level to it. It's not one of my longer novels, but it punches above its weight to a certain extent, and I think that's to do with the structure. I've always been very aware of how structure can help a novelist tell a story, and I've learned that a fractured structure can help you get more into a novel than an orthodox chronological narrative.

Is that why the book doesn't have chapters as such? Because on top of all that they would be too much?

The italicized sections are titled, so it would be easy to locate a specific bit of Hope narrative that way, if required. I was also aware of a slight literary-modernistic tendency operating in me; there was first person, third person and the italicized sections. Structurally, I was 'pushing the envelope', as they say in Hollywood. So I felt chapter numbers might make it look a bit archaic – or, as you say, be too much.

Hope also says in the prologue, 'This is where I have washed up, you might say, deposited myself like a spar of driftwood.' There's a sense that all these parts of her narrative have washed up alongside her.

That was in my mind, yes. A kind of reflection: what does my life add up to, where did I go wrong, what can I see now that I missed then? She's shoring these fragments against her ruins, as it were.

Coincidence or not, I'm intrigued by this recurring image of a solitary figure on a remote beach. Hope ends up on the edge of Africa, just as Todd ends

up – twice – on the edge of Europe. You don't simply test these characters, you strand them, emotionally and geographically. Do you think that's fair?

I think that's very fair. And I wonder if it's to do with my own odd upbringing, that I didn't have a normal childhood or adolescence because I was living in Ghana and latterly in Nigeria, a country that was tearing itself apart in a civil war. A lot of my early memories are associated with beach life on the edge of Africa. In Ghana we were only about half an hour from the sea, and at the weekend we would go down to this amazing place called Labadi Beach which was very much like Brazzaville Beach: no bars, no hotels, just a few fishing villages. And in Nigeria we used to go to this place in Lagos called Tarkwa Bay, where we did live in beach houses and I would fish and sail. As you know, I'm reluctant to overanalyse why I do certain things – ignorance is an asset for a novelist, because it allows you to take risks and make a fool of yourself – but maybe my early life in Africa has made this image resonate with me. It's the same with *Sweet Caress*: you could say that ends up on a beach as well.

What would you say is the overarching theme of *Brazzaville Beach*?

It goes back to the original metaphor: that our intellect and consciousness have allowed us to evolve, but it's only rules and morals that prevent us from being as vicious as the chimps – and you don't need to look very far in human history to see how that viciousness keeps rising to the surface. So that was the big theme: human viciousness, and how we conquer or subdue it so we can live with each other.

Whether in a group or a couple.

Exactly. Looking back, Hope feels guilty about her husband's suicide and thinks she didn't do enough for him, so when, at the end of the book, she sees two of the chimps about to attack an injured one, she shoots them and kills them. It's the ultimate scientific no-go area – it would be shocking for a primatologist to interfere in that way – but it's a sign of how her thinking has moved on. Because of what she's learned about her moral deficiencies she does what she thinks is the right thing, regardless; she's seen the hideous violence that these chimps can inflict on each other and she's not prepared to let it happen again – and that's a very human response, as opposed to a chimpanzee response. That was the overarching point I was trying to make: that we can control the worst elements in ourselves, and on the whole – with notable historical exceptions – we do a fairly good job of it.

The final line of the novel is from Socrates: 'The unexamined life is not worth living.' You also used that quote as the epigraph. How important are epigraphs to you?

Epigraphs are very important to me, and that was a perfect one for this novel given that, as we were saying, Hope is examining her life on Brazzaville Beach. All my novels have epigraphs, and sometimes my short stories as well, because what the epigraph does – or should do – is give the reader a signpost or clue as to how the novel should be read or what conclusion should be drawn from it. The epigraph might not make any sense to the reader when they turn that opening page, but when they finish the novel they can turn back to it and go, 'Ah-ha!' I'm constantly noting potential epigraphs. I already have a brilliant one for my next novel. Sometimes it comes quite late, but often it arrives before you've even written Page 1, and that means the novel is taking shape in your head and you know what you'll achieve by using that quote. It's like a stamp of approval on the whole enterprise.

You adapted the book into a feature film script. Has that ever come close to being made?

The novel was published in Spain a year or two after it was published in Britain, and I got a call from Pedro Almodóvar saying he was very interested in making a film based on it. I was a great fan and he's a delightful man, but I somehow thought that *Brazzaville Beach* and Pedro Almodóvar didn't really go together. He was obsessed with Africa and interested in the idea of two strong women, Hope and the wife of the project leader, isolated in the jungle studying chimpanzees and vying against each other. I had a meeting with him in London where he said to me, 'This is going to be my first English-language film,' then he went off to Cannes and I never heard from him again – and, interestingly, he still hasn't made an English-language film. Then a man called Coco Brown, who was the son of a Hollywood producer and had dabbled in the film world, wanted to option the book and make a movie from it. I remember him saying, 'Will, I want to give you some money,' and I said, 'No, Coco, we're friends, I'll write it for you for nothing.' So I wrote the script on spec, we polished it a bit, he took it out to a few people – and then he fell ill and died. And it never got any further than that. But it would be easier to make now, technically speaking. Back in the '90s you were talking about animatronics and children in chimp outfits to try and replicate the chimpanzee violence, because if it didn't look realistic it would have been fatal for the film. Now you could do it fantastically well: you wouldn't know what was real and what was fake.

The screenplay is set entirely in Africa, the English sections have completely gone, and Hope's former husband is only referred to twice. Was that an immediate choice?

It was my first decision. You couldn't do both halves of Hope's story, because you'd take all the air out of the African sections when you went back to England. At one stage the BBC seemed interested in doing it as a TV mini-series, and if you had six hours you might cross-cut between Africa and England or flash back several years to Hope's marriage, because long form television gives you some of the freedom that the novel gives you to breathe and explore and not be so narratively on-point. But for a two-hour movie it seemed to me you had to take the African element and make that the story, and Coco Brown agreed with me. It was about the movie *in* the book, not the movie *of* the book.

The Blue Afternoon is another novel made up of disparate elements: surgery, aviation, architecture, colonial war, serial murder and a love story. How exactly did those things come together?

It started as an interest in surgery. According to family legend my father was advised to become a surgeon because he was very good with a scalpel, but he didn't, so maybe my interest in the profession came from that. I was particularly interested in the era when surgery stopped killing people, which happened around the turn of the century with antisepsis and then anaesthesia, because up to that point surgeons were basically butchers. Having started with this idea of wanting to write a novel about a surgeon, I then asked myself where that surgeon would be living and practising. Initially, I thought I'd set it in the Boer War, around 1902, but then I thought, 'I mustn't go to Africa again.' I remembered that when I'd interviewed Gore Vidal for the *Isis*, the Oxford University magazine, in the mid-'70s, we'd had a discussion about the American war against Filipino insurgents – the Philippine–American War of 1899–1902 – which he said was like Vietnam but sixty years earlier: a big occupying army fighting a small guerrilla force, imbalanced and brutal. Once I started doing my research I realized this was another of these gifts from history that you get, as a novelist, from time to time, like *An Ice-Cream War*. There had been Filipino novels written about it, but nobody writing in English had ventured into this area. All wars throughout history have their horror stories, so it was probably timeless in that sense, but it was also a very modern, racist war. The

American soldiers had Stetsons and carbines, they were hardened killers from the wars against the Plains Indians, and they massacred entire villages without thinking twice about it. So as I answered my questions about era and locale, the novel built into this complex story of colonial war, and all these other things became part of the narrative: the love story between Salvador and Delphine, the serial murders of American soldiers – and early powered flight, which was another of my interests at the time. And that's how it came together.

Did you need to do a lot of research?

It's the only time I've hired a researcher. This was pre-Google and most of the information I needed was in America, so I hired an American researcher who got me all the books and documents – and a street map of Manila in 1902, which is now framed and hanging in my house. I also found lots of photographs and built up a very authentic picture of what the city was like and how society operated, with its hierarchical structure of Americans, Spaniards and Filipinos. The Filipinos were so pleased to be liberated from Spanish rule by the Americans, then the Americans turned around and replaced the colonialists who had been dominating them with another set – themselves – and the Philippines remained an American colony until World War II. So I steeped myself in the period, but I never set foot in the Philippines. I did think of going there, to the extent of booking a flight, but then a volcano erupted near Manila and all flights were cancelled, and I thought, 'This is a sign that you don't need to go: just send your imagination.' Apparently, Manila was something like the second-most bombed city of World War II, and the old city barely exists, so if I'd gone there I wouldn't have found anything anyway. But after the book came out, I got a letter from the head of the advertising company J. Walter Thompson in Manila, and this letter said, 'Dear Mr Boyd, I loved your novel *The Blue Afternoon*, and I'd like you to know that we give a copy to every new client to explain something of the fraught history of our beautiful country. May I ask, when did you live in Manila?' There's no higher compliment than that.

The first sixty and final forty pages of the novel aren't set in turn-of-the-century Manila, they're set in Los Angeles and Lisbon in 1936. Why did you choose to frame the story with those two bookends?

I wanted the novel to be narrated by Salvador Carriscant's daughter, so the story she was telling was at one remove from her. My model was *Wuthering Heights*, which is a story that's told to somebody who tells it to us – there are three levels. Because I'd written *Brazzaville Beach*, I thought I'd start with this feisty young woman in Los Angeles in the '30s, and this old bloke shows up one day and says, 'I'm your father,' and off we go with the story. There's a mystery at the heart of the novel about who's killing these American soldiers in the Philippines, and if I'd related the story in an orthodox way then I'd have had to identify the killer, but because Kay was narrating I could leave it vague and let the reader guess at the truth. As I recall, Salvador tells Kay a lie which the super-alert reader is meant to pick up on and realize that it's the clue to who did it. He tells her – and us – something that he couldn't possibly know unless he's somehow implicated in the murders. It's so oblique that it's never worked as a device, and I'm not even 100 per cent sure I know the right answer, although I had to make a decision in writing the various screenplays.

That reminds me of Raymond Chandler, when the makers of *The Big Sleep* asked him who killed the chauffeur in the novel: 'Damned if I know.'

That's right. But it doesn't get in the way of the story. Chandler was actually a considerable influence on that opening section; I have a wonderful book called *Raymond Chandler's Los Angeles*, with black-and-white photographs of that world – and a friend of mine had a little Streamline Moderne house in Silver Lake, east of Hollywood, which I used as the house in the novel. In Chandler's time Silver Lake was a very fashionable place to live, all swimming pools and country clubs, but when I knew it in the early '90s it had become unfashionable – and now it's fashionable again. Looking back at the novel I was surprised to see how long the Los Angeles section is, but you need to get to know Kay in order to trust her narrative voice when she tells the story of her father's life.

Given that the mystery element remains oblique, despite a series of murders and a gallery of suspects, what did you see its thematic purpose being?

To be honest, it was pragmatic rather than thematic: it added to the Chandleresque complication of the narrative.

It's often the needs of the narrative that make me introduce these plot elements, and in this case I was taking something from genre fiction and bringing it into literary fiction to make the story as compelling and intriguing as possible. The richer the brew the better, as far as I'm concerned.

Is that why you made Kay an architect, despite architecture playing no further part in the plot?

I needed to give her a reason for going off with Salvador, and that reason was the collapse of her dreams: seeing this beautiful house that she designed being demolished in front of her eyes. There were very few women architects in the 1930s, so choosing that as a profession for Kay embodies the kind of person she is – single-minded and independent – and it's her disappointment at being thwarted by more powerful forces that sends her off on this wild goose chase with this strange man who's obviously her father.

And a man who's similarly single-minded, independent and thwarted by more powerful forces.

Exactly. He's a modern surgeon, she's a modern architect, so there's an echo there. I also wrote a short story, 'Loose Continuity', about a German woman architect from the Bauhaus who winds up in Los Angeles designing hotdog stands. There's another one in 'The Things I Stole', about a guy who recounts the thefts he's committed through his life; he's an architect as well. Even in my play *The Argument* one of the characters is an architect. So it's clearly a recurring theme. And it's a very interesting job: are they artists or are they engineers?

Several of the characters in *The Blue Afternoon* are pursuing improbable dreams: Kay in architecture, Salvador in surgery – and his friend Pantaleon in aviation.

Yes, I think that's true. I can't say now what made me introduce aviation into the story; it just added to the historical texture – and, again, it was the right era. The Wright Brothers got their plane off the ground in 1903, but when you investigate the history of powered flight there are many so-called 'lost flights', where people claim to have flown for five minutes and managed to land again but unfortunately had no witnesses. But powered flight became a dream of human endeavour, and once those two bicycle manufacturers from the Midwest had made this technological breakthrough, there was the most incredible acceleration. The Wright Flyer took to the air in 1903, and in 1969 Americans were walking on the moon; if you were very old, you could read about Neil Armstrong stepping out of the Apollo lander and remember reading about Orville and Wilbur Wright at Kitty Hawk, North Carolina. The moment in history when all that starts gives you a resonance throughout your narrative.

The same moment that surgery developed and war became mechanized – a moment of seismic change.

Yes. It's extraordinary how modern the world had become. I realized this when I wrote *An Ice-Cream War*, which starts in 1913, just a few years on from *The Blue Afternoon*. So many of the things that we take for granted now, from refrigeration to central heating to mass communication, were already present in the early twentieth century. It's always intriguing as a novelist, going back in time and seeing how accelerating technology affects human lives and human interactions. My next novel starts in 1799, and until Georgian times not much had changed for centuries, then suddenly the railways came and communication got faster and everything changed. Computing is the thing that's utterly transformed our lives, but it's still a form of communication, it's just got super-fast and super-efficient. It's similar looking back at surgery in 1902. Someone like Salvador, as a modern surgeon, had antisepsis and anaesthesia, he kept his surgery clean and wore a gown – but he still didn't wear gloves, which meant that operating inside the body was almost a death sentence.

The way you introduce Salvador in the Manila section – 'Dr Salvador Carriscant, the most celebrated surgeon in the Philippines' – reminded me of Mario Vargas Llosa's novel *Aunt Julia and the Scriptwriter*, which you adapted as a movie three years earlier. Every alternate chapter of *Aunt Julia* is the first episode of a different radio soap opera written by the eponymous scriptwriter, all opening with a florid pen portrait of the male lead. Chapter Two, for example, describes 'a famous physician of the city, Dr Alberto de Quinteros'. I wondered whether Vargas Llosa, and the chaotic polyglot Lima he depicts in that novel, were

an influence on the vibrant characters and setting of *The Blue Afternoon*.

That's interesting. You're right, that style is very South American. I wouldn't have said that Vargas Llosa was a conscious influence on the story – it's more that the Hispanic nature of the locale demanded something like that – but I am a great admirer of his realistic novels, *Aunt Julia* in particular, and the stuff that you imbibe can filter down in all sorts of ways. My interest in South America is as much to do with its music as its literature. I've always loved samba and salsa, mariachi and fado; that's why I wrote the story 'Never Saw Brazil', imagining this minicab driver fantasizing about living in South America, fuelled by the music he listens to. And then you've got to factor in my own exotic upbringing: I've been listening to world music, particularly African and South American music, almost my whole life. Also, of course, because it's being narrated by Kay, Salvador's story *is* novelized, in a way.

And yet Kay isn't a novelist. Do you ever give any thought to the eloquence of your narrators, or do you see it simply as literary convention?

The latter. It's a convention that's as old as the novel: Moll Flanders writes remarkably like Daniel Defoe. Characters may speak demotically, but their interior life is that of a sophisticated novelist. So I don't give it any thought at all. She's a middle-class architect; why shouldn't she have a fully formed vocabulary?

Like *Brazzaville Beach*, the novel opens with a short prologue. Kay asks her father what it's like to pick up a knife and cut into human flesh, and Salvador hands her a scalpel and tells her to close her eyes . . .

. . . and she thinks she's cutting into the rind of some cheese or the skin of a melon, and actually she's cutting into her father's forearm. That was a later addition. I realized about halfway through writing the novel that it would be a great way of getting into the story. And it was part of my fascination with surgeons. What happens to you as a result of doing that job every day? How do you come to see the human body?

Also like *Brazzaville Beach*, you echo the epigraph at the end – specifically, Wallace Stevens's poem 'Landscape With Boat'. Again, was it a post hoc decision to loop back to that quote – which also inspired the novel's title – or was it planned?

I think it was post hoc – *The Blue Afternoon* was a late title choice – but one of the very first short stories I wrote, 'The Laubnitsch Upright', was a take on an absolutely wonderful Wallace Stevens poem called 'Sunday Morning', so I've been a huge fan of his since I was an undergraduate. I was looking for a way of uniting certain sensory moments in the novel, particularly when Salvador notices this change in the light, which is a symbol of the intensity of his feeling for Delphine – 'magic hour', as they call it in the movie business; that moment at sunset when everything is somehow aquiver. I remembered the

Wallace Stevens quote and thought it perfectly fitted that sense of epiphany – and at the end of the novel, Salvador is almost in the situation of the poem, sitting on a terrace with a glass of wine. It's quite manipulated, but that's part of the construction of a novel. It doesn't just pour out perfectly onto the page; there's a tremendous amount of second, third, fourth and fifth thoughts as you look at what you've written and decide what to cross out and what to rewrite and what to reposition. You're trying to create a work of art, and works of art don't just happen. They require a lot of graft and thought, and all these elements – the title, the epigraph, the ending – are part of that process.

And, as we've discussed before, the chapter headings. The chapters in Part One, 'Los Angeles, 1936', have numbers. The chapters in Part Two, 'Manila, 1902', have titles. And the chapters in Part Three, 'Lisbon, 1936', have dates. What determined that difference in headings?

I wanted to distinguish between Kay's third person narrative – her novel about her father, as it were – from her two first person narratives. And at the end you're in the present – or rather, *her* present – so the dates have their own relevance. It's another of those technical decisions you make, real nuts-and-bolts writing, but it does help the reader in their analysis of the book, just as epigraphs do.

Despite the disparate elements of the novel, does it, again, have an overarching theme for you?

Yes, it does, and it's a theme that I've come back to again and again in my work: it's about recognizing the importance of love, and not underestimating the good fortune that brought love into your life. That's why the epigraph is so telling, because to be 'touched by blue', to quote the poem, is to be touched by love. The thing that's kept Salvador going through thirty years of incarceration is the knowledge that he had that, and when these two old lovers find each other at the end, when Salvador's search and Salvador's yearning pays off, they achieve a kind of serenity that's very satisfying. It's in *Any Human Heart* as well, where the love of Logan's life is killed in World War II, but at the end of his life he knows he was lucky to have had that experience, because lots of people don't. So that's the message of *The Blue Afternoon*: that love will sustain you, and give your life validity and meaning, even if everything else is going to hell in a handcart. It's a theme as old as the hills, but it's one of those things that bears repeating.

You mentioned 'various screenplays' based on the book. How many versions have there been?

I originally wrote it on spec for Nicholas Hytner to direct. Nick's a friend of mine and had made a couple of movies, *The Madness of King George* and *The Crucible*, and his movie directing career was almost overtaking his theatre directing career. So I wrote the screenplay for him and – I think – for Pathé, and he and another friend of mine, Steve Clark-Hall, who produced *The Trench*, went on location recces in Malaysia and Australia looking for somewhere to shoot Manila. And then Nick was offered the job of Artistic Director of the National Theatre. So, you know, what can you say? 'Congratulations!' Then somebody told me that Brian De Palma was obsessed with the novel, and we got in touch with each other, and I ended up rewriting the screenplay for him. He wanted me to take it back to the book as much as possible, which I did, and he was also keen on the serial killer element, so I beefed that up considerably and made it explicit that the killer was Salvador's friend, Pantaleon. I then took this script, with Brian De Palma attached, to a company and producer I'd been working with, Potboiler and the late Simon Channing Williams. I thought it was a sure thing, but as another producer, Lorne Michaels, once said to me, which is now drilled into my brain: 'There are no sure things, Will.' And, sure enough, it all fell apart. It was only resurrected thanks to Sally Woodward Gentle, who produced *Any Human Heart* and my Shakespeare film, *A Waste of Shame*. She loved the novel and said, 'Let's do this for TV,' so now we're on the road again.

Leaving aside the frustration of projects repeatedly falling apart, is there a satisfaction in reshaping your work in different ways?

If you park your novelist's brain and engage your screenwriter's brain, then it is satisfying – and creative. You know this better than anybody: when an adaptation is working at full throttle it can be transformative and breathe new life into material that might seem unfilmable. I always quote Nabokov on this. Kubrick didn't like Nabokov's screenplay of *Lolita* and rewrote it, and Nabokov didn't like Kubrick's version but wasn't going to slag it off, so he described it as a 'vivacious variant' – which is a very good description of what happens when you adapt a novel for the screen. The film has to be a variant of the novel; you can't just reproduce what's on the page. And the more vivacious it is, the better. What's happening in the pilot episode of *The Blue Afternoon* is exactly that. It's taking the novel and trying to make a variant of it which is as vivacious as possible.

Thinking about the longish first section of the novel, in Episode One of the TV script you interleave that section with Salvador's story in Manila.

That's a perfect illustration of the difference between the two art forms. If I reproduced the sixty pages of Kay's life in Los Angeles in the screenplay, the audience would be switching off in their tens of thousands, so I need to prefigure what's coming up while sustaining their interest. In an eight-part television series your pilot episode is crucial. That's the one where you have to hook your audience. All my efforts with Sally and her team have been to create a pilot that's so intriguing and compelling that you're gagging to find out what happens in Episode Two. It's a narrative imperative imposed by the different art form. Long form television is like the serialization of a Victorian triple-decker novel. Make 'em laugh, make 'em cry, make 'em wait was Dickens's algorithm, and it worked.

You returned to Los Angeles in the title story of *The Destiny of Nathalie 'X'*, a movie-making tale which feels appropriately cinematic.

That story and *The Blue Afternoon* were probably the tail end of my Los Angeles obsession, which started in the '70s with my first short stories, and they also coincided with the end of my Hollywood film career. I went there two or three times a year in the early to mid '90s and had the full Hollywood experience, good and bad. I never stayed longer than a week; I always stayed in the same hotel, the Bel-Air, which was a classic LA place in those days; and because I don't drive I'd get limos to take me to meetings. My then Hollywood agent said to me, 'Think of it as a golden river. Every now and then you come down to the bank and dip your hands in and scoop up some gold and go away.' So I worked for several studios, I wrote quite a lot of films and some of them got made: *A Good Man in Africa*, *Stars and Bars*, *Mister Johnson*, *Aunt Julia and the Scriptwriter*, *Chaplin*. It was the collapse of *The Gunpowder Plot* project that made me think, 'Sod this for a game of soldiers.' There are certain projects where you shrug your shoulders and say, 'It wasn't meant to be,' but there are others which you run in your head and think, 'God, that would have been great,' and *The Gunpowder Plot* was one of those. We had Antonia Fraser's book, we had Daniel Day-Lewis as Robert Catesby, Pat O'Connor was going to direct it – a *Stars and Bars* reunion – and if we'd made it then it would have been an incredibly prescient film about state oppression nurturing the cancer of terrorism. For a while the wind was behind us – I did about six months' free work polishing it because I was enjoying it so much – then there was a corporate upheaval at Universal and everybody got fired from the head of the studio on down, and I didn't go back to Hollywood for about twelve years. 'Nathalie "X"' was my attempt to sum up that whole Hollywood experience in thirty pages or so. I wanted to write about Hollywood but it had been written about so often, so I had the idea of making it into a kind of fairy tale and using different characters, different voices, to tell this story about an African auteur coming to Los Angeles.

The way the story moves between third person and first person is like a documentary narration interspersed with interviews.

A faux-documentary with address to camera, exactly.

The idea of various Hollywood players trying to advance their careers by brokering a studio remake of an independent film, while that film is still being shot, seems perfectly plausible to me.

I think it is perfectly plausible. It's a very accurate portrait of Hollywood life. When I wrote the script of it, I updated it a bit – different types of cars, mobile phones instead of fax machines – but I didn't change anything about the story, even though the whole industry had changed by the time I went back. In the '90s, I was working with a senior vice president at Universal who could commission scripts up to the value of 200,000 dollars with no questions asked. He said, 'I can make a writer's year, once a week.' When I told studio executives that in 2012, they looked at me as if

I'd just come from Mars. Everything had to go up to the top. I pitched for a couple of jobs, but it was such a rigmarole. There was one quite interesting rewrite job, and in this film, which was a thriller, somebody had to fake their own death. I came up with a brilliant way of how you can do that, even today with DNA and everything, and one of the executives said, 'We need details, Will, we need details.' And I said, 'I'm not giving you any details because you'll just steal them. Commission me to write the script and you'll find out.' So that never happened. I realized that there were probably three or four other writers up for this job, and that these harassed executives were just taking notes and reporting back to the head of the studio. That was my last moment of trying to deal with Hollywood studios, although I am still writing films for independent producers.

Did you have a potential script in mind when you were writing the story?

I didn't, actually. A Dutch producer approached me about it, so I wrote a script on spec; we got a director on board, Lucy Blakstad, an excellent documentary film-maker; and we were going to shoot it in LA as a sort of guerrilla film, which would have fitted the story very well. But the Dutch producer moved on to another project and Lucy became pregnant, so that was that. A young director called Miguel Sapochnik was also attached to it. He has subsequently become a highly regarded director, but I think he was worried that if his first feature was a film sending up the industry he wanted to join he might be shooting himself in the foot, so nothing came of that either. It may never see the light of day, but we got fairly close. I also tried at one point to make a short film based on my story 'The Care and Attention of Swimming Pools', which, again, is set in LA. We put together a cast and crew and were going to make it as a non-union film during one of those technicians' strikes; then the strike ended and all these guys who were going to work on our short went back to their normal jobs. Many of these experiences fed into 'Nathalie "X"'.

The irony of the story is that the African auteur, working outside the system, manages to make not one but two films, and make them in exactly the way he wants, while the various Hollywood types are still trying to get their remake off the blocks.

Exactly. Everything is possible. You can make a film on your phone, but there's no money in it. I've had producers saying, 'We'd love to make this film but it's too cheap, which means we won't get any significant fees.' What kind of an excuse is that? 'Too expensive' you can buy, but 'too cheap' seems crazy. But there you are. That's the weirdness of the business.

Looking at the titles of some of the other stories in this second collection – 'Transfigured Night', 'Never Saw Brazil', 'The Persistence of Vision' – fleeting moments and unrealized dreams seem to be common themes.

I think that's true, but it's probably true of my novels as well. I've also written a lot of stories about real people, and 'Transfigured Night' is about a true event in the life of Ludwig Wittgenstein. He was a very wealthy man and gave away a lot of his money to artists, and one of the artists he chose was the poet Georg Trakl, who was also a drug addict. It's quite adventurous in literary terms, in the sense that the narrative is fragmented and the voice is never identified as Wittgenstein's, apart from in the epigraph. The stories allow me to pursue those sort of things; subjects that I'm obsessed with or can see potential in but don't want to write a novel or a film about.

'N is for N', on the other hand, feels like it's about a real person but they're actually fictional.

'N is for N', in a way, was the spark for *Nat Tate*. In the story I invented a fictional Vietnamese, francophone writer called Nguyen N. Then, after the story was published, somebody came up to me at a party and said, 'I'm really interested in this writer Nguyen N – can you still get his books?' and I suddenly realized how easy it was to make something totally fictional seem totally real. So when *Nat Tate* came along I was ready for all kinds of trickery, and then *Nat Tate* led to *Any Human Heart* – and that page-and-a-half story, *N is for N*, was the beginning of it, because this person absolutely thought I was writing about a real author.

It's also a valuable lesson in brevity: a whole life in a page and a half.

Part of my short story writing life is to see what you can do with narrative and how you can get a quart into a pint pot. 'Nathalie "X"', for example, may only be thirty pages but it contains enough material to fill a medium-sized novel.

Another place you return to in this collection is Nice: there are two more stories, 'The Dream Lover' and 'Alpes Maritimes', featuring your 'evil twin', Edward Scully.

He's also in the title story of *Fascination*, and another story in that collection, 'Adult Video'. He ends up at Oxford, gets unhappily married, has a child and becomes a failed writer. It's quite interesting following a character like that, and, again, part of the pleasure of the form. I wouldn't want to write a novel about Edward Scully but I can write half a dozen short stories about him, in the same way that Hemingway wrote a series of Nick Adams stories. It's funny: I've written sequels to my short stories but I've never written one to a novel, even though people have asked, 'Why don't you write a sequel to *A Good Man in Africa*?'

The final story in this collection, 'Cork', is one of the most elliptical. How would you describe it – and your script of it, *Nobody's Heart*?

I've always described it as a strange erotic love story set in the 1930s. I think that encompasses all its elements. In more detail, it's about identity, and a journey from bereavement to fulfilment – and rebirth. I became very interested in Fernando Pessoa, who's the T. S. Eliot of Portuguese modernism, a huge figure in their twentieth-century literary landscape. He wrote poems that were stylistically different depending on the fake poets he became to write them, whether it was a right-wing nationalist poet or a fey nature poet or a cynical modern poet. He had masses of these 'heteronyms', as he called them, but there are four or five well-known ones that he repeatedly returned to, and the idea for the story was, 'What would it be like to have a love affair with somebody like that?' Pessoa was a lonely figure – and a massive drinker; he died of cirrhosis of the liver and his fame was entirely posthumous – so I imagined a story narrated by this woman, Lily, who finds herself in an affair with this man, who I call Boscán, but every time they meet up he's turned into one of his other heteronyms, so each liaison is different from the last. I also came across a little monograph in the London Library about cork, published in 1904, and the more I read the writer's observations about this material, the more it seemed strangely human. So I stuck extracts from the book into the narrative to justify the title and to show that Lily's journey was about trying to achieve the same qualities of lightness and elasticity and impermeability that cork possesses. Boscán opens a door for Lily and dares her to come through it, and in so doing he frees her from the awful shock and grief at the death of her husband and she rediscovers herself and her soul. It's quite a redemptive tale, even though Boscán dies at the end.

And it's really Lily's story, even though Pessoa inspired it.

That's right. And it would be Lily's film, because she's in every scene and everything is seen from her point of view. But Boscán is still a dream role for an actor: you get to play at least five different people. I've been working on the script for so long that I've almost forgotten the original story, and it's had goodness knows how many directors attached to it. Antonia Bird was going to direct it, but she died tragically. Anand Tucker was attached for a long time, then he had a clash with another film. It's like 'Nathalie "X"': you're trying to keep all these balls in the air and one keeps thudding to the earth. It would be fantastic if we could pull it off at some point; it has all kinds of potential.

The Destiny of Nathalie 'X' and On the Yankee Station were republished in a single volume as The Dream Lover in 2008. Why did you want to bring the two collections together?

A chapter of corporate accidents made me leave Penguin, who I'd been with all my working life, and move to Bloomsbury for four novels – and because Penguin had let the collections go out of print, Bloomsbury's thinking was, 'Let's repackage them in an omnibus edition.' So I gave it a new title and wrote an introduction to make the book different. I'd similarly moved hardback publisher before *Nathalie 'X'* came out. My first editor at Hamish Hamilton, Christopher Sinclair-Stevenson, set up his own publishing imprint, and I moved to his company for *Brazzaville Beach*, *The Blue Afternoon* and *Nathalie 'X'* – then Sinclair-Stevenson was amalgamated into Random House and I went back to Hamish Hamilton for *Armadillo*.

Armadillo, your seventh novel, started life as a script for the director John Schlesinger – is that right?

The inspiration came from that. I got to know John and was very fond of him, and we decided to do a film together. John said, 'Why are there no great British thrillers? Surely we can come up with one?' and I said, 'Let me see if I can.' I had friends who worked in insurance and I'd heard it was all based on trust and heard a story that you could commit a massive insurance fraud once in your life and get away with it. So I wrote this script called _Thicker Than Water_ about a senior Lloyd's agent – respected, married, children – who realizes he has a one-time opportunity to make tens of millions of pounds. It's about how an honest man becomes corrupt. Then John went and made _The Falcon and the Snowman_ and didn't need to do another thriller. We stayed in touch and had mutual friends – Jim Clark, who edited _Midnight Cowboy_, also edited _The Trench_ – but we never got to make a film together. But this idea of an insurance scam was the source of _Armadillo_.

Along with another rich stew of strands: loss adjusting, ancient armour and sleep disorders, for starters.

All those interests went into the hopper of the novel and came out at the other end as a story. In the course of researching the script I learned that there's a whole army of ex-special forces types who adjust loss on insurance claims. It also happened that a jeweller friend of mine was the victim of an armed robbery, and he put in an insurance claim for the two or three million pounds' worth of jewels that were stolen, and this tough South African came to see him and said, 'We're going to give you a million pounds, and that's it. Otherwise, see you in court.' And my friend said, 'What could I do? I couldn't sue my insurance company.' I thought that was a fantastic background for a novel, and my favourite theme of good luck and bad luck played into it perfectly. The myth of insurance is that you can protect yourself against bad luck, which you can't, of course. This multi-billion-dollar industry is based on a fantasy, which is a wonderful metaphor for human fear and human need. Armour is also a metaphor: insurance is an armour that supposedly protects you from life's slings and arrows. I have a slight obsession with arms and armour, particularly helmets, so I just stuck my obsession in the novel and gave it to Lorimer Black. And, of course, armadillo means 'little armed man', which is what Lorimer is – but he's not confident about his armour.

The helmet that Lorimer buys doesn't protect him, for example, because it's so thin. It only provides the illusion of protection.

That's right. It's a decorative helmet, not a proper one.

What it does do, though, is conceal most of his face, which ties into two more of your favourite themes: identity and duplicity.

Lorimer is a kind of chameleon. His real name is Milomre Blocj and his family comes from Transnistria, a real place on the borders of Moldova and Ukraine which doesn't officially exist – so he's effectively a man from nowhere.

He creates this persona, Lorimer Black, which is one of many personas in his loss-adjusting life. Whoever he's adjusting he becomes just like them, and becomes a person that they trust. That's the secret of his success, until he's swallowed up in this scam.

But there's already an underlying sense of existential restlessness, even before he stumbles on a hanged man at the start of the story, embodied by the insomnia that he chronicles in his journal, which he's titled 'The Book of Transfiguration'.

'The Book of Transfiguration' is Lorimer's dream diary, if you like, and was a narrative device that I found extremely useful. It punctuates the novel as we move from third person to first person, and it reflects on what's just happened and what's going to happen, a bit like *Brazzaville Beach*. I'm not an insomniac but I know insomniacs, and for some reason I got interested in sleep and dreams. Every human being since the beginning of time has had to sleep, but it wasn't until about 100 years ago that people started studying it and realized that there are two types of sleep: deep sleep and rapid eye movement sleep – REM sleep. REM sleep is when people dream – you can see their eyes moving under the eyelids – and you think, 'Why had nobody spotted that in three millennia?' There are theories that deep sleep, where you're semi-paralysed, is your body repairing your organs, monitoring your defences; and rapid eye movement sleep, when you're starting to surface, is the brain synapses firing, revving up the engine. And that's when you dream. But *why* do we dream?

Nobody really knows, but everybody has experienced it. So I decided to make Lorimer a chronic insomniac and send him to a sleep clinic so I could throw in all this stuff, which is really interesting and utterly universal.

The sleeping ties into the armour, doesn't it, in the sense that when you're asleep, you're armourless?

Yes, that's true. And you're not just armourless, you're vulnerable to whatever your psyche throws up in the course of that particular night, which can be beguiling or terrifying. It's a strange moment in your life, those hours you spend unconscious or semi-conscious, and I've thought of revisiting the idea of sleeping and dreaming. I haven't found a way of doing it yet, but it was certainly intriguing to do it in *Armadillo*.

And, to extend the metaphor, Lorimer's meetings with Flavia Malinverno are the only times when he consciously removes his armour and reverts to his own persona.

Exactly. She becomes the beacon of hope that he feels compelled to follow. It's all one way: he's massively, obsessively committed to her, and we don't even know at the end whether she's committed to him. But it's enough to give his complex, unravelling life some sort of central meaning – which is also the theme of *The Blue Afternoon*, in a way. So all the ingredients of this comic brew pertain to the theme that we will never be safe, and all we can do is try to meet somebody like Flavia Malinverno.

Your previous three novels – *The New Confessions*, *Brazzaville Beach*, *The Blue Afternoon* – had all been fairly weighty. Was this a conscious decision to write something a little lighter?

I certainly hadn't written a comic novel for a while. There's a lot of comedy in *The New Confessions* but you wouldn't call it comic, so I did want to write something that had a vim and vigour to it. Also, I'd lived in London for a good while by then and had come to grips with the city to a certain extent and wanted to explore it in all its strangeness, which is why I started with a deliberate echo of Dickens's *Our Mutual Friend* to set up the tone and get things rolling. Dickens is *the* great novelist of London, so I wanted that echo to resonate.

It is a very specifically London novel. Whenever Lorimer travels around the city, you take great care to describe precisely what route he takes.

That's possibly because I don't drive. When I'm not on public transport I'm being driven around in cabs, so I see London from the back of a car. We had a minicab firm near our first house in Fulham and I got to know all the drivers, and one of them is now an executive chauffeur and is still driving me around almost forty years later. We must have covered hundreds, if not thousands, of miles of London. I put all that into *Armadillo*: the drivers are drawn from life. So I'm always very aware of the journeys I take, and being that precise seemed to me to be a way of stitching the city together. London is a character in the novel, just as the Thames is a character in *Ordinary Thunderstorms*. But whereas *Ordinary Thunderstorms* is a following-the-river novel, *Armadillo* is a four-points-of-the-compass novel. I've been all round London twice over, researching those novels. It's a fascinating city, if not the most fascinating on the planet.

Do you ever worry about being *too* specific? That if you're not British or don't live in London, you're less likely to understand the references?

I don't think you can worry about that as a novelist. You write your novel and it gets translated to the best of the translator's ability. *Trio* has had fantastic reviews in the States, and it couldn't be more English: provincial Brighton in 1968. If I was writing for international audiences, it just would become generic. I do think *Armadillo* is the most underrated of my novels – or the least referred to – possibly because it came out relatively swiftly as a miniseries before having any sort of life as a novel.

For me, even though your adaptation is fairly faithful, the miniseries has a different feel to the novel – but I can't quite put my finger on why.

It may be to do with the casting of James Frain. Lorimer is a faceless, shapeshifting character, so when you cast somebody as vivid and as confident as James, it changes and becomes a different thing. But that's in hindsight. At the time of making it, I was delighted with it. I still am.

Maybe it would have become a different thing regardless of the casting. When you read a novel you don't

necessarily have a fixed image of a character in your mind, but when you watch a film or TV series the character becomes concrete in the shape of the actor.

That's a consequence of any adaptation: every reader has an impression of a written character, and when they become a physical actor it can jar horribly. Some people find it ruins their retrospective enjoyment of the novel and they'll never watch, for example, *Any Human Heart*, because they don't want to see Logan Mountstuart portrayed by Jim Broadbent or Matthew Macfadyen or Sam Claflin. But it comes with the territory; there's nothing you can do about it. And I was really happy with the casting of *Armadillo*: not just James, but also Stephen Rea as Lorimer's boss George Hogg, and Hugh Bonneville as the awful Torquil Helvoir-Jayne, and Catherine McCormack as Flavia.

On the other hand, the dream sequences translate well to the screen, as do the scenes of Lorimer driving around the city, which have a semi-documentary feel heightened by the vibrancy of the soundtrack.

That's *mise en scène* again: three pages of a novel can be a few seconds on screen. I'm against dream sequences in films as a rule, but when they work they're much better than dream sequences in novels. On the page they feel a bit laboured, but when you photograph them they look effortless. And the soundtrack was also a great plus: something film brings to those scenes that you don't get on the page.

In the course of its lengthy journey from the film script for John Schlesinger, to the novel, to the TV series directed by Howard Davies, to what extent did the story retain its original thriller pulse?

Underneath everything that's going on, Lorimer's inadvertent involvement in this insurance fraud is still the motor-drive of the novel, and the thriller element gave the story a natural shape. I've often borrowed from genre to power my narratives, like the serial killer story in *The Blue Afternoon*, because I'm a great believer in narrative compulsion – in making the reader want to turn the page.

Four

Screenplays 2

Mister Johnson (1990) – *Aunt Julia and the Scriptwriter* (1990)
Chaplin (1992) – *The Trench* (1999)

A Good Man in Africa was your second African-set collaboration with director Bruce Beresford. How did you come to collaborate on your first, Mister Johnson?

An independent producer called Michael Fitzgerald approached me – a very intellectual man who'd made two films with John Huston, *Under the Volcano* and *Wise Blood* – and I think he'd read my introduction to a Penguin Classics edition of the book. Bruce was attached to direct, having just made *Driving Miss Daisy*, and he had lived and worked in Nigeria right at the beginning of his career, so we both had this Nigerian connection. So we teamed up and I wrote the adaptation with great pleasure – and then there were the usual hassles in getting it made.

Why do you think that Joyce Cary's novel is considered a classic?

It's one of the few novels set in Nigeria that's written by a non-Nigerian. There are masses of novels by white writers about East, Central and South Africa, but hardly any great or enduring ones about West Africa. There's a very good book called *No Joy of Africa*, written in the '50s, by a man who's completely forgotten now, W. R. Loader. And there's Graham Greene's classic, *The Heart of the Matter*, but Greene hadn't been in West Africa for very long, so I don't think he understood it in the way Cary did. Cary was a district officer in Nigeria in the 1920s, so his understanding of Nigerian society at the time is quite acute. He understands the local potentates as well as the colonial administrators, and the Nigerian characters are as prominent in the narrative as the white characters – and at the centre of it all is this great comic character, almost like a Nigerian Tom Jones or Don Quixote. As someone who was born and raised in West Africa, it rings true to me – and it rings true in an unsentimental, unpatronizing way. I remember talking to the Nigerian writer Ken Saro-Wiwa about it, and I think Nigerians recognize it as being authentic, too. Cary managed to get rid of his colonial baggage and, through his novelistic empathy, enter the head of this character and locate something timeless and universal, which is a rare feat for a white writer. Now it might be called appropriation: why is this white Irishman writing about a Nigerian character? But it's done with tremendous insight, and that's what makes it a classic.

There's an introduction in the Everyman edition by Joyce Cary himself, who describes Mister Johnson as 'a young clerk who turns his life into a romance, a poet who creates for himself a glorious destiny'. In other words, he's constantly deceiving himself and others, which doesn't always make him a likeable character – but having the character inhabited by

Maynard Eziashi in the film makes him much more sympathetic than he is in the novel.

That's a very good point. Cary's attitude when he wrote the book probably wasn't as sympathetic as ours when we made the film, and Maynard's presence on screen perhaps embodies a version of Mister Johnson that's different to the character in the novel. He's still lying and covering up, but his guileless naivety is incredibly engaging and his death at the end is really poignant. It was inspired casting by Bruce, because Maynard was totally unknown: it was his first role, and he ended up winning the Silver Bear for Best Actor at the Berlin Film Festival. Pierce Brosnan, who'd just come off *Remington Steele*, is also fantastic in it as the colonial administrator, Rudbeck.

The novel is set in the 1920s, was written in 1939, and was filmed in 1990. Did you need to modify its colonial attitudes in any way for modern sensibilities?

If I was writing the screenplay today my woke antennae might quiver more, but at that time I was simply trying to be true to the spirit of the book, which is a completely clear-eyed account of colonial life. Young middle-class people like Cary went out to the colonies and saw what they were doing as something that you just got on with. With hindsight, of course, you can see how invasive it was – and in *A Good Man in Africa* I was far more conscious of that colonial legacy – but at the time Cary's novel was written, pre-World War II, I don't think there was much criticism of colonial ambitions, because every European country was trying to grab their bit of the

Earth. At the same time, it's not saying, 'The sun never sets on the British Empire, isn't that a wonderful thing?' There's this uneasy alliance between the local rulers and the colonial power to keep things ticking over, and everybody's making the best of a bad job. It's very aware of human frailty and fallibility, which is why it's such an interesting novel.

There was a cycle of films and TV series in the '80s and '90s about the British and the Empire which was dismissively dubbed 'heritage' cinema by critics. Would you say this film fits into that cycle?

I wouldn't, because it's very unglamorous. It's not *The Jewel in the Crown*, it's about a remote outpost in Nigeria. Any period film could be described as 'heritage', but there's no sense in which *Mister Johnson* is putting a gloss on colonial life. The opposite, if anything: it's showing the brutal reality of administering a vast district on your own with no communications, and acting as judge, jury and, sometimes, executioner.

What were the hassles in getting the film made?

The night before principal photography started, Michael rang me up and said, 'We're a million dollars short. Everyone has to defer their fee,' and because it was a passion project we all said yes. Then, when the shoot was under way, it looked like the film would have to shut down. It was made in northern Nigeria, and the crew was paid in cash. Every week these suitcases of money would come up from Lagos, and one week the money didn't arrive.

Michael and Bruce were complaining about this terrible shortfall to the owner of the only restaurant in town, who they'd got to know very well, and he said, 'I can take care of it.' And, amazingly, this Lebanese restaurateur paid for a week's filming and was reimbursed once the cash flow sorted itself out. Then, on the last day, Michael, Bruce and his daughter Trilby, who'd come out to visit the set, were driving back to Kano to catch the plane to London and had a hideous car crash. All three of them crawled out of the wreckage with bruises and scratches, but it could have been the ultimate nightmare: producer, director and baby daughter killed in car smash on death-trap road. So it was a real *African Queen*-type film-making experience.

Did you also visit the set?

I didn't really need to go. I was in London, watching the rushes with the editor. It was all shot on film in those days, and the footage was flown out from Kano and put on the Moviola back in London. I'm very proud of the film, but like *Stars and Bars* it got caught up in Hollywood politics. The guy at 20th Century Fox who commissioned it was fired, and the film was barely released. Bruce said it was the best-reviewed film of his career, and it was shown in one cinema in London. But he and I went on to make *A Good Man in Africa* together and forged a firm friendship, and the film is there to be seen and appreciated. It's now part of the Criterion Collection in a deluxe remastered edition, and I still think it's very true to the spirit of the country and the times.

Aunt Julia and the Scriptwriter, released the same year, also performed less well than it was reviewed. How did you become involved in that project?

That was a more straightforward commission. A producer called Mark Tarlov had optioned Mario Vargas Llosa's novel, and David Puttnam, who was still running Columbia at this point, said to him, 'You should get William Boyd to write it.' I'd read other books by Mario but I hadn't read that one, and I really liked it. I think it's his best book, because it's basically his story: he had a love affair with his aunt and they ran off and got married. The novel is set in Lima, Peru, but the one thing I'd been told was that there was no way the film could be set in Lima, Peru, because the studio wanted to make an English-language film. On the flight to New York to meet Mark, I was racking my brains and came up with the notion of New Orleans, which I'd visited when I was researching *Stars and Bars*. I thought, 'If there's one place in the US that can replicate multicultural Lima in the 1950s, it's New Orleans.'

I've never read another novel quite like it. Would you describe it as magic realism?

I'm not sure that Vargas Llosa has really written in that tradition. He's always quite grounded in history. There are other South American writers who are far more fantastical. In *Aunt Julia*, the fantasy is fenced in by the structure, and therefore it doesn't penetrate the rest of the novel. It's actually quite a realistic story about a young man's obsession with an older woman, interspersed with these bizarre and increasingly surreal soap operas that are being written by this mad scriptwriter.

Mario in the book becomes Martin in the film, played by Keanu Reeves, while the scriptwriter, Pedro Camacho, becomes Pedro Carmichael, played by Peter Falk. Pedro's stories and Martin's romance are more directly linked in the film, to the extent of Pedro orchestrating Martin and Julia's meetings to give him material.

That's right. In the novel there are thirteen different soap operas and I rewrote it as one soap opera, and Martin begins to realize that things he's done and words he's said are popping up on the radio, so there's a much stronger connection between the love affair and what's happening in the soap opera than there is in the book. It's a pretty audacious novel, and we sort of got that on the screen. Mario and I had dinner together a few times and he said to me, 'Just do the best you can.'

The tone of the film is quite broad, and the look of it is similarly vivid. To what extent can you determine those things – determine, if you like, the mood of the film – when writing the screenplay?

The look is something that you can't really determine in a screenplay – the visual aesthetic will be created by the director and the art director – but if the tone you want is present in the script it will probably end up on the screen. Working with directors now and seeing the 'mood board' aspect of film-making, it's interesting that the visual impact of a film is derived from the script but is also independent of it. I was talking to a director and she said she really likes following shots; she thinks the backs of people's heads can be as eloquent as the front. That might not be in the script, but she'll shoot scenes in that way. She also said, 'I really like long takes. I'm sick to death of cut, cut, cut.' Again, that's an aesthetic the director brings. And that's all very well, but there are still the narrative demands of the story. All your 'lovely visuals', as Dickie Attenborough used to call them, may end up on the cutting room floor if nobody can understand what's going on. So it's a collaboration, and sometimes a compromise, but the essential tone of a film, whether it's ironic or comic or absurd, will be in the script. You can't impose that as a director if it's not already there.

It's an unusual film, from an unusual novel, but a very enjoyable one. Why do you think it didn't do better business?

When David Puttnam left Columbia, the project was put into turnaround and picked up by a smaller studio. Jon Amiel was attached as director, hot from *The Singing Detective*, and the film came together fairly swiftly. It was shot at the Dino De Laurentiis Studios in Wilmington, North Carolina, and we had this fantastic cast: Peter Falk, Keanu Reeves – and Barbara Hershey, who was great as Julia. There were also lots of cameo roles in the soap opera, so we had all these amazing people popping up to do a day or two's work on the film. Susan and I flew out for a week or so, and because there was only one decent restaurant in

Wilmington we had dinner every night with Peter Falk – a delightful man, who was enjoying making the film and very pleased with his performance. So everybody had a ball, and everything looked set fair. Mario really liked the finished film, it got phenomenal reviews, and we were booked to go on a tour to promote it in America. Then the producers, thinking they had a hit on their hands, decided to change the title to *Tune in Tomorrow.* I made myself very clear to them, and to Jon, that I was totally against this. This was in the days of faxes, and I sent them a fax saying, 'If you change the title, the following things will happen: Mario Vargas Llosa will have nothing to do with the film, and every single review will start, "What idiot changed the title?"' And I wasn't happy that I was proved right. Mario pulled out of the US publicity tour, because nobody was going to associate *Tune in Tomorrow* with his wonderful novel; and it was released as *Aunt Julia and the Scriptwriter* everywhere else in the world, because *Aunt Julia and the Scriptwriter* is a wonderful title and *Tune in Tomorrow* is a crap title. It was a real blunder by the producers, but dollar signs got in their way. One of them said to me, 'Will, we're talking fat city here.' They opened it in 400 cinemas and thought they were going to make a ton of money, and they were wrong.

How do you feel about the film now?

Apart from the persisting anger about the title change, it was a really enjoyable experience – and I've seen Mario since, and there's no bad feeling between me and him. Both Mark and Jon became firm friends of mine, and

Mark and I made *A Good Man in Africa* together. Mark's producing partner John Fiedler is still a producer and I'm working with him as we speak on the film of 'Cork', so the personal and professional relationships that were established when we made *Aunt Julia* are very strong. It was John Fiedler who persuaded Peter Falk to do it, and I think it was Peter Falk's favourite film. He didn't do many films, but this was the one he was most proud of. And with those reviews, it should have been a hit. But, hey, that's the movie business. *Stars and Bars* and *Mister Johnson* were sunk by studio politics. *Aunt Julia* was sunk by a bad marketing decision.

The next film you worked on, Richard Attenborough's *Chaplin*, had a bumpier journey to the screen – reflected in the screenplay credit, which is shared with Bryan Forbes and William Goldman, with a story credit for Diana Hawkins.

That was another commission. Dickie Attenborough was obsessed with Charlie Chaplin and had always wanted to make a film about him. He almost saw himself as a Chaplin figure: a left-wing film-maker who was both actor and director. So he set up the project at Universal, and his old collaborator Bryan Forbes wrote the script, but Forbes's draft was rejected by the studio.

What did Universal feel was wrong with the Forbes draft?

It was all over the place, as I recall. Chaplin's body was stolen after he died – some thieves disinterred his coffin and try to ransom it back to the family – and I think that's how the script started. It was also far too long. Universal felt it was unfilmable, basically, and they said to Dickie, 'If you want to make the film, we have to hire a new writer and start with a clean sheet of paper.' So it was a new script, not a rewrite.

Although it was based on Chaplin's autobiography, *My Life*, and David Robinson's book *Chaplin: His Life and Art*.

That's right. I'd just finished *Brazzaville Beach* when Dickie asked if I'd be interested in writing it, so I said yes and just plunged in, and read everything I could and watched Chaplin's films. Because of the problems with the Forbes script the studio was very involved in the development of the new draft, and an executive called Barry Isaacson was in charge of shepherding it through to production. Barry came over to London and we talked about the kind of film we wanted to make, and it was a very fruitful collaboration. In fact, I might have been his suggestion to write the script.

And what kind of film *did* you want to make?

We decided to go for broke, and our model was *Raging Bull*, both as a biopic and because of the troubling complexities of Chaplin's persona. The Tramp is still iconic, but people forget the rest: he was bigger than the Beatles but obsessed with underage girls; he was very left-wing but ran his studio like a fascist dictator. In the first draft the big story was: poor Lambeth kid dreams of going to America; goes to America, makes a fortune and becomes the most famous man in the world; then is kicked out of America on suspicion of being a communist. That, to me, was the story of Chaplin's life, and we decided to produce an unsparing version of that, but it was naive of us to think that Dickie was going to do this. He was a bit rocked by our first draft, but he knew that Barry was very keen on it, so in his own nicely devious way he started watering it down. Barry and I said we weren't going to have any cockney cheeky-chappie stuff in the script, and Dickie filled the film with, 'Hello, Charlie, how's the trouble and strife?' But in the first draft we thought we'd push the envelope, and there's still a lot of that draft in the finished film. The scenes between Robert Downey Jr. as Chaplin and Milla Jovovich as his young wife are probably the steamiest scenes that Dickie ever shot, even if it was against his instincts. Anyway, the script went through many drafts, the studio signed off on it, Downey was cast, sets were built and it was ready to go – but by now the budget was something like forty million dollars, which would be about one hundred million today. I was looking at locations in Los Angeles with Dickie when he got a call from the studio – in very early mobile phone days – saying he would have to defer his fee if the film was going to go ahead. And Dickie said, 'I never defer my fee.' So Universal pulled out, and the film collapsed. Only Dickie could have put it together again – and he did, with a company called Carolco, who stumped up the forty million dollars on the condition that the script was rewritten. I'd ended it in the 1950s when Chaplin was kicked out of America, but they wanted the Switzerland years, so they hired William Goldman to add some scenes about Chaplin's later life.

Why didn't they ask you to write the additional scenes?

I think my contract was up, and Dickie had worked with Goldman on *A Bridge Too Far* and *Magic* – both with Anthony Hopkins, who appeared as Chaplin's publisher, quizzing him about his life for his memoirs: 'So that was when United Artists was founded?' 'Yes. And everyone said the lunatics had taken control of the asylum.' It was shockingly bad writing, just blatant exposition. If I ever give a lecture on screenwriting, I'll use that as an example of how not to write a scene. Downey also hated those scenes, because he was only in his twenties and he had to age up to eighty. It took hours of make-up and it didn't look right – but he who pays the piper calls the tune. So the finished film is probably 70 per cent me, maybe 5 per cent William Goldman, and 25 per cent Dickie and his writing collaborator, Diana Hawkins.

Tom Stoppard also did some work on it, didn't he?

Tom worked on it while the film was still at Universal, because he was under contract to them at the time. I think he was simply meant to, as they say, put it through his machine – add a bit of wit, sprinkle some Stoppardian magic dust on it – but he actually got quite involved and did, if not a rewrite, a substantial polish. Dickie and I didn't fall out over it, but he was less than honest about Tom's arrival on the scene. Dickie hated doing anything that would make people dislike him, so he would try to finesse it or pretend it wasn't him – when the best way to deal with any problem in life is just to be honest. He blamed it on Barry, but I rang Barry and said, 'What the fuck is going on?' and Barry said, 'It's nothing to do with me.' Then it was all thrown out anyway and we went back to my script plus William Goldman. There isn't any of Tom's work in the Carolco version.

Which brings us back around to the three-way writing credit.

That was the final chapter. As you know, when there's more than one writer on a film, and more than one of them is claiming a credit, it goes to arbitration at the Writers Guild of America. It's a sort of star chamber and you don't know who the jury is. The first writer almost always gets a credit in these arbitrations, so the credit ran William Boyd, Bryan Forbes, William Goldman – although, in reality, the third writer on the film was Diana Hawkins, not Bryan Forbes. But Bryan was so bitter about his script being rejected, after he had spent so much time working on the project, that he was determined to get a credit. It caused a lot of bad feeling between Dickie and Bryan, but they eventually made it up. Then I met Bryan and we got on extremely well, and all the bad feeling dissipated. I wasn't able to tell the full story until both of them had gone on to the great screening room in the sky, but now I can. It was the usual messy business of film-making, but I think – and this sounds like faint praise – it's a very interesting film.

I don't think it entirely works, but I agree it's very interesting.

Downey's performance is mesmerizing, particularly in the early days of the Tramp. I got to know him quite well during the making of the film. And Dickie and I remained close. I was incredibly fond of him and thought he was a wonderful man. It's the biggest film I've been involved in and he brought me into every aspect of it. I went with him and the production designer, Stuart Craig, to see Chaplin's old studios in LA, which had been bought by a record company, and when we went into Chaplin's actual office there was a bust of Gandhi there. Maybe the record company executive admired Gandhi, but for Dickie Attenborough to be standing in Charlie Chaplin's office and seeing a bust of Mahatma Gandhi – he was lost for words. So it was an extraordinary couple of years, working on that film.

Again, why do you think the film wasn't more successful?

It's funny, because it got fantastic scores at the test screenings, yet it was a flop. It wasn't particularly well reviewed, either. I think it was a case of too many cooks: it lost its edge. But Downey was nominated for an Oscar, and although it did no business I get the odd cheque from it, so it's still being watched. If people ask what films I've written, *Chaplin* is the one they've heard of. Downey's career has made it interesting, a bit like Daniel Craig's career has made *The Trench* interesting. There's a retrospective glow.

The Trench was your first and, so far, only screen work as director. What was the inspiration for it?

It was two things: a) my abiding interest in World War I, and b) *The Gunpowder Plot*. Off the back of that unhappy experience, where so much work was wasted, I said, 'I'm not going to do that again. I don't have to go to Hollywood. I can work in Europe.' Round about the same time that those thoughts were whizzing around my mind, I saw the original TV version of *Das Boot* and thought it was fantastic: the claustrophobia was phenomenally well realized. I have this obsession with authenticity, and I had the conviction that World War I hadn't been done properly on screen at that time. The original film of *All Quiet on the Western Front* is good but it's not realistic, and the great Stanley Kubrick's *Paths of Glory* is a joke in terms of realism: the trenches are like motorway cuttings so he could get these huge dollies into them. Watching *Das Boot* was a Damascene moment: 'The way they did World War II is how you could do World War I. Stay confined, never open up, and you can make something totally realistic but relatively cheap.' So that was the inspiration for *The Trench*.

I'd argue that Simon Gray's adaptation of the J. L. Carr novel *A Month in the Country*, and Allan Scott's adaptation of the Pat Barker novel *Regeneration*, released in 1987 and 1997 respectively, are both great World War I films, even though they mainly don't take place in the trenches.

A Month in the Country is a great film – directed by my old friend Pat O'Connor – and *Regeneration* is also very good.

But the fighting is only at the beginning in both of those films, and my ambition was to show the trench experience – or as close to it as I could get.

Why did you decide to direct the film as well as write it?

As directors had dropped out of other projects I'd written – and because I had on-the-job experience of how to make a feature film – people would say to me, 'Why don't *you* direct it?' So for this I teamed up with another old friend, the producer Steve Clark-Hall, and we set it up together with me as director. It cost a million pounds, dead cheap for a war movie; we shot it very quickly, in about twenty-five days; and I called in all my markers from people I'd worked with and assembled an incredible crew. They were all friends of mine and I leaned on them very heavily, and I was ludicrously over-prepared myself. I storyboarded the entire film: paperback versions of my storyboard were printed off for all the department heads so they knew what was going to be in every frame of every scene.

The film takes place in the two days leading up to the Battle of the Somme and focuses on one platoon preparing to go over the top, which means it has a tight timeline but an episodic structure. How did you balance those two elements?

Well, we had the ticking clock of the attack that's going to happen – they're due to be in the fourth wave, holding the front line – so that gave the film a sense of forward momentum, and from that timeline I hung the various events and backstories and relationships. I wanted to give a sense of what it was like to be a soldier in the trenches in 1916, about to go into battle. From everything I know about it, they were just ordinary young lads – very young, some of them – and what do you do when you're eighteen or nineteen or twenty and bored witless? You eat, you drink, you talk about girls. So the story is structured as a series of episodes: being on sentry duty, being sniped at, the obligatory rat, the rum ration. There was an incident I took from Robert Graves's classic World War I memoir, *Goodbye to All That*, where someone drank all the rum ration and the sergeant drowned the perpetrator because it was such a heinous crime. So I pinched that – although I didn't have Daniel Craig drown Danny Dyer – along with the fact that the rum was incredibly powerful and these lads were basically pissed when they went over the top. Then there's this growing sense of things going wrong – the sniper, the artillery noise building in the background, the shocking scene where two of the men are blown to pieces – which ratchets up the tension. And then they get the news that they're going over in the first wave. So all of those episodes, building up to that crescendo, provided the narrative pulse.

Was it a fairly short screenplay, ninety pages or so, to produce a ninety-eight-minute movie?

It was probably slightly shorter than ninety pages; I always try to write to length and not overwrite. There was one scene that we shot but didn't include, where the soldiers are extending a latrine sap – there was a wonderful line from one of the Scots: 'I didn't come all this way to dig a shithole' – and they find the buried corpse of a French African soldier, because they've taken over the trenches from the French army. They disinter him and cart his body off on a stretcher, but it freaks them out because he's not just a dead soldier, he's a dead Black soldier, and he seems surreal and alien to them. It was an interesting scene and the kind of thing you can do in a novel, but it didn't lead anywhere and slowed the film down, so in the first assembly we realized it had to go. Often the edit is unsparing in revealing your bad ideas.

How did you set about achieving the authenticity you wanted?

I got a historical advisor on board, Martin Middlebrook, a hero of mine who's written books on World War I and World War II – and two books on the Falklands, one from the Argentine side. His first book, *The First Day on the Somme*, is phenomenal. He visited the World War I battlefields in the late '60s and thought, 'Some of these guys are still alive and somebody had better talk to them before they all die.' He went and interviewed 400 people who'd been at the Somme and wove their testimony into the history of the battle, and the book was an instant classic. One of the other books that most influenced me was *Her Privates We*, by Frederic Manning, which is *the* great novel of World War I. There's an unexpurgated version called *The Middle Parts of Fortune*, which was privately printed and has all the swear words in: you name it, they say it. I said to the actors, 'If you want to say "fuck" or "shit", go ahead, even if it's not in the script, because that's how soldiers talk.' And, sure enough, they all swear like troopers. I also said to them, 'Don't put on your actor's voice. Speak in the accent you'd use to speak to your mother.' So Paul Nicholls has a Bolton accent, and Daniel Craig has a Liverpudlian accent because he's from the Wirral. We actually took the actors to boot camp before the shoot, which was a bit hair-raising – and we had a couple of deserters. We also had them dress themselves on set, so some of them were neat and tidy and some of them were a hopeless mess. It was all in the interests of making everything seem as real and as naturalistic as possible.

There's a class element to the accents, too. The officers, Julian Rhind-Tutt and Adrian Lukis, are upper class, whereas the privates and NCOs are all working class.

There was a monstrous divide between the officer class and the enlisted men, which is often overlooked in films but you read about in memoirs. The interesting thing about Frederic Manning's book is that he was an academic, an intellectual, but he didn't want to be an officer, he wanted to be a private. So you have this refined sensibility in an atmosphere where he would have seemed like a toff, which makes his insight all the more valuable.

The cast also includes Danny Dyer, James D'Arcy, Cillian Murphy and Ben Whishaw – a very impressive roster for a low budget movie.

It's extraordinary, looking back: several of them have gone on to stellar acting careers, but at that time, in 1999, they were barely even familiar faces, let alone household names. I said to Steve Clark-Hall, 'I don't want any movie stars,' so the most famous person in the cast was probably Paul Nicholls, who'd been in *East-Enders* for a couple of years; the rest were either unknown or had no profile. I also wanted everybody in the cast to be young. Daniel Craig was one of the oldest actors, and he was only about thirty at the time. Ben Whishaw was still doing his A Levels, I think. The doyenne of casting directors, Mary Selway, got all these incredible guys in: I saw about a hundred and thirty different actors, and ended up choosing a platoon of thirteen plus a few extras, so I could have cast the film several times over. Again, what I was looking for in the auditions was naturalism, and I rejected some very well-known actors who didn't quite cut the mustard.

Would you say that the film is seen through the eyes of the Paul Nicholls character, Billy Macfarlane, or did you regard it more as an ensemble piece?

I'd say it's both. It's Billy Macfarlane's film because it starts and ends with him – and there's no doubt that the relationship between him and his brother, and him and the sergeant, are the key emotional axes – but at the same time it was inevitably going to be an ensemble.

The final image of Billy being shot is reminiscent of Robert Capa's famous photograph of a soldier dying

during the Spanish Civil War, which Peter Weir also recreated in his film _Gallipoli_. Presumably you had both of those reference points in mind?

Yes. I like _Gallipoli_ – which _is_ a realistic World War I film – and I know that Capa photograph very well. Capa's photograph also appears in _Sweet Caress_, where it's accused of being fake, which is how it's generally regarded now. I always planned to end with the death of Billy, and I always envisaged it as a freeze-frame. It's quite interesting how we did that. A rope was attached to Paul's back, he started to run, then he was pulled backwards. We then took out the rope in post-production, and it looks brilliantly authentic, because Paul didn't know when to expect that jerk back.

Talking of fake images, I notice that the film-maker from the War Office Cinematograph Committee who films the colonel's pep talk to the platoon is Harold Faithfull, John James Todd's unscrupulous rival from _The New Confessions_.

Nobody's picked up on that apart from you. Even I'd forgotten it! But yes, that moment is pure _New Confessions_. Harold Faithfull is very much, 'I can fake this up back at base, sir,' but John James Todd actually wants to get out into no man's land, hide in a shell crater and film the real thing. Cameras were banned from the trenches until 1916, so there's no footage of British trench warfare before the Somme. The first newsreel pictures were taken then and stitched together with fake stuff to produce a feature-length documentary, _The Battle of the Somme_, and it played to packed houses because nobody back home knew what it was like out there.

The relationship between director and cinematographer is key in movies, particularly for a debut director. How did that relationship work with your director of photography, Tony Pierce-Roberts?

It worked extremely well. Tony was presented with the challenge that we were going to build most of the trenches in the studio, and I said to him, 'How do we film with freedom in something six feet wide and eight feet deep?' I thought we would use a Steadicam, but with that you still need a cameraman in the trench, so Tony came up with this idea of a camera on a boom, controlled by joysticks and a monitor outside the set. It was a brilliant invention, because the camera was also on a track, so you could move up and down, and on a gimbal, so you could pan 360 degrees. Genuine 360 degree pans are very rare in films because usually your camera crew gets in the way and you have to fake it, but in *The Trench* nobody can spot the joins because there are no joins. Possibly my favourite scene is when Tam Williams gets shot: the camera movement in that scene is fantastic. It's panic and mayhem and it's all being done on Tony's contraption. One of my only post-mortem niggles is that the lighting in some of the scenes is just a little too lush. I deliberated with Steve for a while about whether to leach the colours out, but then I thought that was a bit of a cliché. The whole point is that it's World War I in Technicolor, not in black-and-white like we're used to.

Also, if we'd had more money, we might have dug more trenches and sheeted them over with a roof so you wouldn't have been able to spot that we'd moved from the built trenches, but it was a low budget art-house war movie and we had to work within those parameters. For *1917*, they had the advantage of digging actual trenches on Salisbury Plain, but that wasn't an option available to me – although we did go to a field in Berkshire and let off real explosions. We also used early CGI for the walk across no man's land, to make a few dozen extras look like a cast of hundreds.

Perhaps using built instead of dug trenches was an advantage after all: the claustrophobia is heightened by the fact that we rarely see above them.

That was the *Das Boot* influence: you get very few glimpses of the sky and it's often shut out by these curious bridges that they had in the trenches. The only time it really opens up is when they go over the top, and you're almost glad to be out of that relentless brown labyrinth. The other benefit of shooting in a studio was that we didn't have to worry about rain or aeroplanes or cars passing by. We actually finished early because it was so well planned. We had about a day and a half to fill, and went around doing pick-up shots of the trench floor and people walking; shoe leather we could stick in if we had an editing issue. God knows what we'd have done if it had rained the day we went over the top: we only had one day to shoot it and didn't have any weather cover.

Your editor and production designer, Jim Clark and Jim Clay, are both distinguished in their fields. What was your experience of working with them?

Jim Clark was editing the film on set and would send us little notes saying, 'I need a close-up of his hand.' If we went a whole day without receiving one, I'd say to the script supervisor, who oversaw the continuity, 'We haven't had a note from Jim Clark today!' Jim Clay also did a brilliant job. The Somme, in July 1916, was a quiet sector of the trenches: it hadn't rained for months and no man's land was a meadow of chest-high grass. We couldn't find a suitable meadow, but apart from that the look of the trenches is completely authentic – and then, of course, ill-informed critics said, 'Where's the mud?' One of the reasons I opened with real black-and-white photographs of the trenches was to show that they were dry and well constructed and nobody had any mud on them, and then the photographs bleed into colour to make it seem seamless. There's also a scene where Paul Nicholls goes to pick up the rum ration, and it looks like the trenches go on for miles; but he's basically walking down the same stretch, we just changed the signposts and moved a few sandbags.

The score was composed by Evelyn Glennie and Greg Malcangi, who had done very little screen work up to that point. How did you come to choose them?

I knew Evelyn Glennie's work, and I thought if we had a percussive score it would get away from the violins and accordions associated with World War I films. Evelyn is a brilliant percussionist – and Greg Malcangi, her then-husband, was the technical expert – so I pitched it to her and she was absolutely thrilled. We did end up putting in a bit of synthesizer, but it's not your typical score and I think it's great – although she said to me, 'It's the most conventional music I've ever written.' Scoring is a mysterious art, it seems to me, and I learned a lot on *The Trench*. During the scoring of *A Good Man in Africa* we kept firing the composers, and I realized that it's almost counter-intuitive: you think there should be music when there shouldn't, or you think it should be jaunty when it should be serious. There's a contemporary tendency to over-score films – they sometimes seem to have music running under every scene – but a good score makes a huge contribution to the film as a whole.

Would you like to direct again?

It was a great experience and I enjoyed every aspect of it – apart from getting up early in the morning – so I would like to have at least one more stab at it. Shortly after *The Trench*, I wrote another script for myself to direct and Steve to produce – a thriller called *Stone Free*, which all takes place in one building over one night and would also be shot in the studio – but we've both been busy with other things and haven't managed to get our ducks in a row. That would still be the one I'd direct if I could, but to be honest my film-making life is satisfied by the role I have now as writer/producer: I'm involved in the casting, the editing and the scoring – and, as a lazy novelist, I can go to the set whenever I want.

You said earlier that, as directors have dropped out of other projects you've written, people have asked, 'Why don't *you* direct this?' So why don't you – particularly if it's an adaptation of one of your own novels or short stories?

As I've said, I have this slightly purist idea that original screenplays are what you should be filming, not adaptations. Even though two-thirds or three-quarters of all films are adaptations, they're almost, by default, compromises, whereas if you write something expressly for the screen then no compromises are necessary. Also, having written a novel or short story, it wouldn't be so satisfying to direct it, somehow. Never say never, but I feel that if I do direct again I would only direct something written for that ninety- or hundred-minute slot, something that plays to the strengths of the art form without always having the source material lurking behind it.

Is it your experience that the more challenging the material is, the harder it is to get a project off the ground? Or is it just luck?

At the end of the day I think it's luck, and I've had lots of strokes of luck in my film career. *Stars and Bars* got made because David Puttnam became head of Columbia Pictures. That was a stroke of luck. A few years ago I wrote an adaptation of Graham Greene's last novel, *The Captain and the Enemy*, which I thought was dead in the water, but that's suddenly heated up again because a director, Asif Kapadia, read it and loved it. That was a stroke of luck. As a screenwriter you choose interesting stories and hope that producers are attracted to them, but the catalyst that makes them happen is the talent. Art-house movies are an endangered species now, and you need to have a director or an actor attached that will make financiers relax. Everybody may love the script, but nobody will give you five million dollars to make it unless they can be reassured that they will get their money back.

Five

Fiction 3

Any Human Heart (2002) – *Fascination* (2004)
Restless (2006) – *Ordinary Thunderstorms* (2009)
Waiting for Sunrise (2012)

The subject of *Any Human Heart*, Logan Mount-stuart, first appeared in 'Hôtel des Voyageurs' in *The Destiny of Nathalie 'X'*. Did you have any idea when you wrote that story that you would later devote a whole novel to this character?

No, I didn't. That story was inspired by Cyril Connolly, who's one of my favourite writers. Connolly kept a fragmentary journal in the 1920s, which was published and edited by David Pryce-Jones, and I was very engaged by the tone of it and wrote 'Hôtel des Voyageurs' as a sort of pastiche, with Logan as a Connolly figure. There's a lot of Connolly in Logan: constantly falling out with people or falling in love with people. So that may be when the journal idea seeded itself. And, of course, I used Logan again in *Nat Tate*.

In fact, at the start of *Nat Tate*, which was published four years before *Any Human Heart*, you

note that you are 'currently editing' the journals of Logan Mountstuart.

It's probably fair to say that *Any Human Heart* was already looming behind Logan's presence in *Nat Tate*. *Any Human Heart* cohered when I picked up, in a shop in Paris, a book called *A. O. Barnabooth* by Valéry Larbaud. Larbaud is a fascinating figure, a dilettante *littérateur* who's best known as the translator of Joyce's *Ulysses* into French, and he wrote this little book in journal form about a rich American in the 1920s. Again, it's very engaging, and it led me to the decision to write a long novel in that form. So that was the sequence of inspirational moments behind *Any Human Heart*, and it then took me four years to figure out and research and write it, because of the acute technical challenges it presented.

Nat Tate also includes two photographs of Logan – or two different men who you identify as Logan – a group photo from 1947 and a portrait photo from 1959.

Not many people have realized that there's a portrait photograph of Logan Mountstuart in *Nat Tate*, but you're right, there he is – although I slightly regretted that once I'd reinvented him in *Any Human Heart*.

Given Bernard Levin's review of *The New Confessions*, in which he talked about 'riffling through the pages for the photographs', did you ever consider using photos in *Any Human Heart*?

That review triggered me into collecting photographs: I'd buy discarded albums in junk shops and antique sales and raid them for photos, and out of one family album I might get two good photographs. I decided not to use photographs in *Any Human Heart*, because *Nat Tate* had rather stolen its thunder, but I did use them later on in *Sweet Caress*, for which I bought two thousand photographs and used seventy-three.

Which made sense, since *Sweet Caress* is about a photographer.

Exactly. Photographs suited that endeavour better. Whereas the paraphernalia of *Any Human Heart* – the footnotes, the index, the editorial presence – was all literary.

We've discussed the theme of good luck and bad luck in relation to previous novels, but it seems to me that *Any Human Heart* is the book in which you most clearly articulate it. Would you agree?

Absolutely. Again, I try not to overanalyse myself, but looking back I can see it's an abiding theme, and for some reason I decided to foreground it in the story of Logan's life. And I think people who read the novel pick up on that and apply it to the ups and downs and forking paths of their own lives.

One of the things which makes it so engaging and, in the end, so powerful, is that Logan spends half his life berating himself for not writing a great work when in fact he's doing it all along: what he thinks of

as a simple chronicle of good and bad luck becomes his biggest artistic achievement.

Yes, I think that's true. I also think it's true of a lot of the great journal keepers, whether it's Boswell or Pepys or Kilvert or Virginia Woolf. Woolf's novels are strange, fey, unsatisfactory things, but the record of her life in her journals is absolutely fascinating and enduring. There's something about the journal form, written innocently day by day, that bears witness to a life better than anything else.

Was that one of the technical challenges the novel presented?

That was the biggest challenge: it took a lot of artifice to make it seem artless. The best journals are those written without an eye to posterity. That would include all those people I mentioned – except Virginia Woolf, who had a beady eye on posterity, which you can spot. The other journal keeper who I really like is the artist Keith Vaughan, and when Logan tries to commit suicide in Paris he replicates what Vaughan did. Vaughan was writing his journal as he died, and you can see the pen tail off on the last page as he loses consciousness. But that journal wasn't written for posterity, and similarly Logan's journals aren't written for anybody apart from him to read. So I did a lot of thinking about how to make them feel natural and guileless and honest, and I deliberately made mistakes and repeated things and put in stuff that was boring. At the same time, I wanted people to be curious about what happens next – for it to have the momentum of a novel and yet look like the random happenstance of someone's life – so I set a lot of narrative hares running up front, the friendships and relationships that endure and recur: like Peter Scabius's wife, Gloria, who he encounters earlier on and who comes back into his life to die, or the French poet, Cyprien, who leaves him the house that he winds up living in. It was carefully constructed to give the book a shape even though it's supposed to be shapeless.

The novel comprises eleven sections: a preamble, an afterword and nine journals – School, Oxford, First London, Second World War, Post-War, New York, African, Second London and French – plus editorial summaries of Logan's life between journals. Were they a way of limiting the novel's length?

It's the same with all these 'whole life' novels: if you were going to do it properly you'd have a 3,000-page book, so you have to decide where you cut and what you elide. With the editorial interpolations I could easily fill in the gaps, and deal with five years of Logan's life in one paragraph. I usually have a pretty good idea of the length of the novel I'm writing – to within, let's say, twenty or thirty pages – and *Any Human Heart* was always going to be a long one. I didn't set out to write a 500-page novel, but it turned out to be almost exactly that – and I suspect the novel I'm going to write next will be close to 500 pages as well, because I know how much matter I have to cover. Sometimes I'm surprised. I thought that *Trio* would be shorter than it was, but as I wrote it, more stuff went into it.

The epigraph from Henry James which gives the novel its title – 'Never say you know the last word about any human heart' – is echoed in a line from your short story 'The View from Yves Hill': 'Other human beings, however well you may think you know them, are utterly opaque, utterly mysterious.' In other words, people are endlessly multifaceted.

Exactly. And related to that is the idea which Logan articulates in his preface: that we're not simply one individual, we're a collection of selves, and as our life moves on our personality mutates and transforms at some elemental level. I find that idea very intriguing: that the person you were at eighteen is a stranger to the person you are at sixty-eight. That's certainly true in my case, and the evidence is there in my journals. I started keeping a journal in my first year at university, and I've been keeping one since 1981 when my first novel was published. There's a gap of about eight years in between but it's now millions of words, and when I went back to my teenage journals I didn't recognize that person. If you'd said, 'What were you like when you were eighteen?' I'd have given you a totally false impression. I'd have said, 'Oh, I was lazy and easygoing,' and actually I was anxious and hard on myself. All that went into *Any Human Heart*: the sense that Logan changes through the different journals as things happen to him. So that's another big theme of the book.

You've said that you're not an autobiographical writer, yet the various sections of *Any Human Heart* are all set in places that have played major parts in

your own life: public school, Oxford, London, New York, Nigeria, France. Which begs the obvious question: is there a great deal of you in Logan?

I don't think so, but maybe I'm not the best person to judge. He does go to a lot of places I've been, but the same is true of *Love is Blind*: the places that Brodie Moncur goes to are all places I know well or have visited. Logan is born abroad, as I was, but his relationship with his parents is completely different to mine. He's much lazier than me, and more neurotic than me. So no, he is a fictional character. If he's like anybody, he's like certain types of English writers that I'm rather obsessed with: Cyril Connolly, Lawrence Durrell, Henry Green – lazy, drunken, slightly dodgy types who somehow managed to finesse a literary career. And the ultimate model was William Gerhardie: a huge literary star in the 1920s who published his last book in 1938 and died in 1977 after thirty-nine years of silence. He's a fascinating case study, and a terrible warning of how it can all go wrong. Logan's career is very like Gerhardie's, and Yves Hill is based on him too.

You've had considerable and consistent success as a writer for forty years, yet you've written a number of times about artists whose early success is followed by a steady decline or premature death: John James Todd, Nat Tate, Logan Mountstuart – and later, in your short stories, Yves Hill. Is that because failure is more poignant than success?

Yes, I think it is. You can't write a novel about someone who's fit and happy and successful, and everything goes well for them and they die in their sleep aged one hundred and four. For stories to work, things need to be at stake. To put it bluntly, stuff has to happen. Even if it's interior stuff, there has to be some forward motion. And the more things that go wrong, the easier it is to produce that forward motion. It's elementary storytelling.

Logan's experiences at boarding school are a lot less harsh than Todd's in _The New Confessions_, or your own as described in _School Ties_ and depicted in _Good and Bad at Games._ Was that deliberate?

I didn't have any intention of making it a more benign portrayal of boarding school life, but it may well be, because they're senior boys and can engineer an easy life for themselves within the school's demands. The friendships formed there carry on through the rest of the novel, so it was more to do with the larger narrative plan than anything I wanted to say about boarding school – which, in any case, I'd already said. Some incidents are based on my experience – the military exercise, for example – but a bigger influence was probably the diaries Evelyn Waugh wrote when he was at Lancing College. He comes out of them as a very unpleasant young person – as he's the first to admit – but you get a glimpse of the man who would emerge from the boy. If I was trying to reflect anything, it was that precocious intellectual disdain you can have at the age of seventeen or eighteen. I'm trying to remember if there was a model for every journal of Logan's, a deliberate echo of other diaries, but I don't think there was.

There was clearly a model for Logan's friend and fellow writer Peter Scabius, and that's Graham Greene.

I'm a great admirer of Graham Greene. I've written a lot about him, and some of his novels have been hugely influential on me. As I read a writer's canon I find that I become interested in the writer's life, and Greene is a very complex figure. His Catholicism, for example, was highly suspect – something I think he switched on and off as required – so a lot of his equivocation went into Peter Scabius, and Scabius's novel *Guilt* is reminiscent of Greene's *The End of the Affair*. Peter Scabius is like a nastier Graham Greene: totally amoral and self-serving, with an eye for the main chance. But there are many writers like that, so you could have modelled him on all manner of people.

There are several episodes in the novel – his entanglement with the Duke and Duchess of Windsor, his internment during World War II, his involvement with the radical fringe in the 1970s – which have a surreal, almost Kafkaesque quality.

This comes back to the idea that I'm essentially a comic novelist, that I see the world, in all its cruelty and injustice, through an idiosyncratic comic lens, and those episodes are very good examples of my natural tendency to shift into black humour or absurdity rather than po-faced seriousness. There isn't anything particularly funny about the Baader–Meinhof Group, but I thought there was something quite funny about our English equivalent, the Angry Brigade, who only managed to slightly injure somebody once in all their bombs and outrages; so Logan's encounter with the Angry Brigade and the Baader–Meinhof girls is surreal, but with dark undercurrents because they're still trying to kill people. I'm fascinated by that whole era, and I've gone back to it in a TV series I've written called *Finzi's Game*, which is a contemporary thriller but has its roots in Italian urban terrorism of the '70s and '80s: the 'Anni di piombo', as they're known, the 'Years of Lead'. Terrorism was ever-present as I was growing up, so that's why I'm interested in it and why it's filtered into my work.

It strikes me that Logan keeps getting involved in other people's battles – not just with the Angry Brigade, but in the Spanish Civil War, with the Windsors in the Bahamas, in the Biafran War, and with his neighbour in France – often at the expense of getting a grip on the struggles in his own life.

Good point. I hadn't thought of that. You're absolutely right, but that's a reflection of his impulsive nature: he doesn't stop and think, he just barges in. Like when he has an affair with his son's ex-girlfriend: not a good idea. It's the same with the widow in France and her father's dubious criminal past – which is actually a true story. That's the nature of the man: things happen to him and he has to employ massive damage limitation to sort it all out. In a way, the portrait of Logan is a portrait of any individual: sometimes he behaves badly and lets himself down, other times he behaves well and acts courageously, but he's not consistently one or the other – as none of us is. People are very complex, and that's what interests me.

Any Human Heart is the novel of yours that people seem most likely to know. Are you aware of it being particularly close to readers' hearts?

It's curious how novels resonate with readers. I wrote an introduction to Alasdair Gray's novel *Lanark*, which is like the *Ulysses* of Glasgow, saying that readers have unique relationships with novels: that the person you were when you read them – where you were, how happy or unhappy you were – all colour the way that you read them. I've had more letters about *Any Human Heart* than about any of my other novels, so there's no doubt that it affects readers more than the others – although some of the others, like *Sweet Caress* and *Brazzaville Beach*, do generate an extra readerly response, where people particularly identify with the story or the characters. *Any Human Heart* actually got quite mixed reviews when it came out, but it's probably my most-read book, and read by people who aren't always regular readers. It's read out at weddings and funerals, and I get letters from people saying, 'I've called my son Logan.' As an author you just thank your lucky stars that something you wrote resonates in that way; that this person you invented, this unusual, individual life, seems to touch real people's lives. With *Any Human Heart*, I think that's because a) it's a journal, so it's very intimate, and b) it's a whole life, so you know everything about this character. That's what makes it different from other novels.

Your TV adaptation of the novel takes a bold approach to dramatizing the 'whole life' concept,

starting from its dreamlike opening, with the three older Logans standing on a riverbank looking at young Logan in a rowing boat, then turning to look at each other like passing a baton.

That's pure cinema, really. Often on screen, where there's meant to be a seamless transition from a young person to an older one, they haven't taken the trouble to get the match even close, and it bothers you. Given the nature of the novel, we decided to set up our conceit at the very start – these are the people who will be embodying the different ages of Logan – so that when one morphs into the next, people don't have a problem with the fact that they don't look anything like each other. And there's that great scene at the end where the camera tracks across the kitchen, and through the magic of cinema Jim Broadbent turns into Matthew Macfadyen and then into Sam Claflin and then into the little lad. It's something the novel couldn't do, and the series pulled off with incredible gracefulness.

The opening also establishes the use of voiceover, which is absolutely central to the adaptation working.

Exactly. It came with the territory. It wasn't tacked on in post-production, it was intrinsic to the script. Voiceover is still a crude tool compared to what you can do in a novel, but it's a very useful way of giving exposition and getting inside the characters' heads.

Of the four episodes, totalling four and three-quarter hours, Sam Claflin appears for three-quarters of an

episode, Matthew Macfadyen for two episodes and Jim Broadbent for one and a quarter episodes, more or less. Did you find that structure through the various drafts of the script, or at the editing stage?

A lot of that was in the script, but certain decisions were taken in the edit, as they always are with film. The edit is such an important moment to rethink a project; you can do extraordinary things with the material you've shot. There was much discussion about when we would move from Sam into Matthew, and from Matthew into Jim, and how we would finesse that. I would say that Matthew is centre stage and Sam and Jim bookend his narrative, and I think Sam and Jim would acknowledge that what happens to Matthew is the meat of the story. Matthew's part was the key one to cast, and when we got him we went looking for the older and younger Logans. In fact, we cast it pretty effortlessly – and it's fantastically well acted. From its commissioning onward the whole experience was very good, and I was really pleased with the result.

The school section of the novel is the first major omission from the TV version, although you did conflate some of the incidents from it with the Oxford section. Was that a difficult or an easy cut to make?

Easy, I think, because we'd have needed another, younger Logan, which would have been five actors, so we thought we'd start when the characters are in their early twenties rather than in their teens. Also, because I'd already done two films about public school, I thought I might be repeating myself and it might be a bit dull. The whole Nigerian section was cut as well, because we'd have had to go to Africa to shoot it. One bold decision there and you save a huge chunk of the budget. When it was commissioned, by Liza Marshall at Channel 4, I said, 'It has to be six hours long. I can't have it any shorter than that,' and she said, 'Fine!' In the end, as you say, it did turn out to be shorter, but we were given a lot of scope and that made a big difference. But you still can't get all of the novel into five hours, so it was a question of what worked best. The love story with Freya was obviously central, so that got a lot of attention. We thought we could attract interesting actors to play the Duke and Duchess of Windsor, so we made the Bahamian section more important. These very simple narrative choices determined what was in and what was out. The remarkable thing about the TV series is that even though it's a totally different art form and maybe 40 per cent of the novel isn't in it, it has the same effect as the novel. People feel that they've seen a life lived from beginning to end and have a familiarity with Logan that's unusual in film, as it's unusual in a novel. It's amazing how, on screen, less can be more; how you can treat something in a fleeting way but people don't see it as fleeting. A glimpse of the Spanish Civil War does a lot for you in the series, whereas in the novel it's dealt with in a far more significant way. So that's another thing that film does well: elision.

You've not only taken things out, you've also put things in, including one dramatic addition: Logan's discovery that Freya was pregnant when she was killed.

It's very easy for films and TV series to sag narratively; that's why I put in new stuff at the end of the TV version, to give the ravening maw of film something to chew on. Nothing much happens at the end of the novel. Logan's living in his house, he's going shopping in the village, he's got his cat and his dog. That doesn't make for exciting film-making. So I invented the revelation that there was another child which he lost when Freya died, because otherwise nobody would carry on watching this old geezer living out his quiet life in the French countryside. A decision like that is straightforward when you're trying to do the best adaptation you can rather than be slavishly faithful to the book, which is almost always a mistake.

When you're adapting one of your novels for film or TV, do you ever go back to ideas you considered and discarded when you were originally writing them?

I don't go back looking for solutions for the script, but I do sometimes recognize in scripting the adaptation that certain things would have worked very well in the novel. The discovery of Freya's pregnancy is a good example: it adds a poignancy to the end of Logan's life that isn't there on the page.

The TV series has a flashback structure which takes the place of the editorial presence in the novel: the older Logan is sorting out his papers at his French house, and whereas the novel is divided into different journals according to his location, Logan organizes his papers to reflect the woman most central to each

section of his life. What was your thinking behind that structure, both dramatically and thematically?

That's a good example of how something that works perfectly well in a novel doesn't work very well on screen, therefore you have to find something that works better. I had the idea early on that the older Logan is setting his house in order, and we see him laying out all this stuff on trestle tables; and because people are more interesting than places – and because we had all these amazing actresses playing the different women – we decided to make it character based rather than location based. That was a good decision, I think, and allowed us to give a unifying structure to Logan's life, looking back at it through the relationships he had. Love is one of the biggest themes of the novel: Freya is Logan's great love, and somehow that love irradiates his life after she's dead, even though he has other relationships. He says something like, 'I loved her and she loved me and that's all I need,' which is something that crops up again and again in my work.

Watching it the other day, more than a decade after it was made, the section set in London in the 1970s, in a country Logan describes as angry and divided, had a real resonance for Britain in the early 2020s.

It was a strife-torn period, and part of my own memories of being a student in the '70s is going on marches and demonstrating for and against various causes. I vividly remember the miners' strike and the three-day week – and the 1979 general election, which is when Logan leaves the country, was the beginning of a revolution that we're still living through. Sometimes you think you're living in the worst of times, but a bit of historical perspective can make it seem less bad than you thought.

The ending of the TV series is almost more affecting than the ending of the novel: the final tracking shot through a bookshop towards a table piled with books and into close-up on a copy of *Any Human Heart*: *The Intimate Journals of Logan Mountstuart* with a photograph of Matthew Macfadyen on the front – his account of his life becoming a palimpsest of your account of his life. It's meta, but it's moving.

I actually have that very copy on my mantelpiece. But you're right, it winds the whole thing up brilliantly. In the novel you're only told about Logan's death, but in the series you see Jim keel over, with that wonderful image of backlit thistledown. That's one of the great strengths of film: photography. You see him die and then you see what he's written and you don't need any words to explain it. As you say, it's a bit meta – the series is called *Any Human Heart*, and there's the book it's adapted from – but it delivers emotionally: catharsis is arrived at and you suddenly see what the life you've been learning about ends up being.

There are a handful of deleted scenes on the DVD, mainly short scenes from the linking structure, and in one of them the older Logan throws an empty box file labelled *Octet* onto a bonfire and says, 'I've written it.' In other words, he realizes that his journals

are his great work – which would have made him too self-aware, and would have undercut that final shot.

That may be another example of, 'Don't try to faithfully adapt the novel.' I was looking at the ending of the book the other day, and it says in the afterword, 'No trace of the novel *Octet* was found, but Jean-Robert remembers helping Logan build a bonfire a week before he died.' And that didn't work filmically. We hadn't seeded it throughout, and it would have taken far too much effort to explain the significance of the scene. Also, how do you film somebody writing a long novel? Yawn. So it was a very easy thing to let go.

Conversely, if you had adapted the novel into six or eight episodes, which is now much more common, is there anything you cut out that you would put back in?

It's an interesting thought experiment. What would I have done if I'd been given eight hours? Would we have taken Logan off to Africa, which is a bit of his life I really like, and got him out of Europe and America? I don't know. The thing you get with six or eight hours is a leisureliness, in the best sense. Film is usually cut, cut, cut, get on with it, get on with it. Long form TV allows you to take the time to establish a scene or a relationship. I suspect if we'd had six or eight hours to make *Any Human Heart* it would have been exactly the same story, but that extra time would have been enriching for the performances and the cadences of the narrative. But if you're writing a narrative-driven thriller like *Finzi's Game*, you don't want leisureliness, you want non-stop, heart-in-mouth, what's-gonna-happen-next? So different genres exploit the time available in different ways. Either way, you'd better have a lot of narrative to hand, otherwise you can suddenly find yourself running out of stuff to write.

From long form to short form: your third story collection, *Fascination*. The interval between *Fascination* and *Nathalie 'X'* was five years less than the interval between *Nathalie 'X'* and *Yankee Station*, yet there are seven more stories in it. Does that mean you were writing more short stories during that period?

I have lots of vague ideas for short stories floating around my head, but I don't just write them and put them out there, I wait to be asked, and it's the commission that makes the ideas coalesce. *Le Monde*, for example, wanted a very long short story for their summer issue, and that became 'A Haunting', which they translated and I think is my longest short story. Similarly, the reason for the slight increase in output was that a friend of mine, Bill Buford, who had been the editor of *Granta*, became the fiction editor of the *New Yorker* and started asking me to contribute stories. I came across a story the other day which was in the first issue of the *Literary Review*; I'd forgotten I'd written it and I'm thinking of putting that in my next collection. So it's pretty random, but it's quite a continuum underneath the other work that I do.

When we talked before about 'Varengeville', which I compared to 'Killing Lizards', you identified the artist

in the story as Georges Braque, who also appears in
***Nat Tate*. Why, then, is he unnamed?**

I do that all the time, in my novels as well: little allusions
that are there not to make me look smart, but to give a bit
extra to readers who pick up on them. At the end of *Love
is Blind*, Brodie Moncur is in Trieste and meets James
Joyce and his brother Stanislaus, but they're only named
as Shem and Stan. If you know about Joyce, you'll think,
'Of course, he was in Trieste at the time,' but if you don't
know that, they're still a couple of very funny Irishmen –
and if you don't know anything about Georges Braque,
he's just an old painter and it doesn't affect your enjoyment of the story. He's always been in Picasso's shadow,
Braque, and he ploughed a lonelier furrow, but he's an
extraordinary painter – and Nat Tate does indeed go to
visit him in his studio and then commits suicide after seeing his amazing late paintings. Braque lived in Varengeville
at the end of his life, and I got a letter a couple of months
ago from a man who arranges tours of Braque's studio.
He'd stumbled across *Nat Tate* and assumed that I'd been
to Varengeville and wondered where that photograph of
Braque was taken, so I had to disillusion him that it was all
fake.

**'Varengeville' not only harks back, it also looks for-
ward: the story ends with the boy watching a woman
on a beach with a dog, and later in the collection you
have a story called 'The Woman on the Beach with a
Dog' – which, in turn, is obviously referencing the
Chekhov story 'The Lady with the Dog'.**

Inevitably, as time goes by and the body of work gets larger, the web of interconnections becomes more obvious – and more intriguing, perhaps. The commission in that instance was for the magazine *Modern Painters*, to write a short story inspired by an Edward Hopper painting, and it was published in the magazine with the picture. The one I chose is of a woman sitting alone on a sunlit bed, looking out the window.

Hopper's pictures are redolent with loneliness.

Yes, exactly. When you think of those Hopper images – a man at a gas station, a woman sitting on a porch – they seem quite banal on the surface but you can invest them with all manner of emotions. Even his landscapes and townscapes – because they're always done at a certain time of day, when the shadows are long and the buildings are clearly defined by the low sun – are replete with potential. The template for the story is modelled pretty closely on 'The Lady with the Dog' – an affair that's rumbling on but will never be fully requited, with one of those wonderful open-ended Chekhovian endings where the reader can make of it what they want – but that last image of the couple in the hotel room separated by their anguish is quite Hopperian. His pictures encourage narrative speculation.

You mentioned that Edward Scully reappears twice in *Fascination*. You also introduce two new characters who recur in your next collection, *The Dreams of Bethany Mellmoth*, beginning with the unnamed film-maker who pens 'Notebook No. 9'.

I've written two stories featuring this embittered British director, 'Notebook No. 9' and 'Unsent Letters', and he may crop up again if I want to vent my frustrations about the movies. I've spent forty years in and around the movie business, and I've got a whole host of anecdotes and opinions about it, so it's inevitable that it appears in my fiction – *Trio* being a case in point, or *The New Confessions*, or 'Nathalie "X"'. It's like my boarding school experience: a huge chunk of my life that I've observed at close range.

Even stories not directly about film-making are sometimes inflected with it: 'The Persistence of Vision' in *Nathalie 'X'*, 'Loose Continuity' and 'Visions Fugitives' in *Fascination*.

And 'Adult Video', which uses the labels on a zapper as a way of advancing and reversing and pausing the story. I've watched as widely in the art form of film as I've read in the art form of fiction, so it's completely part of my cultural and intellectual landscape and manifests itself in ways I'm both aware of and unaware of. 'Visions Fugitives' was a challenge I set myself, an attempt to write a short story in the form of a French New Wave film, with jump cuts and repeated images and so on. You'd be a fool to try and do that at novel length, but I'm really pleased with how it works as a short story. I always say, though, that devices which may seem cinematic were actually present in novels before cinema was invented: close-ups, cross-cutting, ripple dissolves, slow motion – it's all there in *Madame Bovary*.

I'd say that 'Visions Fugitives' is one of your most complicated stories: there's cinema, there's music, there's the past, there's the present – it's a very rich tapestry.

It shows what short stories can achieve: they can contain multitudes. Going back to my theory that there are seven types of short story, I would describe 'Visions Fugitives' as a ludic short story, in that you're playing with different elements and saying, 'How do these parts relate to each other?' They do, but you have to figure them out. Nabokov is great at that kind of story, like 'Spring in Fialta', for example, where you baffle and beguile the reader and urge them to decrypt the narrative.

Another story in the collection, 'The Ghost of a Bird', was turned into a short film, *Patient 39*, written and directed by Dan Clifton. It's the only work of yours that you've allowed somebody else to adapt for the screen – why that one in particular?

Dan and I worked together on another project that never got off the ground – *City of Lies*, based on Hugh Trevor-Roper's book *The Last Days of Hitler*. In this case, his approach was very professional, the film was financed and ready to go, and all he needed was my approval, so I just thought, 'Let's go for it and see what happens.' I've allowed radio adaptations that I haven't written, and somebody did a stage adaptation of *Good and Bad at Games* which I didn't see, so occasionally I say yes – and *Patient 39* was a good experience. I went to the shoot one day, and I went to two early screenings, and it's a very good adaptation of the short story.

The second recurring character who first appears in _Fascination_ is the writer Yves Hill, and 'The View from Yves Hill' is like a chapter from the later life of Logan Mountstuart.

It's not so much Logan as one of the inspirations behind him, William Gerhardie. Like Logan, Gerhardie peaked too early. His first two novels were huge hits; he wrote his autobiography when he was in his thirties; Evelyn Waugh, Graham Greene and Anthony Powell all acknowledged their huge debt to him; but his last novel to be published came out just before World War II, and afterwards he slid into neglect and oblivion. Michael Holroyd championed him, and his books were republished in the 1970s, but it made no difference. He was a forgotten man and became poorer and poorer and more and more eccentric. So in the same way that 'The Pigeon' is a portrait of Chekhov, 'The View from Yves Hill' is an imaginary version of what William Gerhardie was like at the end of his life, when he would buy one hundred tins of mandarin oranges at a time and had a massively irritating but very close relationship with his cleaning lady. He pops up in the Bethany Mellmoth stories as well, and there's another story in that collection, 'Humiliation', about the young Yves Hill. He's a bit like Edward Scully, a sort of alter ego: imagining a future where everything has gone hideously wrong and nobody wants to publish your books any more.

Hard to imagine, in your case!

I do know older writers who cannot get published despite hugely distinguished careers. It's very odd how tastes or fashions or perceptions change and your category becomes obsolete. There's an expression that a friend and I share: 'Male, pale and stale.' That probably happens to every writer at some stage in their life: you're suddenly seen as past your sell-by date and the commissions dry up.

'The View from Yves Hill' isn't a sad story, though. He's still writing, living – loving, in his way – right to the end, and the final line of what feels like his self-penned obituary is strangely upbeat: 'He looked on the world and its denizens with a curious and not unkind eye. Most things he saw amused him.'

He's not in decline, he's a feisty, self-confident old geezer. Again, that was modelled on Gerhardie: his spirit of absurd humour was very Chekhovian. Gerhardie was born in Russia, spoke and read Russian and wrote a superb little book about Chekhov, and I think he introduced Chekhov into English literature. He was a friend of Katherine Mansfield, and Katherine Mansfield pillaged Chekhov, so you can see the spreading tentacles of Gerhardie's influence.

You've also adapted the story into a spec play, part monologue and part three-hander: Yves, his cleaner, and an academic who comes to interview him. Why the hybrid structure, rather than one or the other?

I originally conceived of it as a one-man show – and there's a whole genre of that, like Simon Callow doing Charles Dickens – but I thought it was funnier and worked better with these two women characters in it. I've written a play about Jean-Jacques Rousseau, *The Language of Love*, and in that Rousseau turns and addresses the audience. It's a common device in the theatre – and even in film, when a character breaks the fourth wall, nobody's bothered by it. It's a tool in your toolkit and you can use it if it's appropriate, so I didn't worry about the hybridity of the play. Like the story, it was stimulated by an intense familiarity with Gerhardie's life and its vicissitudes, and a desire to reinvent this literary figure in fictional form.

The same kind of familiarity, I imagine, which stimulated the final story in the collection, 'The Pigeon' – even though Chekhov is, once again, unnamed.

That's right. It's always interesting to get to know the individual behind the work that seems to speak to you, and I've become so immersed in certain writers that I almost feel like I've met them: Waugh, Greene, Dickens to a certain extent, Shakespeare, Shelley . . .

Gerhardie.

Exactly. I've written and read so much about them that I can imagine them walking into the room. I had that sense about Chekhov, and I also had this theory that the one woman he loved was a woman called Lika Mizinova, so I thought I'd write a story based on their on-off affair: he wouldn't commit to marrying her, so she eventually had an affair with his best friend to stir him up, got pregnant and had a child, and they resumed their relationship after that. He was a very sexually active man and several of the women he had affairs with wanted to marry him, but he would just dally with them and then dump them when it all got too intense. I suspect it was because he knew he was going to die young. He was a doctor, he had his first tubercular haemorrhage when he was twenty-three, and his brother died of tuberculosis at the age of thirty-one, so there was no sense in which he could kid himself. He did get married towards the end of his life, to the actress Olga Knipper, and it was not quite a marriage of convenience but certainly a marriage of distance, because they spent so much time apart. By then he knew he only had a couple of years left, and his family wanted him to get married, but she was at the theatre in Moscow and he was convalescing in Yalta. So I think that knowledge of his terminal illness made him a commitment-phobe, but I also think it shaped the clear-eyed view of human nature that you see in the stories. I don't know why I should be this arrogant or hubristic, but I really feel that I've got to grips with the kind of person he was, and that the voice in the story is almost Chekhov's voice speaking from beyond the grave.

There were four years between *Armadillo* and *Any Human Heart*, with *Nat Tate* in between, and there were another four years between *Any Human Heart* and *Restless*, with *Fascination* in between. Is it fair to say that *Any Human Heart* was a challenge to follow?

It was a challenge to write, there's no doubt about it. It's probably the longest I've ever taken to research, plot out and assemble a novel. But I wasn't thinking, 'That's it. I've climbed Mount Everest.' I just got on with the next one. In fact, it was the research into the world of spying that I'd done for *Any Human Heart* – Logan working with Ian Fleming and the Naval Intelligence Division during World War II – that made me come up with the idea for *Restless*. I became very interested in the Cambridge Five, particularly Kim Philby, and *Restless* is an attempt to understand what happens to you as a person when you have to live a double life and what kind of psyche you have to have in order to maintain this duplicity. Its thesis is that as a spy you can't trust anybody, because trusting people puts you at risk, yet you can't live a normal life without trusting people, so you become dehumanized. It's no wonder that most of them, like Guy Burgess and Donald Maclean, cracked up under the pressure. Philby was extraordinary; he maintained this facade for twenty-three years in spite of the fact that he was very nearly rumbled on at least two occasions. His three wives didn't know. His close colleagues had no idea. Hugh Trevor-Roper, who adored Philby, practically had a nervous breakdown when he defected, and John le Carré wrote a piece about Philby which is almost biblical in its rage and condemnation. Philby fooled them all. So the inspiration for *Restless* was imagining Philby triumphant: what if he hadn't defected to Russia but had become an Anthony Blunt figure – who was knighted and made Surveyor of the Queen's Pictures. Then I came across this reference to Winston Churchill's dirty tricks organization, British Security Co-ordination, and what they got up to in America in 1940–41, and I began to research that – and it was another of these gifts from history that you sometimes get as a novelist. I thought, 'That's the background to my story.' I also thought, 'Let's make it fresh and have a woman spy at the centre of it.' So the narrative motor is Eva Delectorskaya's relationship with this double agent, Lucas Romer, and how she ultimately gets her revenge on him.

Helped by her daughter, Ruth, in the chapters set in and around Oxford in 1976 – whose flirtation with radical, particularly German, politics presumably also came out of your research for *Any Human Heart*.

Yes – Logan's involvement with Baader–Meinhof is one of my favourite episodes in *Any Human Heart*. That seemed to me a good way to frame the story and, again, make it fresh, to have it narrated by two women in the third person and first person: Eva feeding Ruth her third person memoir to explain the life she's led and why she needs her daughter to help her bring about closure, and Ruth's first person story as she discovers that her mother is somebody totally different from the person she believed she was – and her understanding of what her mother went through beginning to trickle down into her own life. There are little autobiographical nods in there, too, in that Susan and I were living in Oxford during that blazing summer of 1976, and Ruth's flat above a dentist was our flat – which also appears in 'Adult Video'.

***Brazzaville Beach*, *The Blue Afternoon* and *Armadillo* all contain thriller elements, but *Restless* is your first novel which could actually be called a thriller. Would *you* call it that?**

I always call it a spy novel. It's squarely within that genre. But it's a very rich genre: a whole century and more of literary novelists have turned to it, starting with Joseph Conrad with *Under Western Eyes* and *The Secret Agent*.

Were you particularly influenced by any other spy novels when writing it?

There was a general literary influence, but I wasn't borrowing from any particular writer. For me, the key aspect of a successful, well-constructed spy novel is that it should be creatively baffling: you know that something's going on but you don't know what, and the basic allure is that you might get to the truth before the author reveals it. Le Carré, at his best, is brilliant at doing that: giving you glimpses and hints, and teasing you into reading on in an attempt to arrive at that conclusion.

So the journey that Ruth and Eva go on in *Restless* is like the journey any reader goes on in the course of a spy novel?

Exactly. Ruth is being fed this story piecemeal and is trying to get to the bottom of it, and when Lucas Romer is revealed as the traitor it should come as a huge surprise: the reader realizes it as Eva realizes it, because he makes one crucial mistake and gives away something – so she suddenly knows that he's going to kill her and she's got to go on the run. That's part of the pleasure of writing a spy novel, that 'Oh, my God!' moment.

During the novel you quote a line from Chekhov, which you also used as the epigraph for 'The Woman on the Beach with a Dog', and used again as one of the two epigraphs for *Trio*: 'Most people live their real, most interesting life under the cover of secrecy.' You seem to be intrigued by that notion.

I think that's why spies are appealing, because they do that by definition. In a way, that interest or insight or feeling reaches its fruition in *Trio*. I didn't think I'd be going down that road again in my fiction, having written about it in *Restless*, *Waiting for Sunrise*, the Bond novel, *Solo*, and the TV series, *Spy City*; but in fact I've got another novel in mind which occupies the same terrain, so it's definitely something I find very intriguing. Your inner life, however banal or shocking, is sacrosanct: no one can gain access to it apart from you, so it must make up some crucial element of your being. That's another reason why the novel is such a powerful art form, because only in a novel can we understand what people are really thinking and feeling. Other people are fundamentally unknowable – they might be lying to us or we might be getting them wrong – and Chekhov understood that. It's one of the things that makes his stories seem so modern.

The epigraph for the novel is taken from Volume Three of Proust's *À la recherche du temps perdu*: 'We may indeed say that the hour of death is uncertain, but when we say this we think of that hour as situated in a vague and remote expanse of time; it does

not occur to us that it can have any connection with the day that has already dawned . . .' Quite heavy for a spy novel.

But very relevant to the story. I'd been reading Proust, who's a much racier novelist than his reputation might indicate, and I was struck by this passage. As I've said, epigraphs are incredibly important in novels because they give the reader a clue as to how the novel should be read, and if you start a spy novel with a quote from Proust, it's saying, 'This is not lightweight.' It explains Eva's disquiet, her restlessness, because she doesn't know what's going to happen, or when. When I started writing the novel there was a case of an MI6 spy who had been in the heart of the IRA, and when he was outed after the Good Friday Agreement he went off to a remote cottage to hide – but he knew that one day there'd be a knock on the door. And there was: he was killed by a hit man with a shotgun. That's what made me choose the title, because it made me think of that life: once a spy, always a spy; once a stool pigeon, always a stool pigeon. Even if you're in the best witness protection programme in the world, at the back of your mind there must always be this terrible doubt. You're going to pick up the kids from school, but you don't know whether this is the afternoon you might die. That's what I wanted to suggest with the Proust quote. It's a wonderful comment on the random nature of our fates.

Does the title refer to the restlessness in Ruth as well?

I think so. She becomes infected with her mother's distrust. There's a moment during Eva's training when she goes to a bus station in Edinburgh and she's looking at the people around her and she realizes that this shift has occurred: she's no longer an ordinary person, she's now a spy, looking at the world in the way a spy does. And as Ruth understands that about her mother, it begins to contaminate her as well. She doesn't become as restless as her mother, but she's not quite at ease any more. That's what happens when you surrender trust: you've lost the ability to be at ease. The French title is interesting. 'Restless' is a hard word to translate because it has more nuances in English – it could just mean you can't get to sleep or it could mean some deeper anxiety – so in France it's called *La vie aux aguets*, which roughly translates as 'life on tenterhooks'. That's very much Eva's state of mind. That's what I was trying to pin down.

Restless was the first of four novels published by Bloomsbury during your eleven-year hiatus from Penguin, and was later reprinted in their 'Modern Classics' series. What do you think makes a book a classic?

The simple answer is posterity and consensus: if people are still reading the book and liking it after a certain amount of time has passed then it becomes a classic, and there's no way at all of predicting that. Contemporaries of Dickens like Mrs Humphry Ward and Edward Bulwer-Lytton were selling as many books as he did, if not more, but who reads them today? Posterity and consensus have made Dickens a classic writer but have consigned those two to the scrapheap of forgotten novelists – where we may all end up, of course. As the stoics say, 'Posterity is not our business.' But I think that's what makes books endure. It's nothing to do with the novel's ambition or scale, or when it was written or published, it's to do with its afterlife – or its half-life, like a radioactive isotope. Will it fizzle out or will it persist?

The novel was a bestseller and won the 2006 Costa Book Award, so it's no surprise that it was soon televised. How did the creative elements of the TV version come together?

It's one of the swiftest script-to-screen experiences I've had. I'd worked with the producer, Hilary Bevan Jones, on a short film called *The Three Kings* which Richard Eyre directed, one of a series of ten-minute films for Sky. They were basically silent movies, in that you could have sound effects but no dialogue, so I wrote this film about three special forces soldiers trying to rescue a downed pilot in Afghanistan, and they can only talk in sign language because if they speak they'll be discovered. Hilary's company, Endor, then suggested adapting *Restless*, and it was very quickly picked up by the BBC. We also cast it relatively quickly, and the cast was tremendous. Charlotte Rampling took a bit of persuading but she's fantastically good in it, and Hayley Atwell, who'd been in *Any Human Heart*, was sensational as the young Eva. We shot a lot of it in South Africa, which has amazingly varied landscapes: New York was Cape Town, Scotland was just outside Cape Town, Holland was somewhere upcountry. It was a very smooth and sunny experience, and I'm really pleased with the way it looks. It's had a substantial DVD life, and was streaming on Amazon quite recently. One of the downsides of writing for TV is that it sometimes feels a bit ephemeral in comparison to novels, which can have a very long shelf life. *Armadillo* is now available on DVD, but for a long time it wasn't, so nobody could see it. But now, with all these streamers, stuff that seemed lost is available. Even *Stars and Bars*, which never even had a VHS life, is streaming on some platform somewhere.

The 1940s sections of the TV version have a real film noir feel, and the part where Eva flees New York after the death of Morris Devereux reminded me of *Three Days of the Condor*.

Three Days of the Condor is a brilliant film, an inspirational film for me. I know exactly when I first saw it: Susan and I had just moved to Oxford, and on our first night there we went to the movies, so that would have been 1975. And I was blown away by it. I love film noir, too: *Chinatown* is possibly my favourite film. Film does thrillers really well: the genre plays to the medium's strengths. A lot of the films I like best are complicated thrillers, and those complexities often find their way into my novels, whether consciously or unconsciously.

One of the things that film allows you to do is cross-cutting, which is particularly effective in creating a climax at the end of Episode One, where Ruth and Eva are both going to vital meetings.

That's true. *Restless* was made in the two-times-ninety-minute format, which was very popular ten years ago and is now very unpopular, bizarrely. It's like making two movies, and you're very conscious of how you're going to end the first half of your drama, so you need a cliffhanger. That's probably what determined the cross-cutting: to make you tune in next week.

Even with three hours to play with, you still had to leave things out – including most of the '70s politics. Do you think removing those elements of Ruth's story shifts the balance of the narrative to Eva?

Yes, I think it does. It's another example of what you can do in a novel but you can't do on screen because of time and budget constraints. Also, if you're offering the public a spy thriller, they're expecting suspense and jeopardy rather than a leisurely investigation of radical politics in 1976. The other bit we left out was the Canadian sequence, when Eva is in Ottawa, which covers quite a long period of time in the novel even though it's not a large number of pages.

On the other hand, you added a sequence in London where Romer recognizes Eva by chance and chases her through the East End during an air raid, which brings together a number of elements in a very visual and dramatic way.

Exactly. It's the same reason I invented Freya's pregnancy in the adaptation of *Any Human Heart*: what's interesting in a novel isn't necessarily the stuff of filmed drama, so you have to think about upping the ante. Once Eva is back in England she becomes Mrs Gilmartin and assumes the life of an ordinary provincial housewife, so we needed something exciting to fill that gap.

You've also conflated characters: Ruth's PhD supervisor, and the academic he refers her to who knows about wartime spying, become one character, who's more mysterious than in the novel: you're not sure whose side he's on.

Again, that was to emphasize Ruth becoming infected by her mother's suspicions. But a lot of decisions you make are pragmatic. If you can conflate two characters, you have a juicier role for one person rather than two less juicy roles for two people. It's also to do with the industrial nature of film-making, and the demands of budgets and schedules and casting and so on.

The ending of the novel harks back to John James Todd on the beach in *The New Confessions*: Eva standing at the end of her garden, scanning the woods through her binoculars, wondering who or what might be coming for her. Towards the start of the TV version, Ruth actually sees someone in the woods looking back at her, although it could be a walker or a poacher. To what extent is the reader of the novel and the viewer of the TV version meant to think that Eva's fears are based purely on paranoia?

Well, it's a possibility. The whole thing may be a result of her terror. Every time that MI6 guy in the remote cottage in County Mayo saw a car winding up the valley he must have thought, 'Uh-oh, here they come,' but it might just have been people going for a picnic. That's what made me so curious about Philby: once you enter that world of paranoia and suspicion it can ruin your life, but he somehow kept it up for all those years and nobody suspected him. There's a slightly pedantic need in a film to see a figure in the woods because you can't so easily suggest that it's in all Eva's mind – or in Ruth's – but the last image of the TV version is still very potent: that great shot of the restless trees as the camera cranes up and away.

Your follow-up to *Restless*, *Ordinary Thunderstorms*, was again pegged as a thriller, but it feels to me like one of your most unusual and ambitious novels.

Ordinary Thunderstorms was an attempt to write a novel that did for modern London what *Our Mutual Friend* did for Dickens's London, following the Dickensian model of looking at every stratum of society, from the millionaires and the aristocrats to the prostitutes and the crack addicts. It also follows the course of the River Thames, starting at Chelsea Bridge and ending on the Hoo Peninsula – which is where *Great Expectations* begins – so the Dickensian echoes are carefully planted, if that's not mixing a metaphor. I'd used multiple voices in novels before, but there was usually a single point of view, whether it was first person or third person, and I think that's what makes *Ordinary Thunderstorms* feel different: you keep jumping from one character's point of view to another. It's very multicultural, too, although it never specifies anybody's ethnicity and it's up to the reader to decide if a character is Black or Chinese or Eastern European. It's not fixed in any one year, either, so it's just as contemporary now as when it was first published. So there's no doubt it has that pseudo-Victorian 'all human life is here' feel about it, like Dickens – or like the Trollope novel, *The Way We Live Now.* And, in fact, *Our Mutual Friend* is also a kind of thriller: it's about an inheritance and who's going to get the money.

It has a distinct John Buchan feel about it, too, with Adam Kindred as a modern-day Richard Hannay.

The Buchan echoes are deliberate: nice young chap gets in a pickle and has to sort things out. That's the plot of *The Thirty-Nine Steps*, and of many thrillers of that sort which flourished in the first half of the twentieth century. A man falsely accused of murder; how many novels have started that way? If it had been a Buchan novel, Adam would have headed up to the Scottish Highlands and lived in a cave, but in fact he goes down to the lower depths of the city. So they're old tropes, but with a new spin, I hope.

In the same way that Hannay returns to London from Africa, Adam has relocated from America – and before he left, he was working on a project to create the weather. In other words, trying to control something that cannot be controlled, which is presumably why you chose climatology as his profession?

I've always looked for a proper job for my protagonists, and I'm a bit of a weather obsessive: I've got books on clouds and books on rain and books on wind, and I was interested in this idea of cloud seeding, that you can sow some kind of oxide in dense clouds and trigger rainfall beneath. It's random, weather, and it plays into my view of life being fundamentally uncertain; so Adam's job is, as you say, an attempt to regulate something that's inherently unregulatable. In the same way that I made up the preface to *An Ice-Cream War*, the epigraph at the front of the novel, about how ordinary thunderstorms morph into multi-cell and super-cell storms, was cannibalized from various sources to produce something that would fit my purpose.

The title obviously ties into Adam's job, but also into his circumstances – and the circumstances of the other characters, who are all weathering their own storms.

It's also an oxymoron. Is there such a thing as an ordinary thunderstorm? Aren't they all unique in their own way? So there's a challenge in the title, too, which is then explained by the epigraph.

***Our Mutual Friend* and *The Way We Live Now* could both be described as 'state of the nation' novels, and Dickens's work was driven by what you might call a campaigning zeal. Did you have any particular socio-political agenda for this book?**

Only insofar as I wanted to portray contemporary society as accurately as possible. If you want to make a political point, write a manifesto, don't write a novel. But I was very interested how you can disappear in this age of mass surveillance: 200,000 people go off the radar in Britain every year – that's the size of a large provincial town.

Instead of running away, Adam goes to live among this underclass of non-people, because if you're sleeping rough and scavenging and paying cash, the modern world can't pick you up. You can walk in front of a hundred CCTV cameras on any given day and nobody will know who you are unless you leave an electronic trail. It's more like being a medieval peasant than living in the twenty-first century. I was also looking for an antagonist, and big pharma did the job nicely. Licensing a new drug is a licence to print money, and if you're in a position to make billions of pounds' worth of profit then the temptation to take shortcuts can be overwhelming. I wasn't making that point out of some burning sense of injustice – although everybody knows that the appalling scams of big pharma are legion – I just needed a shameless, conscienceless villain figure.

The villains do seem more overtly villainous than in your previous novels – the mercenary, Jonjo Case, for example.

That came from the research I did. These defence contractors, as they're called, are usually posh ex-SAS types, recycling their skills and making tons of money. I've met a couple of them and they're unbelievably plausible, but they're often functioning on the very edges of legality. That was another interesting lid to lift, but it wasn't so much campaigning zeal as narrative expediency that made me go down these roads. It's also quite a comic novel, which I sometimes pushed into surreal absurdism, so that's another reason why the characters may be drawn with bolder strokes: because it fits the mood and tone.

In a sense, it's like a companion piece to *Armadillo*, which was a black comedy with thriller elements, whereas this is a thriller with black comedy elements, with identity a key part of the plot in both.

Yes, I think that's a fair comparison. That theme of changing identities, the sense in which your identity is something you can put on or shed as required, is present in many of my novels. Even in *Love is Blind*, Brodie Moncur changes his name when he's living in Biarritz. In this case, it fitted the thriller element: Adam has to change his identity in order to figure out who the people are that have brought him low.

Adam's name was obviously carefully chosen: both his Christian name and surname, Kindred, give you a sense of him being an Everyman figure.

And a sense of 'There but for the grace of God'. That feeling, again, of the randomness of the universe: how one generous act ends up destroying his life. Little does he know, as he strides along Sloane Avenue to return Philip Wang's lost file, that Jonjo Case is doing Philip Wang in.

It's good luck and bad luck, going back to *Any Human Heart*.

Absolutely, although there's a slightly different emphasis here. In *Any Human Heart*, Logan's bad luck is random.

When the V-2 rocket falls, it kills whoever is underneath it, but it's not aimed at them. In Adam's case, there's a causal connection between why his life is going wrong and who's responsible for it. Jonjo is on his trail, and Jonjo is responsible for the death of Mhouse, which makes Ly-on an orphan – there's a domino effect. Adam initially seems to have the worst luck in the world, buffeted by powerful forces he can't understand; then, slowly but surely, as he takes back control of his life, his luck begins to change.

To the extent that by the end he's assembling a new life with Ly-on and the river cop, Rita Nashe.

He finds love, which is the great redemptive force in my novels, so it's quite an epiphanic ending. He's clear of the murder rap and full of hope, even though Jonjo is still alive and clinging to an empty cooking oil can 10 miles offshore.

The love story starts comparatively late in the narrative, yet somehow you don't feel that it's come out of nowhere: the elements cohere in a logical and pleasing way.

I think that's because we've been in Rita's head quite early on. There's something brewing between Adam and Mhouse, but that's cut off by Jonjo killing her. Then, when Adam goes to the morgue to identify Mhouse's body, he meets Rita and off that goes. It was a complicated book to write because of all the interlocking parts, and the way that they had to complement each other and be consistently interesting until they eventually meshed.

Armadillo borrowed the opening phrase of *Our Mutual Friend* – 'In these times of ours' – and *Ordinary Thunderstorms* opens in a similarly Dickensian way: 'Let us start with the river.' Counting *Stars and Bars*, that's the third time you've opened a novel with one or more paragraphs of omniscient narration. Have you ever considered writing an entire novel in that form?

Having done it twice, I thought, 'It's a good device, I'll use it again.' It signals the authorial presence, that the pieces on the chessboard are being manipulated by the author's sensibility. But I don't think I'd ever write an omniscient novel. It's full of traps, and there's a terrible temptation to have your cake and eat it that offends my neat and ordered mind. *Ordinary Thunderstorms* is probably as omniscient as I'll get, in that I jump from character to character, but I do it chapter by chapter, not paragraph by paragraph.

Did you know which chapters were going to focus on which characters before you started writing?

I planned it very thoroughly, as usual, so I knew exactly when I was moving from Adam to Jonjo to Mhouse to whoever, but there were moments when, with hindsight, I interpolated a short Rita chapter because I felt we hadn't seen her for a while. So I did do a bit of housekeeping later on, but a lot of it was determined by the way the narrative was going.

It's not just the point of view that changes, the language changes too. In Jonjo's chapters, for instance, there are a lot of masculine clichés, of the sort that someone of his type might use.

But I hope they're all in the dialogue rather than in the linking prose! Because what I was striving for – which also occurs in Victorian novels – is that the dialogue is in the character's voice, even when it's reported speech or their thought processes, but the prose sections are in the author's. Mhouse and Ly-on barely speak English sometimes, they speak in this curious patois, and in one of the Mhouse chapters there's a paragraph about the architectural history of the Shaftesbury Estate, which she clearly wouldn't be remotely interested in. Similarly, when Jonjo visits Risk Averse's offices, you see some of it through his eyes but there are other bits that he wouldn't notice: he wouldn't notice that Tim Delaporte had a gold silk tie, but the author does. When you move from the author's overview into the character's sensibility, the language changes, and it shouldn't be intellectual if that character isn't intellectual.

The Shaftesbury Estate is fictional, but other locations are clearly real. How much research did you do for the novel, and how did you decide which places to make up?

I did a lot of research – and I travelled a lot around London, as I did with *Armadillo*. I went to Putney Vale Crematorium. I went to Canvey Island, which is a strange place. I wandered through Thames Barrier Park, near where Jonjo lives. I hung out at City Airport, which I'd never been to at the time of writing the novel. I first went to that bit of East London, Silvertown, for *Armadillo*, and it was a wasteland with a couple of condos being built. Now it's apartment city. Sometimes you do need to see places if you're going to write about them properly – if you haven't been there you may not get the richness or authenticity – but, equally, some things you just have to make up. A retired superintendent checked my police procedure, and I'd sometimes ask her odd questions like, 'Would a detective inspector call a woman police constable "darling"? – for example, "Hello, darling, how are you today?"' – and she said, 'Yes, he probably would, but he shouldn't.' Even she couldn't get me access to the Marine Support Unit at Wapping, so I just built an annexe to it, a Portakabin where the morgue is. The same with the hospital which I built in Southwark. I don't know if you've been in a hospital recently, but it seems to me they're becoming almost like shopping malls – brightly coloured cities of ill health – and I used my imagination to think what the next generation of hospital would be like, which is how St Botolph's came to be. Part of the godlike power of being a novelist. You accumulate this massive aggregate of material and the skill is choosing the one or two details that will do the work for you. You can't just pile it on, and that's something you learn as you go.

The novel has been in development as both a film and a TV series, and both versions make one major change: the fifth principal character in the book, Ingram Fryzer, the head of the big pharma company,

is more villainous. **In the book he doesn't know that there's a problem with the new drug, or that his business partners have ordered a hit on his chief scientist; instead he gets an unrelated medical condition and ends up reconciled with his son. That's very different to the journey he makes in the scripts, where he becomes a key player in the conspiracy.**

Again, it's the economy that film imposes on you. You're right, in the novel he's not actually a villain, he's just a rather hapless Sloane Ranger who runs a drug company but doesn't really know much about drugs – and then his bad luck arrives in the shape of this hideous brain disease. It would be hard to tell that story in a movie, so I had to make him part of the conspiracy – although he sort of falls into it, because he's about to make vast sums of money. When Wang says, 'This drug is killing people,' well, what does a chap do? You go to your friend in the defence contracting business and say, 'Could you take care of my chief scientist who's going to fuck everything up?' And so the snowball is pushed down the mountain and the avalanche duly arrives. But it's the neatness, and the need to contract, that you get in writing a screenplay which necessitates these narrative changes.

Something else that struck me about both versions of the script, possibly because it's more of a thriller than others of yours I've read, is that it's written in a much more staccato style.

My screenwriting style is evolving in that direction anyway. If I look back at my *Hitler* scripts, which I wrote nearly twenty years ago, I wouldn't write them like that now. My early screenplays were much more verbose, but as I've written more screenplays – and read more scripts by other writers – I've come to think that pithiness is very much the best style, because you're trying to make the jaded reader sit up and take notice. In my experience it's often the commercial screenwriter, the writer of big Hollywood movies, who has a handle on a way of writing that best serves movie-making – and I include TV in that. That punchy, epigrammatic style works really well for a reader, and I try to make my screenplays good reads. When you're reading them, you're seeing the finished movie.

Variety reported in 2011 that your adaptation of _Ordinary Thunderstorms_ was number two on the 'Brit List', a rundown of the best unproduced British feature film screenplays. So why hasn't it been made?

It was optioned before publication by David Thompson's Origin Pictures, a screenplay was commissioned by BBC Films, and shortly thereafter Pascal Chaumeil was attached to direct, who was a hugely successful director in France. I got on very well with both Pascal and David, but it fell apart because of corporate dysfunction. A change of personnel at the top of BBC Films initiated a period of endless delays and regular rewrites; Pascal couldn't understand the prevarication and became increasingly disenchanted, as did I; and then he became ill with cancer and died aged fifty-four, which cast a cloud over the project. When the option lapsed I didn't allow Origin to renew it, because it was clear to me that there was no enthusiasm at BBC Films to take the project forward, and I subsequently rewrote it on spec as a six-part TV series – which is now in development with Ecosse Films.

You've also adapted your follow-up, *Waiting for Sunrise*, as a TV series – which isn't surprising given how much material it provides. It's set in the period 1913 to 1915, and you get a real sense of the birth of the twentieth century: psychoanalysis, modern art, organized espionage and mechanized warfare.

I can trace the origins of that novel precisely. I was writing a piece about one of my favourite artists, Egon Schiele, and I was sent to the Leopold Museum in Vienna, which is dedicated to his work. It was my first time in Vienna and one day I visited Freud's apartment and consulting rooms, and apart from the cars in the streets that bit of the city is very much unchanged. You go into a courtyard, then up some stairs, and there are two doors – one to Freud's consulting rooms and one to his apartment – and when I was standing there, looking around me, I thought, 'I could be standing here in 1911, waiting to see Dr Freud.' It was a moment of time travel, and that was the inspiration for the novel. We're all Freudians now, but at the time psychoanalysis must have seemed the biggest kind of mumbo-jumbo; so I wondered what it would have been like to go and consult Freud, and I wanted to make it feel strange again, and new. The choice of Vienna as a locale also had a lot to do with one of my favourite writers, Joseph Roth. His novel *Radetzky March*, which I've developed as another TV series, is a masterpiece – a word I use very rarely – and along with its sequel, *The Emperor's Tomb*, is a hymn of praise to the old Austro-Hungarian Empire. He died in 1939 and only remembered it as a child, but it had a symbolic significance for him. I've been to Vienna many times since, and I'm fascinated by that period before the cataclysm of World War I. Certain cities at certain points in history take on a world importance, like London in the 1850s or Paris in the 1890s or New York in the 1950s, and Vienna was the place to be in the 1910s. And then it all ended: the Hapsburg Empire, which had existed for hundreds of years, was suddenly over. So it wasn't going to be a spy novel, it was more about how the world was changing. That transition from the Victorian to the Edwardian to the modern, and how quickly it happened, is very intriguing.

How *did* it become a spy novel?

It was part of my interest in espionage that had arisen as a result of *Any Human Heart* and *Restless*. Spying is as old as history, but I think Britain's Secret Service Bureau, which was established in 1909, was the first official government intelligence service, and I got interested in the beginnings of that secret world. I'd also read Somerset Maugham's 'Ashenden' spy series, and Maugham was recruited by the embryonic service and sent to Geneva, so the story built up in my mind as I explored these pathways I was intrigued by. I've been using actors more and more as my protagonists, so I thought of this young actor, Lysander Rief, who has this problem, anorgasmia;

loses his head over this flighty young woman, Hettie Bull, whom he meets outside Freud's consulting rooms; and is then reluctantly entrapped into joining the secret service. And that's how it became a World War I spy novel.

It is an intriguing juxtaposition, because psycho-analysis is about revealing secrets while espionage is about concealing them, so there's a contradiction between why Lysander goes to Vienna and what he ends up doing there.

Yes. And this question of what you lose when you become a spy, how dehumanized you become, is a very interesting psychological problem – and another reason why I was intrigued to explore Lysander's journey. Who can he trust? What lies is Hettie telling? That's the attraction of the spy genre: it's very much about the human condition.

What's the relevance of the title?

I had trouble with the title. With some novels the right title doesn't come until the end, and in this case it came very late on. I was going to call it *The School of Night*, referring to the atheistic group around Walter Raleigh, but that was an odd title and wrong for the book. Then I decided to go for dawn rather than night, and I think I used the phrase 'waiting for sunrise' when Lysander is in prison, hoping that everything will be better in the morning. It seemed evocative, and it sort of fits, but it does have a vaguer correlation with the narrative than I usually aim for.

The epigraphs correlate more closely: 'A thing is true at first light and a lie by noon' from Hemingway; 'Truly, to tell lies is not honourable, but when the truth entails tremendous ruin, to speak dishonourably is pardonable' from Sophocles.

Well, one is cynical – everybody's lying – and the other is saying that sometimes expediency demands you tell a white lie or an untruth in order to stop something worse from happening. I wanted to establish a sense of this miasma of half-truths and cleverly constructed lies, and start building doubt – that actually everybody is hiding something.

The novel moves between third person and first person narration, and Lysander's 'Autobiographical Investigations' is a similar device to Lorimer's 'Book of Transfiguration' in *Armadillo*. Why did you decide to tell this story in that way?

Something I learned from *Brazzaville Beach* was that shifting pronouns from 'I' to 'she' – or from 'he' to 'I' – can pay dividends in giving you intimate access to the inner life of the character. Of course, you can access the inner life of any character in a novel, but the first person has a different impact on the reader than the third person. The third person restricted form is the author telling you what's happening. The first person confessional form allows you to hear the character's own voice. Also, a first person narration can be unreliable or only partially informed, and the reader can be in the position of knowing more than the character. It gives your narrative an extra dimension and richness, in the sense that you can switch tone of voice as well as point of view. It's a win-win situation, if it works.

The novel is similar to *Armadillo* in other ways, too: Lysander and Lorimer are both seeing doctors for medical conditions, and Hettie, like Flavia, is capricious, impulsive, destructive – a classic femme fatale.

Well spotted. No one else has picked that up. And it's true. Lorimer and Lysander are also both actors, in a way: Lorimer plays different roles to help his loss adjusting, just as Lysander pretending to be other people makes him a better spy. I don't know why these themes come up again and again, and I think it's good that I don't know why they do, but I also don't think I should resist them if they're on my mind. The unattainable, or only partially attainable, love object is something else that strikes a chord in me, for some reason: the idea that there's an intense emotional connection between two lovers but that somehow fate or accident or personality contrives to separate them. It's not something I've experienced in my own life, but it's something that really intrigues me: what if the one thing, or the one person, that could make you totally and utterly happy is forever out of your reach? Like, 'That way madness lies.' It's there in *The New Confessions*, and it's in my next novel as well. It's just one of those things that gets my brain ticking over.

In the same way that you've been a successful author for several decades but repeatedly write about unsuccessful writers, you've also been happily married for

several decades but repeatedly write about unrequited love affairs. It's as if you continually write about the opposite of you.

As my friend Freddie Raphael said, who's been very happily married for ever: 'If you're adrift on a life raft in a shark-infested sea, you can't help imagining what it must be like to fall off.' I think that's what it is for me. If you're the kind of writer who uses your imagination, you can explore places in your fiction that you would never want to go in your own life. There's a lot of my life in my novels – it creeps in under the radar – but it's not the raw material for them. The raw material is almost always something imagined, and the trigger that fires my imagination is often banal or random or out of left field. But I do recognize, as you've recognized, that there are inevitably repetitions in the canon.

The first chief of the Foreign Section of the Secret Service Bureau, Mansfield Cumming, appears in the novel – and Lysander, like Maugham, is sent to Geneva. Did you base other characters on real people?

I read a very good biography of Mansfield Cumming, so a lot of the stuff about the War Office is based on fact. Lysander's Uncle Hamo is vaguely based on Siegfried Sassoon, who did have a brother called Hamo. You obviously couldn't come out in 1914 but some people were phenomenally audacious – think of Oscar Wilde and Bosie – hence Uncle Hamo living openly with his Black lover in Winchelsea and to hell with everybody else. I remember reading about Ellen Terry, who lived a rackety life in Rye – 'living in sin', as they called it then – so I borrowed certain elements of genuine theatrical lives to make mine seem authentic. East Sussex seems to be one of my favourite landscapes: it keeps popping up in my novels.

Again, the novel has an omniscient opening – but this time it closes that way, too. It puts the reader in the shoes of a watcher, implying that Lysander was on the secret service radar before the story began, and will remain on their radar after it ends.

Yes, exactly. Once they knew he was going to Vienna, they had him – and I made that more explicit in the TV version, because I had a returning series in mind for broadcasters.

What's the current status of the TV version?

I originally wrote it as a movie, and it was going to be produced by Lorne Michaels, this legend of American TV, who loved the novel. I made dramatic changes to fit the book into one hundred pages, then after a couple of years of working on it Lorne said, 'You know what? It should be TV.' So I said, 'You're right,' and rewrote it as a six-hour drama. Then, very much like *Ordinary Thunderstorms*, it went down various alleyways that weren't satisfactory to me. I kept having to invent new episodes and new plot twists, and it got further and further away from the novel, and I thought, 'The six-hour version is true to the book. That's the version everybody's interested in. If it ain't broke, let's not try to fix it.' So I've now set it up independently with a German producer – and reset it in Munich rather than Vienna in the interests of casting and finance – and Lorne is on board as an executive producer. But Germany has a different TV culture, I've discovered, and moves in mysterious ways, so we'll see. I've actually thought about making it into a trilogy; I've already blocked out narratives for Seasons Two and Three – or Volumes Two and Three. *Waiting for Sunrise* is Volume One and ends in 1915. Volume Two would be called *The Demon at Noontide* and deals with the Russian Revolution. And Volume Three, *Blood Red Sunset*, would end up at the Paris Peace Conference in 1919. So maybe if I live long enough, I'll sit down and write my thousand-page epic about World War I. Something to look forward to!

Six

Screenplays 3

Sword of Honour (2001) – *Man to Man* (2005)
A Waste of Shame (2005) – *Spy City* (2020)

With three novels and nine hundred pages of source material behind it, *Sword of Honour* is probably your most ambitious screen adaptation to date. How hard was it to compress Evelyn Waugh's trilogy into two ninety-minute episodes for TV?

It was quite a tall order. You probably wouldn't have thought the trilogy could be shoehorned into a three-hour miniseries, but if somebody who knew the novels watched it and you said to them, 'What did they leave out?' I don't think they'd be able to tell you. It was originally going to be six hours, but then Channel 4 – God bless them, who paid for the whole thing – said, 'Let's do it in three.' So I had to do a lot of filleting. But I think we got the best bits into it and a coherent narrative out of it, and the final version is remarkably true to the spirit of the books. The trilogy is quite uneven because it's autobiography thinly disguised as fiction: *Sword of Honour* is basically Waugh's war. He was originally only going to write two novels, then the third panel of the triptych arrived some years later, and you can tell which bits engage him and which bits don't. The books are notable in the canon of his work, but more because of the light they cast on his life than because they hold together as a trilogy about World War II.

The three novels – *Men at Arms*, *Officers and Gentlemen* and *Unconditional Surrender* – were collected and revised as *Sword of Honour* in 1965, and in his preface Waugh describes the trilogy as 'a description of the Second World War as it was seen and experienced by a single, uncharacteristic Englishman' and 'an obituary of the Roman Catholic Church in England'. How did you view it when you adapted it?

We're all trying to create the taste by which we will be appreciated, and I think that's what Waugh was doing in that introduction. He was a genuine convert and his zeal was irreproachable, but I feel that the Roman Catholic stuff in *Sword of Honour* is bolted on. It particularly comes to the fore in the last section of the trilogy, the Yugoslavian section, when he was deeply bored and had to make it more interesting. The novels were simply a way for him to write about his experiences from 1939 to 1945, with comedy and a love affair and a lot of observation of army life; the overarching theme about values, and the death of the Catholic Church, was superimposed rather than intrinsic. Waugh battered his memoir into that shape – Guy Crouchback joins the army to fight against the forces of evil but ends up witnessing the triumph of communism and the West allying itself with Stalin's godless regime – so it had a kind of significance.

That would explain why the books are uneven, certainly in terms of tone: broad yet bitter, solemn yet satirical. Did you try to even that out?

Not really – because, as you say, the books are like that. They veer between classic Waugh comedy and autobiographical truth, and there's a sense in which he's using the comedy to conceal the autobiography. So, in a way, filleting out the film from the novels allowed the film to achieve a fictive integrity which maybe the novels don't have.

Given that the novels are thinly disguised autobiography, and Guy Crouchback is therefore an idealized depiction of Evelyn Waugh, Daniel Craig isn't necessarily the first actor you'd think of to play that part.

Daniel was my suggestion, because I thought that if Guy Crouchback was like the character in the novels, weak and stuttering, it would fatally handicap the film. I said to the producers, 'We need a real man,' and that counterintuitive casting really paid off, not least because there's a real, powerful love story between Guy and Virginia, played by the wonderful Megan Dodds. The scene where Guy reads the letter about Virginia's death and the tears begin to run from his eyes always astonishes me; it's incredibly moving. It's like certain scenes in *The Trench*: they're done with subliminal emphasis rather than anything histrionic and are all the more powerful for it. He's a brilliant actor, Daniel, and we were lucky to get him.

The whole cast is brilliant: a who's who of British character actors.

It was a lavish production, and the money is all up there on the screen. Wonderful cast. Fantastic locations. We shot a lot of it in Mallorca, which doubled for Africa, Crete, Yugoslavia and even for Scotland, although we shot in and around Edinburgh as well. The director, Bill Anderson, did a wonderful job on it, especially the retreat from Crete, which is really epic – and in some ways the most interesting bit of the novels, a very intriguing and still much-disputed episode in Waugh's life.

The novels end with two of Guy's social circle talking about how he's remarried and adopted Virginia's child, but the adaptation ends with him meeting the little boy for the first time. Were you aiming for something direct and affecting, rather than a scene which takes place at one remove?

Yes, that's right. The novels chart Guy Crouchback's growing disillusion: he tries to do the right thing but circumstances prevent him, and his individual human response is the only consolation he has. His father – wonderfully played by the late Leslie Phillips in the film – has this repeated phrase in the novels: 'We must not repine.' However awful things are, however ghastly the world is, we must continue on our steadfast path, and that's what that last scene shows you: Guy forgives his unfaithful wife and accepts her illegitimate child as his own. It gives a closure to his war that you don't get in the final novel, and it's more emotional than the novel, which is dry and ironic. The shot of Daniel holding the child, with that incredible score by Nina

Humphreys as the camera cranes away, is a very emotional bit of cinema. It really delivers.

How would you say *Sword of Honour* fits into your own canon?

I would say that a lot of war novels and war movies have an agenda – they want to emphasize heroism and human dignity and so on – but the reality of a war zone is almost the complete opposite. What I've always tried to do in my accounts of wars – whether it's in *An Ice-Cream War*, or *The New Confessions*, or *Brazzaville Beach*, or *The Trench* – is to convey its utter, absurd, anarchic cruelty. And the cynical, satirical, anti-heroic tone of *Sword of Honour* does exactly that.

***Man to Man*, on the other hand, is harder to place in your filmography. You share a credit for 'English screenplay' with the director, Régis Wargnier, but the screenplay is credited to Wargnier and two other French writers, based on an original idea by those writers. What exactly was your role on the film?**

Régis is a very good friend and a great fan of my novels, and we originally met at his instigation to write a movie for Catherine Deneuve. They'd just made *Indochine*, which was a huge hit and won the Best Foreign Language Film Oscar, and she said to him, 'I'd really like to do a comedy.' So we wrote this film called *À l'aventure*, set in a fictional former Soviet Republic, and Catherine's role was a French diplomat who gets embroiled in a caper. But it turned out she didn't want to do a comedy after all, so Régis rewrote the script and turned it into a movie called *Est-Ouest*, which Catherine had a cameo role in but I had no credit on. He then concocted this story about the human zoos of the nineteenth century and the search for the missing link, and asked if I could turn the outline, which was in French, into a screenplay in English, because he wanted to make an English-language film. Régis speaks excellent English but he isn't bilingual, so the screenplay was effectively written by me, based on the outline he'd written with these other two French writers, and of course it changed dramatically as it went through its various drafts. Then, when the film was made, one of the original writers said he wanted a co-writing credit on it. I pointed out that the script was written in English and he didn't speak English, and said that he should have a story credit because he invented the story, but he couldn't understand the division between somebody who comes up with the idea for a film and somebody who writes the film. It was all perfectly amicable, but it was like talking to a brick wall. He then sued everybody – the producers, Régis, me – and at that stage I backed off. It wasn't a passion project of mine, it was just a job for me and a favour to Régis, so it's something of a curio in my filmography.

'Curio' is a good description of the film. Almost unknown in the UK despite its cast – Joseph Fiennes, Kristin Scott Thomas, Iain Glen and Hugh Bonneville – and tonally uneven to the point of melodrama, particularly at the end, but a perfect fit for you in terms of subject matter: Africa and anthropology.

I think that's why Régis thought I was the perfect person to anglicize it: I was very at home in that world and knew these types of English characters. But nineteenth-century French culture is totally different from nineteenth-century English culture, and there was a culture clash between French perceptions of nineteenth-century British relationships and what I knew to be the reality of them. It's a really good film up until the last few minutes, when the Hugh Bonneville character goes mad. I said to Régis, 'The end of the film is all wrong. People will laugh in the cinema.' He said, 'That's impossible.' I said, 'I can fix it in the script before you shoot it,' but he didn't want me to do that. Then he shot it and I said, 'I can tell you how to fix it in the edit,' but he didn't want to do that either. And when we went to the first screening in Paris, people laughed at the end of the film. It opened the Berlin Film Festival in 2005 and was shown all around the world except in the US and the UK, and this is an English-language film with British stars. So it's a sort of secret film, and a disappointment and a lesson for me, however much fun the collaboration was. Maybe I'm more pragmatic and Régis is more romantic, I don't know, but there was a real forking path when it came to our understanding of the tone of the piece. What he thought of as dramatic and moving, I knew an anglophone audience would see as farcical and silly, and nothing I could say would make him change his mind. He was adamant that he was right and I was wrong, and he was the auteur; it was '*un film de*'.

To be honest, I'm not sure that the actors were on the same path, either, in their understanding of the tone

of the piece. There are some scenes where they appear to be acting in totally different films.

That was another culture clash. On French movies there seems to be no rehearsal at all, and the British actors were a bit freaked out by that. There were also no rushes, which, again, I think is normal practice in France, whereas on a British or American film you see the rushes that day or the day after. So when I got to South Africa, where some of it was shot, none of the British actors had seen any of the work they'd done and I spent a lot of time smoothing ruffled feathers. But it was amazing that the movie got made; there were all sorts of terrible problems, including financial plugs being pulled at the last minute. Régis reminds me of John Boorman, who I worked with briefly on *The Galapagos Affair* and got to know a little. With John, it's not enough to make a film, you have to go on an incredible journey at the same time. Régis is a bit like that: all his films are epic journeys. It's not just, 'I should make another movie.' It's more like, 'What will consume me for the next three years?' I salute them, totally, because it's almost an alien way of working in the movie business, given the prevailing commercial imperatives. People who are driven by that kind of passion, and whose vision is so intense, have a much harder job making it as a film director. I'd work with Régis again at the drop of a hat, and *Man to Man* and *À l'aventure* are the only two projects in my film-making life where I've collaborated with another writer, albeit a writer-director.

Later that year you returned to TV with the BBC single drama *A Waste of Shame: The Mystery of*

Shakespeare and His Sonnets **– a film which sits more comfortably in your filmography.**

That was a commission, also. I can't remember if it was my idea to write about the sonnets or if that was what the BBC wanted to do, but having spent a decade studying English Lit I was very intrigued by the subject and I was given licence to tell the story as I saw fit. The controversies around the sonnets are fascinating – who is the 'Fair Youth', who is the 'Dark Lady', who is the dedicatee, 'Mr. W.H.'? – but passions about those identifications run so high that you're walking into a literary-critical minefield. There are two camps, and you're either a Pembrokian [*William Herbert, 3rd Earl of Pembroke*] or a Southamptonian [*Henry Wriothesley, 3rd Earl of Southampton*]. The Southampton camp says you have to invert the initials – that W.H. was a disguise for H.W. – but as I did my research the whole thing seemed to turn irrefutably in the other direction. If it's Southampton, that implies the sonnets were written when Shakespeare was in his twenties; but the sexual experience in them makes it much more likely that they were written by a mature man, therefore W.H. – and the 'Fair Youth' – has to be Pembroke; and once you make that identification everything falls neatly into place. If you were arguing it in a court of law the Pembroke case is far more plausible, whereas people who advocate for Southampton have to go through all sorts of contortions to explain the narrative of the sonnets.

My interpretation was that a mature, sexually ambiguous Shakespeare became besotted with this young aristocrat while at the same time visiting brothels in Southwark – there were Black and mixed-race prostitutes in Elizabethan and

Jacobean England, so it's entirely plausible that one of them was the 'Dark Lady' – and if you read the sonnets narratively, you can follow the story through. The first few are routine sonnets, commissioned by this young aristocrat's mother, on the theme of becoming immortal by getting married and having children; then they go off into this extraordinary autobiography of a mature man with a homosexual obsession, and the object of his obsession has an affair with the same prostitute he visits; and then, in the last, bitter sonnets, the author gets the pox. Again, scholars dispute this – did Shakespeare have the pox, or is it a metaphor? – but I think the evidence is incontrovertible. Our historical advisor was the late Katherine Duncan-Jones, who was one of the world's pre-eminent Shakespeare experts – and she concurred with my identification. We had a memorable evening at the Royal Society of Literature where she and I gave a talk on the film and the sonnets, and when we went to the audience for questions people stood up and said, 'Mr Boyd, don't you realize that Francis Bacon wrote those sonnets?' All these conspiracy theorists came out of the woodwork, and Katherine nudged me and said, 'I told you: it's a snake pit.' She gave me a job when she was a don at Somerville College, Oxford, and I was a young postgraduate student, so it was very nice for me to be able to get her this consultancy job in return. She appears in the film, too, at the end: she has an Alfred Hitchcock walk-on part as an Elizabethan lady, scrutinizing the books for sale outside St Paul's.

She's credited as 'academic advisor'. Was her presence dictated by the fact that the film was produced in association with the Open University?

There was no input from the OU, they just put some money into it. It was more to do with making it absolutely watertight historically and intellectually, so nobody could say, 'That's a terrible anachronism,' or, 'How dare you besmirch the name of our national bard.' If anything in it seemed strange or racy, we wanted chapter and verse to back it up.

I'd have said brutal and filthy rather than strange or racy. The film has an authentically down-and-dirty period feel.

Whatever era I'm writing about or medium I'm writing in, my ambition is always to make it as authentic as I can: this is what it was like to go over the top in World War I, or to take to the air in an early flying machine, or to be a woman photographer in Vietnam. It's something that I respond to as a reader and a viewer, and something that's very much part of my working practice. When I write things that are based on real people and real events, my aim is always to demythologize, to strip away received wisdom and rose-tinted glasses and say, 'What was actually going on?' It may be surprising, it may be uncomfortable, but that's better than some sort of Walt Disney version. I've read so much about Shakespeare, but so little is known about him in terms of documented facts. There's a wonderful biography by Samuel Schoenbaum which looks at every single document where Shakespeare's name appears, and some are as strange as him being called as a character witness for a brothel keeper who'd beaten up a prostitute; yet based on these scanty details, the history of the time and a certain amount of intuition – and the work, of course – you can piece together a hypothetical but well-evidenced story of a real man in London at the beginning of the seventeenth century. So I learned a tremendous amount, even though I'd been reading Shakespeare all my adult life.

I didn't realize until I watched it that Shakespeare never went abroad.

He never left England. He could have done – lots of his contemporaries spent time abroad, and he could have reasonably visited France – but he didn't. And yet his plays are set all over the place, which is an interesting example of sending your imagination instead – or reading the relevant books and borrowing the details you need. The other thing that's interesting about him is that he stopped writing plays. *The Tempest* was his swansong, then he packed it all in and went back to Stratford, bought a big house and became a landlord. It's not a romantic journey; he was clearly a genius but was in it for the money, and there were a good few years at the end of his life when he was just living off his theatrical success.

Did you draw any of your dialogue directly from Shakespeare's plays?

Sometimes I did. His blank verse is stylized and heightened, but the prose dialogue in something like *Henry IV* or *Henry V*, spoken by Falstaff or one his cronies, has an authentic demotic ring to it. That's also true of Marlowe – and another contemporary of Shakespeare's, Thomas

Nashe. I read a lot of Jacobean literature searching for that colloquial voice, because I didn't want the dialogue to be cod-Shakespearean. I was really pleased with the way it worked, and that spun off into a play I wrote – about a play John Dryden wrote – called *Secret Love*, set in the Restoration period. I took enormous pains writing the backstage dialogue in that to make it sound naturalistic but authentic, which is the challenge for anybody writing something set in the fairly distant past. My next novel is set in the nineteenth century, and I'm finding it quite hard to access the actual voice of the period because of the literary conventions of the time.

The film is punctuated by lines from the sonnets, appearing on the screen and then fading away. What were you aiming to achieve with those?

I wanted to foreground the autobiographical evidence that the sonnets provide. But I also thought – and have always felt, from watching television programmes about poets – that to do poetry properly on screen you have to hear and see the text at the same time. Because the film was about the sonnets and we needed to seed them in, rather than just having voiceover we could also have these captions fading in and fading out, which makes all the difference to the resonance of the poetry.

The use of language, the modest size of the principal cast and the small number of locations gives it a theatrical quality. Was that a reflection of its lead character?

No, not at all. I wrote it as a film. But we had a strict length requirement and a very tight budget, so we shot it on location because we couldn't afford to build any sets. Logistically it was a real challenge, and the producer, Chrissy Skinns, did a brilliant job, darting all over the country to Tudor and Jacobean houses; and the director, John McKay, also did a brilliant job, using the angles and vistas he had available to him. If you panned left you'd see a sign saying, 'Please keep off the grass,' so the shots were probably framed tighter than they would have been if we'd been making it for Netflix. It cost absolutely nothing in movie terms, but as a result it does have a real authenticity. We would maybe like to have had more than five extras, but it was a great cast and a great experience and I'm proud of the finished film. One of the producers was Sally Woodward Gentle, with whom I went on to make *Any Human Heart*. And among the cast was Rupert Graves, who had a tiny part in *Good and Bad at Games*. He was in my very first film, then cut to more than twenty years later and here he is playing Shakespeare. He vaguely remembered me, but I certainly remembered him.

Your most recent TV project was a six-part Cold War series, *Spy City*. Was that also a commission?

Yes, it was, but it had the usual rollercoaster history. It came to me because of my friendship with Pascal Chaumeil, who was going to direct the film of *Ordinary Thunderstorms*. Pascal had been approached with this idea – basically spies in Berlin in 1961 before the Wall went up – which at that point was with the French producer and distributor Gaumont, and the plan was that I would write it and he would direct it. When he died, Gaumont pulled out and the German company who initiated the idea, Odeon, took over and rebooted it with a German director attached. Then he left, another German director was attached, and he left in turn. I got on perfectly well with these directors, but the scripts were being shaped by their vision – one of them was an East German, so he wanted to concentrate more on East Berlin – and there were many drafts, some going off in this direction and some in that direction. Finally the third director left as well and we got a Portuguese-German director called Miguel Alexandre, who's very experienced and has made lots of movies and television, and after about five years this stop-start project began to gain some real traction – and I'm very pleased with the way it turned out. Miguel and I worked exceptionally well together, which helped.

Did you draw on any films or books from the Cold War?

Well, it's intriguing. You've got the Berlin Airlift happening in '48 and the Berlin Wall going up in '61, but there's very little written in English about the years in between: it's a moment in Berlin's history which is sort of forgotten. When we think of Berlin we think of the Wall, because the city was divided for nearly thirty years, so one of the fascinations for a viewer is to see the city before it was divided. Before the Wall it was an open city: you might have been stopped and asked to show your papers if you were in a car, but you could just walk through the zones. Billy Wilder made a film called *One, Two, Three* set in

Berlin, and he was shooting it there in the summer of '61. Then the Wall went up, so he had to move production to Munich. But if you watch it, looking at the background, he does cross from the West into the East, and the West is all 1960s glass, steel and concrete, and the East, with its bombsites, wasteland and weeds, looks pretty much like 1945. So I managed to compile a lot of stuff about the Wall going up, but I had to look far and wide to find out what it was like in the summer before it went up. I had a friend who was a young soldier in Berlin at the time, so I could ask him, and we had a historical advisor who was very helpful, but it also draws on the post-Wall thrillers of John le Carré and Len Deighton.

In fact, the character played by Dominic Cooper, Fielding Scott, reminded me of the coolness and insubordination of Michael Caine as Harry Palmer in *The Ipcress File*.

You're absolutely right. I know Len Deighton's novels very well, and I went to see *The Ipcress File* when it opened; I must have been fourteen or fifteen. When you look back, certain films in your history just detonate, and that film was a huge influence on me. Even things like the opening sequence, when Harry Palmer wakes up and makes coffee. I remember thinking, 'What the hell's he doing? You can grind coffee beans?' and I immediately wanted to brew coffee like that. I've watched it many times, and in *Spy City* I was cherry-picking the bits of *The Ipcress File* that I love. If you love movies, I think the films you watch in your teens and early twenties are the ones that burn into your synapses and create the archetypes that you draw on. Even if they're bad you remember things about them, and they shape your tastes and become the key films in your personal library. When I was in my teens I used to go and see three films in a day, and it was magical. I still love films and still surrender myself to them, but there are fewer and fewer that have that profound effect on me, possibly because I'm aware of how they're put together. Now I know how movies are made, there's a part of my brain that's analysing them like a critic rather than enjoying them as a cinephile. A knowledge of the process gets in the way of the pure pleasure of film.

How much research did you do beyond the cinema and literature of the period?

Quite a lot, but I've found that you can do too much research for a script. What's important is getting the story and the characters right, and the historical detail follows from that. Also, the historical detail often isn't in the script, it's in the art direction. There's no point in writing a lengthy description of the clothes a lady-in-waiting is wearing, because that's the work of the costume department. The film I'm writing about the Battle of Arnhem will only work if the story of this individual is gripping, so I've done my reading but I'm not worrying about ranks and cap badges and things like that.

Did the fact that *Spy City* was a German-American co-production, with a British screenwriter and a

Portuguese-German director, cause any issues in terms of conflicting notes?

The real collaboration was with Odeon; Miramax were just putting up a chunk of money to be able to sell it internationally, because it's essentially an English-language show. When Miramax came on board their notes were like, 'Not many people will know that there was ever a Berlin without the Wall, so we need a montage sequence explaining that,' and as a paid screenwriter you dutifully write this stuff and it all gets thrown out later on. We were also getting notes from the German broadcaster, ZDF, because they were more interested in the German characters than the British or American characters, and those sorts of things have to be weighed up in the process. But I'm a collaborator by instinct, particularly in film and TV. Miguel and I really clicked, and I got on very well with the producers from Odeon. One of them, Mischa Hofmann, said, 'Could we have more dead bodies, please?' so the body count is actually very high. But when you write a spy thriller, that comes with the territory – the audience expectation is that there will be death and violence – so I had no problem with it. The relationship between the German couple, Eliza and Reinhart, developed a lot because of things the German producers told me about East German society in the late '50s. I never knew that there had been a near-revolution in East Germany in 1958, when masses of students were banged up in jail, and you think, 'That's interesting. Can we make her boyfriend a student agitator?' Everything was in reaction to what I wrote: 'We really like this,' or, 'Could we have more of that?' I was never given instructions on what to do. In any case, I created the show, so if I said, 'No,' they had to abide by that.

The imminent building of the Wall in Season One is also quite a tight clock.

It's like *All the President's Men* or *The Day of the Jackal*: you know that de Gaulle didn't get assassinated and you know that Nixon did get impeached, but it gives the film an impetus and an energy. There are no real characters in *Spy City* but the historical context is absolutely real, and that's the thing that makes it interesting. It's great fun, in a serious sense.

Like one of Graham Greene's 'entertainments', as he described his thrillers.

Absolutely. That's its function: to be an engrossing, grown-up spy thriller. I get enormous pleasure from watching these kind of shows, so to have the opportunity to write one was fantastic. It's linked with everything I've thought and written about the serious spy novel, and it's exactly the sort of spy thriller I like. It's highly complex and you have to pay attention – and if you step out of the room to make a cup of tea, you may miss the essential bit of information that will explain it all at the end.

Seven

Fiction 4

Solo (2013) – *Sweet Caress* (2015)
The Dreams of Bethany Mellmoth (2017)
Love is Blind (2018) – *Trio* (2020)

How did the commission to write a James Bond novel come about?

It came out of the blue. My agent, Jonny Geller, rang me up and said, 'Are you sitting down?' I said, 'Yes.' He said, 'Would you like to write a James Bond novel?' And I thought for about two seconds and said, 'Yes, I would.' I've written a lot about Ian Fleming and put him in *Any Human Heart*, so I wonder if that was the reason why the estate approached me. Having said yes, you then get interviewed by the Fleming family. They had questions for me and I had questions for them: I wanted confirmation that I was free to choose a location and write a narrative without them trying to shape it or curate it in any way, and I got those assurances. It's a very congenial remit and a rather wonderful gift, to be given this mythic fictional character and offered the chance to run with it. Bond is up there with Sherlock Holmes and Don Quixote as an extra-literary figure. The continuation novels started shortly after Fleming's death with *Colonel Sun*, which Kingsley

Amis wrote pseudonymously; then there were a bunch written by a couple of thriller writers; then the estate decided to ask more serious novelists to have a go, and I was the next in that line following Sebastian Faulks. So having written my World War I spy novel with *Waiting for Sunrise*, and my World War II spy novel with *Restless*, I now had a chance to write my Cold War spy novel with *Solo*. It was an interesting challenge and an intriguing research process, and I enjoyed writing it enormously.

And how did you set about meeting the challenge Bond presented?

You have to respect the conventions of the Bond novels and you have to separate the novels from the films, so I went back and read all the novels and short stories in chronological order, forensically taking notes, which was a fascinating exercise. I wanted *Solo* to be not only a good spy thriller and a good Bond novel, but also a portrait of Bond that Fleming had never put together coherently. If you didn't know anything about James Bond and you read *Solo* you'd get a good sense of his origins and his foibles and his phobias, and they're all sourced in Fleming. All this stuff that might seem rather un-Bondian, like Bond being a nervous flyer or disliking women painting their fingernails, is actually very close to what Bond's begetter wrote.

What would you say that the conventions of the Bond novels are?

You need to have a striking villain. There are usually two love affairs or sexual encounters. And obviously you can't kill him off or amputate a leg or anything like that. The other thing you're aware of when you read the novels is that there's a lot of stuff about cars and clothes and food and drink, and although Bond isn't Fleming, Fleming gave Bond all his tastes: the kind of coffee he likes, the kind of cotton he chooses for his polo shirts, and so on. Bond knows a tremendous amount about women's fashion, which isn't your average spy's forte, and he's also quite well read. Like Fleming, Bond didn't go to university, but he's got a curious taste in literature. Fleming describes Bond's flat as book-lined, and the literary references in the novels go from Milton to Lafcadio Hearn to Eric Ambler. So I took that stuff on board wholesale and put all these little nuances into the novel. What I rejected was the casual racism, chauvinism, misogyny and xenophobia in the novels, which reflect the prejudices and customs of Fleming and his class. *Solo* is set in 1969, and because Bond lives in Chelsea he can step onto the King's Road and see that the world has changed.

Why did you choose to set it in 1969?

Fleming died in 1964, and the last Bond novel, *The Man with the Golden Gun*, was posthumously published in 1965, so I wanted *Solo* to be close enough to that to be authentic. I didn't want to insert a novel into the sequence, as Anthony Horowitz has done, I wanted it to be an actual continuation. And I remember 1969 very vividly: I was seventeen, in my first year of the sixth form, and my eyes were wide open. It was the first time I went to France. It was the first time I experienced London. I had memories of that year which I was happy to recycle, and it was a very interesting year to set it: swinging London and James Bond is a real culture clash. There's a discrepancy in the novels about Bond's date of birth, but in *You Only Live Twice* Fleming finally plumped for 1924, so Bond is a middle-aged man by the time *Solo* opens. Today, forty-five seems quite young to me; but in 1969, if you were born in the '20s, you probably did feel a bit of an oldster. My father was born in 1920, and if I think of him in the late '60s, he always wore a tie, his hair was always neatly cut, he was never remotely unshaven. If you had any kind of military training in the war it seemed to make you prematurely old. So it was fun imagining the late '60s Bond novel Fleming might have written if he'd looked after himself a bit better.

Did you take any account of Fleming's writing style?

Sebastian decided to do his novel as 'Sebastian Faulks writing as Ian Fleming' – as a mask, if you like – but I didn't want to write a pastiche Fleming, and that was something I cleared with the Fleming family. *Solo* is written entirely in my voice and can sit on the shelf with my other novels. It's also different from Fleming's novels because it's written exclusively from Bond's point of view.

And you took no account of the Bond films, either?

Everybody knows the movies – that's why the books are read – but they got further and further away from Fleming as they went on, and by the time you get to the Roger Moore era they're so far from the original material that they're almost farcical. My favourite of the films is *From Russia with Love*, which is very close to the novel. I remember reading the book and seeing the film when I was thirteen or fourteen, and it's one of those movies that stays with you – and, of course, Sean Connery is the first and best Bond. Something else I picked out from the novels is Bond's Scottishness. The Fleming family were Scottish, and Bond is half Scottish, half Swiss. The one influence of the films on the novels is that once Connery was cast – against Fleming's wishes – and Fleming saw how fantastic he was in *Dr. No*, *From Russia with Love* and *Goldfinger*, he re-emphasized the Scottishness in the last two Bond novels, *You Only Live Twice* and *The Man with the Golden Gun*. In *The Man with the Golden Gun*, M offers Bond a knighthood and Bond refuses on the grounds that he's only a Scottish peasant, which is rather wonderful. So that may be Sean Connery's great contribution to the Bond oeuvre, and it's something else I stressed in *Solo*. But even though I've worked with three of the actors who have played Bond – Sean, Pierce Brosnan and Daniel Craig – I completely ignored the films and resolutely concentrated on the novels.

Did you consider how fans of the books might react?

I was aware of the fan base – and I was even more aware of it when the book came out, because every Bond website in the world goes to work on you – but I saw that as a challenge: I'd done so much work on the Fleming novels that I thought, 'Call me out if you can.' One of the things that takes us into real Bond fandom was the issue of the car. Bond famously drove a Bentley, which it looks like he bought when he was thirteen because Fleming is so vague about his dates. Anyway, it's 1969 and Bond is wanting to upgrade his car; I wasn't going to give him an Aston Martin because that's from the films; I'd always admired the looks of the Jensen Interceptor; and I thought, 'This is the kind of car that Bond might fancy.' So that allowed me to tick the box next to the car aspect of the Bond business. Then I got outraged comments on the websites that there was no way James Bond would ever choose a Jensen Interceptor because it had an American engine, which I was able to counter by saying that Ian Fleming was a great admirer of American cars. That sort of stuff had to be right, and it was fun getting it right.

Was Africa your immediate choice for the location?

Once I got the job it was a quite a quick decision. Except for a brief moment at the end of *Diamonds Are Forever*, Fleming never sent Bond to Africa, so it was a new continent and a new experience for him. I took away all the gadgets and he became unaccommodated man, lost in the jungle. *Solo* proves one of my great adages, which is that nothing is wasted. I reused episodes from my unpublished Biafran War novel, *Against the Day*, and I also shoehorned in material from an aborted TV project which I'd outlined, about two African brothers. I thought, 'Why let it wither on the vine?' The novel I'm writing at the moment includes things that I was thinking about in Oxford back in the '70s, ideas that have never had the right arena to be displayed in. I'm sure that's true of all writers. If you have a good idea, you don't just discard it — and when you return to it, everything's changed.

You don't expect a Bond novel to have an epigraph from Wordsworth's *Intimations of Immortality*. Why did you choose that particular quote?

I had a real problem coming up with a title for *Solo*, and I was going to take the title from that epigraph — *Dark Imaginings*, or something like that, which obviously wouldn't have worked at all. But I also wanted to signal the fact that this book was not being written by some hack thriller writer. As I've said, epigraphs are clues to how the book should be read, and the Wordsworth quote did a lot of work for me in setting out my stall, since the novel is about Bond's mortality.

So you saw it very much as a literary thriller?

I think so, because it's not stereotypical. That's how I evaluate a novel: the more stereotypes — whether of language, character or plot — the worse the book. If you've read something a hundred times before, you know the writer isn't trying very hard. It's a curious hybrid, I suppose, in that *Solo* takes a familiar genre and tries to inject it with a sensibility that raises it above a beach blanket bestseller — and, at the same time, undercuts all the Bond baggage.

You also don't expect a Bond novel to open with a dream sequence, much less with a chapter entitled 'In Dreams Begin Responsibilities'.

Well, that's the title of Delmore Schwartz's most famous short story, so it's another literary allusion. The first sentence just came to me – 'James Bond was dreaming' – and the dream is something totally unexpected: D-Day plus one. There are about five references in the novels to Bond seeing action in World War II – a buried story that I don't think anybody else had picked out – so I took that as licence to invent a wartime past for him, and I put him in the special commando unit that Fleming originated in the Naval Intelligence Division. I thought I'd start with that to jolt people into, as it were, my Bond: what the hell is James Bond, aged twenty, doing in occupied France?

He's not just a Bond with a past, but a past which has an impact on his actions in the present.

Exactly. I lifted a quote from Fleming: 'You only live twice: once when you're born and once when you look death in the face.' It could have ended for Bond in an orchard in Normandy in 1944, but it didn't, and that experience has shaped his entire adult life. Again, it set out my stall as a continuation novelist: this wasn't going to be all Bentleys and Berettas, it was intended to be slightly more cerebral.

The ending of the novel also plays with your expectations. The first of the two women Bond becomes involved with, Bryce Fitzjohn, initially seems to be a casual dalliance – but ultimately you hint that he may have fallen in love with her, and sacrifices his happiness to ensure her safety.

You're absolutely right, and I took a lot of care over the ending. Bond has won, but he doesn't know if the villain, Kobus Breed, is still out there, bent on revenge. Bond realizes that anybody associated with him is in jeopardy, because a good way of attacking him is to attack people he feels things for, so he voluntarily renounces the emotional ties that were building with Bryce. She's in her forties – what you might call today 'age-appropriate' – and he's possibly giving up a true relationship with an equal and basically condemning himself to be solitary. In that drive back to London at the end – particularly the last paragraph, which I really like – I wanted to hit the right cathartic, bittersweet note. He imagines her waking up feeling embittered but he knows it's for her own good and he's done the right thing.

Bryce is interesting for another reason: she's a star of Hammer Horror-type films under the name Astrid Ostergard, and you later returned to the British film industry of that era in *Trio*.

A lot of stars of that era were Scandinavian or fake Scandinavian – to have a name like Ingrid or Astrid was a plus – and the home of Hammer Horror was Bray Studios, where we filmed *The Trench*, so I've been on the sound stages where those films were made. When I was at Glasgow University I interviewed this stunningly beautiful Scandinavian actress called Julie Ege, who had a brief flowering of fame around that time; and looking back on it now, sitting chatting to Julie Ege for the student newspaper was somehow more significant than meeting Iris

Murdoch at Oxford. For me, at the age of twenty or twenty-one it was like meeting Faye Dunaway. So for *Solo* I created my own faux-Scandinavian horror movie star, and then, as you say, I revisited that Swinging Sixties world in *Trio*, which is set a year earlier, in 1968.

The second woman Bond becomes involved with, Efua Blessing Ogilvy-Grant, is also unusual in terms of Fleming's Bond, in that she's Black.

That's been done in the more recent films, but I don't think Fleming would have considered doing it for one second – so there's a sense of a contemporary sensibility looking back at this literary construct and thinking how can it be made interesting and fresh, not just recycling the familiar Bond tropes. And since it's 1969, it's in the zeitgeist.

Did the book take you as long to write as your own novels?

It probably took me a year all told, so that's much faster than usual. Because it was a commission, it had a tighter schedule and a precise deadline. I did all this reading beforehand, then I had to submit a detailed outline to the Fleming family, then I wrote it – and then, when I finished it, the family read it to see if there was anything I had got wrong. So it's possibly the shortest of my novels, but it's a good length for a Bond novel. Fleming would write his Bond novels in three months. He'd go to Jamaica for Christmas, write them between January and March, then come back to Britain and hand in the manuscript to his editor, William Plomer. Waugh wrote many of his novels, the first drafts, in under two months. If you've got it all figured out and you write one or two thousand words a day, at that rate you've got your novel in rough shape after fifty days. And then there's the James Joyce model, where it takes you about ten years. It all depends on your writing practice.

What *is* your writing practice?

I write every day, seven days a week, and I tend to write in the afternoon, between lunch and the cocktail hour. That may be my metabolism: I think I'm a slow starter. In the morning I'll research or prepare what I'm writing next, or revise or type up the day before's work. Then I'll break for lunch. In the afternoon I'll do fresh writing; I can write creatively for about three hours before I hit a wall and my brain just stops. Then I'll have supper and a glass of wine. And as a novel is coming to an end and I'm obsessing over it, the day becomes longer and longer and I'll write in the evenings as well, until about midnight. There's a fairly remorseless rhythm to it.

So did the Fleming family think you'd got anything wrong in *Solo*?

They felt that I'd got the Bond/M relationship wrong, which I disagreed with and fought my corner over. I saw it very much as a father–son relationship, and I was able to quote Bond saying in one of the novels, 'M is like a father to me'. There's a scene in *Solo* where M comes to visit Bond in hospital when he's recovering from his bullet wounds, and I freighted that scene with emotion because it was like a father seeing his injured son in bed and the son being visited unexpectedly by this father figure. They felt I'd over-egged that, so I did strip it back – but only marginally.

It seems to me that there are two types of British spy novel. The first are stories of imperial adventure: Childers, Buchan, Fleming. The second are studies in moral ambiguity: Conrad, Greene, Le Carré. In *Solo*, in a way, you blurred the lines between the two.

That's a very fair point. The more literary a spy novel, the more it leans into the moral ambiguities: the price of being a spy, and what it takes to become a traitor. That's the area I've occupied myself with in *Solo* and *Restless* and *Waiting for Sunrise*. There's obviously a lot of action and complex plotting in them, but what's interesting is the psychological machinations of the genre. Bond, in *Solo*, is in exactly that position. He's gone rogue, he's wanting to take revenge and he's dealing with those emotions and motivations. So yes, I'm having my cake and eating it, in that you can read it as an exciting spy novel or you can dwell a bit on the portrait of Bond that emerges from it – and he's a far more complex individual than you might think, thanks to all these clues that Fleming dropped along the way. There's a great line in one of the Fleming novels, I can't remember which one, and it's something like, 'Bond realized that the thirteenth large whisky had been a mistake.' That's about a bottle and a half, so by any definition Bond is a functioning alcoholic.

Another thing the character has in common with Fleming.

Fleming was a complete alcoholic. He was a two-bottles-of-vodka-and-eighty-cigarettes-a-day man. I've made this point before but he was similar to Evelyn Waugh, in the sense that both were hugely successful but deeply unhappy, and both wanted to die but lacked the courage to commit suicide, so both committed slow suicide by drinking and smoking themselves into an early grave. Fleming was fifty-six when he died and Waugh was sixty-two, but they were horrendously ill for the last few years of their lives. There are quite a few case studies like that: successful but unhappy English writers who wilfully shortened their lives. Lawrence Durrell is another, Henry Green is another. It's very curious.

Alcoholism, and its effect on the individual themselves and the people around them, is something you've written about a number of times – including in the novel following _Solo_, _Sweet Caress_, where the heroine's husband, Sholto, does exactly what you've just described Fleming and Waugh doing.

That's true. And if you look at _Trio_, the novelist, Elfrida Wing, is also an alcoholic. There are various reasons for that. I'm not an alcoholic – although I do like a glass of wine – but I've known a lot of alcoholics in my life, and alcoholism seems to be a very writerly problem. There are many famous writers who were chronic alcoholics, some of whom destroyed themselves, some of whom managed to function while being heavy drinkers. You can rattle off the names: Hemingway, Faulkner and Scott Fitzgerald for starters. Then you can throw in Dylan Thomas, Malcolm Lowry, Kingsley Amis. My favourite poet, Elizabeth Bishop, would drink a bottle of eau de cologne if there was no alcohol in the house, yet she wrote these exquisite poems. Somebody once said to me that writers tend to drink more than other people. I'm not sure that's true, it's just that if you're a writer and you have a heavy night on the booze it doesn't matter if you don't get up until mid-day, whereas if you have to be at the office at nine in the morning you probably wouldn't drink as much the night before as Ernest Hemingway would. Who knows, there may be as many alcoholic accountants as there are alcoholic novelists. But it's a part of literary culture I'm certainly aware of, so it does play a part in my novels. When I think back to my childhood in Africa, it was a very drink-fuelled society because drink was very cheap. I grew up in a household where my mother and father would have two gin and tonics before lunch and then drink whisky in the evening, as everybody else did. And if you go back pre-1960s, the amount of booze people drank without a single finger being wagged at them is pretty amazing. Now, if you open your second bottle of wine, it's, 'Uh-oh, slippery slope.'

Having decided to write a 'whole life' novel about a woman, why did you choose photographer as her profession?

Because of *Nat Tate*, I saw how found photographs could play a part in fiction. Also because of *Nat Tate*, I was asked to write the introduction to a book of photographs called *Anonymous*. An American curator, Robert Flynn Johnson, had a huge collection of anonymous photographs, and Thames & Hudson produced this book and I wrote an essay to introduce it called '13 Ways of Looking at a Photograph'. I decided there were only thirteen types of photograph, just as I decided there are only seven types of short story, so I threw that out as a challenge. And since then I've written a lot about photography and photographers: introductions to monographs and articles for newspapers. I've had my photograph taken thousands of times over my literary career, and I always ask the photographer who their favourite photographers are, so I've built up this vox pop archive. I also take photographs myself and am thinking of publishing a little book of them with an essay, and in my next book of collected non-fiction there will be a whole category on photography. So photography has crept into my life, and when I asked myself, 'What does Amory Clay do?' I thought, 'Photographer.' The history of women photographers in the twentieth century is really interesting, because it's an art form that was non-gender-specific: women could become professional photographers in the 1920s, just like men could. Once I'd had that idea and started exploring it, thinking about Amory's trajectory through the century, I started buying photographs again, partly in junk shops and antique sales but largely online, because eBay is a phenomenal source of cheap photographs. By the time I started writing the book, I knew what kind of photographs I was looking for, and it was fun searching for them. For example, when I was writing the Vietnam War section, what I was looking for was snapshots. It was very hard to find photographs of the war that weren't taken by photojournalists and therefore protected by copyright, and I'd have to buy hundreds of photographs and would maybe get two images out of it. But the images I got were great – and occasionally I found ones that provoked narrative additions.

Can you remember any examples?

One that immediately springs to mind is the image of Amory's father doing a handstand as Amory and her sister look on; I gave her father that ability as a result of finding the photograph. There was also an image I liked of Amory on a boat, so I sent her on a boating holiday. I was worried that they might detract from the fiction – that if people saw photographs which purported to show the characters, it would somehow diminish them – but it quickly became apparent from readers' feedback that they added an intriguing extra dimension.

The title is ostensibly drawn from the epigraph, which is attributed to Jean-Baptiste Charbonneau, from his 1957 book *Avis de passage*: 'However long your stay on this small planet lasts, and whatever happens during it, the most important thing is that – from time to time – you feel life's sweet caress.' Except, of course, the epigraph . . .

. . . is completely made up, he's a fictitious character and the book doesn't exist. I did the same thing in *An Ice-Cream War*, where I invented the letter that provided the preface – and the title. The epigraph to *Bamboo*, the Chinese proverb, is also fake: 'Plant one bamboo shoot – cut bamboo for the rest of your life.' I haven't done it very often, but if I can't find the right quote I'll make it up. I was going to call the novel *The Real Life of Amory Clay*, but there's a character in one of Scott Fitzgerald's earliest novels, *This Side of Paradise*, called Amory Blaine, and I didn't want that echo to be foregrounded. So I came up with the title *Sweet Caress*, and then I thought, 'How do I justify it? I know, I'll make up a quote in French and then translate it.' It's actually in an Everly Brothers song, isn't it? 'Your sweet caress', or something like that? I must have listened to it and thought, 'That would be a good title,' and amazingly it hadn't been used.

Did you like its slightly feminine feel?

I think it was more that life is difficult and cruel but there are compensations. That's very true of Amory's life, and that's what I wanted to stress.

The original title morphed into a subtitle: 'The Many Lives of Amory Clay'. *Any Human Heart* also has a subtitle: 'The Intimate Journals of Logan Mountstuart'. And so does *Love is Blind*: 'The Rapture of Brodie Moncur'. What function do they serve?

That's a very good question. I hadn't really thought about it. You could probably write an essay on the use of the subtitle in novels. I'm going to use a subtitle in the novel I'm writing now as well, although I haven't quite decided what it will be yet. Again, it just adds another dimension, and it doesn't need to go on the cover but it can be on the title page. It's a bit like using an epigraph: part of the covert steering of the reader towards the interpretation that you want. It's not there randomly, it's there for a reason, and it's up to you to divine what the reason is.

Sweet Caress covers 1908 to 1983. Any Human Heart covers 1906 to 1991. The New Confessions covers 1899 to 1972. What governed those start and end dates?

The twentieth century, is the short answer. It's my century, in a way. Of course, here we are in the third decade of the twenty-first century, but I was born halfway through the twentieth, and I feel that's my terrain. So that's the reason for the lifespans of those characters – although in the new novel, as I say, I'm going much further back. It has to be a long life, I think, because the longer the life, the more you can get in. If your principal character lives into or close to their eighties they'll naturally live through many decades, and that's what makes the 'whole life' novel so intriguing to readers.

Just as each chapter of The New Confessions ends with entries from the diary of John James Todd, aged seventy-three, on a Spanish island, so each chapter of Sweet Caress ends with entries from the diary of Amory Clay, aged sixty-nine, on a Scottish island. And that similarity points up the essential difference between those books and Any Human Heart: Logan's journals record his life as he lives it whereas they're both looking back.

That's right. The literary form determines the type of story you can tell. *The New Confessions* and *Sweet Caress* are both fake autobiographies, and the difference between autobiography and the journal form is that, in theory, the journal isn't shaped because you don't know what's going to happen; you don't know the significance of things. *Nat Tate* is a fake biography, which is another literary form. And for the novel I'm writing now I've established a different framework, which allows me to incorporate everything from scraps of paper to elaborate reminiscence to editorial interpolation, so it's like a scholarly piecing-together of a life rather than a simple narrative. These devices have always been there in the novel, and you choose the ones that best suit your purpose. You strive to make it watertight and seamless, but you're employing a very artificial construct in order to make something seem entirely natural – which could be the definition of the novel.

It also goes back to your project to make fiction seem both totally real and more powerful than fact.

Fiction does give you that freedom. I always quote my friend Donald Rayfield, whose book about Chekhov is one of the great biographies: 'All biography is fiction, but fiction that has to fit the documented facts.' That's a very interesting definition, because how does anybody know what Chekhov felt or thought? They don't, so they have to imagine it. And autobiography is also deeply suspect, because it's shaped by the person who lived the life. I reviewed John le Carré's biography, which was written by another friend of mine, Adam Sisman. Le Carré authorized the book but was obviously so unhappy with it that he immediately wrote an autobiography to counter it; and if you look at the same events described in both books, it's fascinating how the person who lived through them sees them in one way, whereas the person who researched them sees them in an entirely different way. In other words, biography is a kind of fiction, and autobiography is also a kind of fiction, so the only real truth resides in true fiction, because the author can guarantee its absolute veracity – because he or she made it all up. A rather beautiful paradox.

You employ a device in *Sweet Caress* which you didn't use in *The New Confessions* or *Any Human Heart*: Amory occasionally writes a series of paragraphs all starting 'I remember . . .'

I wouldn't have done that in *Any Human Heart* because it's a journal, but in *Sweet Caress* it's almost a riff, because that novel is slightly more free-flowing than the other two. Amory's memories, as they crowd in on her, provoke this cluster of reminiscences that she articulates. So it works for her character, but it also serves a purpose in that you can cover a lot of exposition in a very neat way.

Free-flowing is a good description of *Sweet Caress*, because while *The New Confessions* is structured around Todd's quest to finish his movie, Amory doesn't have that kind of grand ambition: her life, and hence the novel, is less driven and more haphazard.

I think that's true. I mean, all lives are haphazard. Even though we think we know our direction and destination, we can be thrown off course very easily. But in Amory's case, her life probably is more buffeted and random than John James Todd's – or Logan's. It was interesting adapting the novel for TV, because I started Episode One with the moment when her father drives his car into the lake and tries to kill them both. The fact that Amory survives this event defines the life she's going to lead. She could have died at the age of sixteen but she didn't. Instead she becomes a photographer, is brutalized by Blackshirts in London, meets this alcoholic Scottish aristocrat and becomes a mother, then is a war correspondent in France and Vietnam. The swerves in her life are pretty huge, and she goes with them like thistledown on the breeze, so she's looking back at her journey with a certain astonishment that it's been so varied. That incident with her father at the lake when she was a schoolgirl shapes her, and whatever comes along after that is a bonus because she might not have experienced it.

Although, thinking about it, she could have died at the hands of the Blackshirts or on a road in Vietnam; the threat of mortality is more present throughout her life than in Todd's or Logan's.

Perhaps it is the novel where the thin ice that we're all walking on is most consciously realized. She's very aware of how fragile our well-being or our current state of happiness is, and that informs her view of the world and makes her decide not to take her own life at the end of the novel and to live on a bit longer – because of these transient sweet caresses that life bestows on you from time to time.

If the incident with her father is what shapes her, then World War I is the event that shapes him, and ultimately her life choices – becoming a war photographer, marrying a traumatized World War II veteran – allow her to understand why her father tried to kill them both.

Yes, and she recognizes that parallel: her father was a victim, just as Sholto is a victim, and she's the collateral damage of both men's bad experiences. These kind of stories were part of my family mythology growing up. My father and uncles lived through World War II. My grandfather and great-uncle both survived World War I. They're all dead now, but I look back at them, particularly as I get older, and think what it must have been like to live with these experiences. My uncle Ronnie was at D-Day as a nineteen-year-old able seaman on HMS *Achilles*, down in the magazines of the ship feeding shells up to the guns on the deck. A year later, just after the war, HMS *Achilles* was sent to Athens to help suppress the Greek communist uprising, and my uncle Ronnie was ordered to man a machine gun and open fire if the mob came down quayside – which he did. He never got over what he had to do as a teenager and a twenty-year-old, but he never spoke about it and I only found out about it latterly. These things affect you as an individual, and if as an individual you're a novelist they find their way into the novels you write. In taking Amory's father's trauma of World War I, then having her live through World War II – and, by association, Sholto's trauma of World War II – I dealt with those two vast, monolithic events of the twentieth century and showed how, even if you survive, you're a victim, and that you don't have to be in the front line attacking a machine gun nest to be a victim.

Amory strikes me as a less spiky, more phlegmatic character than Hope Clearwater in *Brazzaville Beach*, or Ruth Gilmartin in *Restless*: the events around her may be vast but she remains fairly even-tempered.

I think that's fair. She still takes risks: her affair with a married American man and subsequent move to America is quite bold. But she does have a sanguine, clear-eyed view of life – again, maybe because she very nearly died at her father's hand, so everything else is a bonus and she's not going to get too upset or fraught about things that don't go her way.

***Sweet Caress* also seems to contain fewer real people than *Any Human Heart*.**

Any Human Heart certainly has many more real people in it, and the new novel is going to have quite a lot of real people in it as well, historical figures that my character encounters along the way. It just depends on the story, really. *Sweet Caress* is more like *The New Confessions*: because of the highways and byways of Amory's life, I tended to take types, characters who could be real people or versions of real people. Sholto, for example, is loosely based on Shimi Lovat, a Scottish aristocrat who Evelyn Waugh knew – and cordially detested – and the uncle that Amory goes to work for is a sort of Cecil Beaton figure. A few real names are dropped, but she doesn't encounter any significant real people.

Although the acknowledgements include both real and fictional names.

I've started doing this in recent novels, putting in gratitude and acknowledgments to people whose brains I've picked for research and without whom I couldn't have written the novel, but I always stick in the odd fictitious figure just to send people scurrying to their Google. In *Sweet Caress*, some of them are fictitious photographers who appear in the novel but others are real women photographers, and one of the reasons for doing that was to rescue them from history. There were famous women photographers in the 1920s, and they're being rediscovered now, but they'd almost been forgotten. So it was part of that exercise to show that Amory's career path was not fanciful in any way, it was entirely realistic.

I find the ending of the book deeply moving. Amory is preparing to commit suicide on her birthday in 1978 before her illness prevents her doing that, but as she takes the pills she starts to change her mind, and when you reach the ellipses at the end of the chapter you don't know whether she went through with it. Then you turn the page and see: 'AMORY CLAY, Photographer, Born 7 March 1908, Died 23 June 1983

(by her own hand)'. It's a great example of how to use elision in a novel.

And it justifies the title of the novel, because she's experiencing things that every person on the planet can experience: stars in the sky, a breeze, surf on the beach. She thinks, 'Now I know how to switch the lights out when I want to, I'll hang on for a bit longer.' The reader thinks the novel has ended, then finds there's another five years that hasn't been written about. It's a nice surprise to serve up.

It's also the last time she dodges death – but the first time it's her choice rather than happenstance.

Exactly. It's done in full consciousness. The disease she's suffering from is motor neurone disease, which is really horrific. Your brain is absolutely fine but you begin to lose all motor function, including, eventually, the ability to breathe. I had a very good friend who died from it, a clever, delightful man who became a kind of ghost person, so that was in my mind. I thought that if somebody like Amory was diagnosed with this hideous disease, somebody who's no fool and knows what's up ahead, she'd think, 'I'm not going through that.' You're right that her whole attitude is level-headed and sagacious – far more so than my two rackety men, Logan and John James Todd, who are railing and fulminating against the universe most of the time. She's also been wounded and has suffered her own share of tragedies, but she's both tougher and calmer about it: she's got things figured out and has a clear view of what's at stake. It's like the epigraph of *Trio*, that quote from Camus: 'There is only one really serious philosophical problem and that is suicide.' Is life worth living or not? And if it's not, what do you do about it? So this philosophical discussion carries on into that novel as well.

How do you regard your third 'whole life' novel now, in comparison to *The New Confessions* and *Any Human Heart*?

It's still selling away merrily, but I feel it hasn't quite achieved what the other two have. Very few of the reviews commented on the photographs, which I thought was completely bizarre. Photographs have been used in novels for a long time – Virginia Woolf and W. G. Sebald are classic examples – but they're usually symbolic in some way, they don't actually illustrate the narrative. I thought I'd done something audacious there, but it just washed over people. I think *Brazzaville Beach* had more impact as the story of a woman's life than *Sweet Caress* did, and yet *Brazzaville Beach* is so odd, with the chimpanzees and everything. I suppose every novelist has two or three novels they grumble about, but it's really a minor grumble – and if we ever make a TV version of it, maybe it'll get a whole new readership and people will see Amory as an interesting character in her own right.

When you're writing a novel, do you ever think ahead to the potential screen adaptation?

If I did, I'd write a sixty-page novel, because you have to throw out so much. I've written the pilot and outline of

Sweet Caress, and there's a hell of a lot in the novel that wouldn't be in those six hours of telly. Anybody writing a novel thinking it's going to be a movie or a TV series is going to write a very simple novel. Interior monologue is impossibly difficult to convey on screen, for example, so you wouldn't give your characters that sort of interior life. I suppose you can see a potential adaptation in almost any novel, but it's never in my mind when I'm writing a novel because I'm only interested in telling a compelling story.

Or, in the case of your fifth collection, *The Dreams of Bethany Mellmoth*, eighteen stories – ten of them about the title character. Where did she come from?

Some years ago this literary magazine called *Notes from the Underground* started up, which was going to be distributed free on the London Tube, and they asked me if I would write something for it. As a favour I wrote this very short story, no more than 1,000 words long, and that was the first Bethany Mellmoth story. At the time Susan and I had a proliferation of young women in our circle of friends and relations – goddaughters, nieces, friends of nieces – all of whom seemed to be drifting. I suppose you'd call them millennials now because they're all in their thirties, but they were in their early twenties then, and I became so familiar with their problems that I thought I'd write this story. And something about Bethany's character clicked with me and I started writing more stories about her, and I just carried on writing them. I wrote another one a couple of months ago – she's now in her late twenties but still as unfocused as ever – and

I'm sure she'll keep popping up as she gets older. I've followed a similar journey with Edward Scully over the years, from being a callow teenager in Nice to getting married and having a child, and it's very appealing revisiting these characters at regular intervals.

Unlike your Edward Scully stories, though – or your stories about Yves Hill, who reappears twice in this collection, as an old and a young man – you grouped the Bethany stories together, almost like a novella.

I've written more Bethany stories than Edward Scully stories or Yves Hill stories, so although they were conceived individually, bringing them together they do form a narrative that works very well. The stories are all written in the historic present – which I've occasionally thought about using in my novels but have always decided against for technical reasons – and it's the perfect tense for Bethany's journey. I've got another four or five Bethany stories which will be published in my next collection, and she's become a good lens to write about contemporary life as I perceive it, particularly the lunatic fringes of the art world.

Incidentally, when Yves Hill first appears, in *Fascination*, it's 1969 and he's seventy-five – so he couldn't really be eighty-seven in the second Bethany story, which is close to contemporary.

You're right! It's like, how old is James Bond?

You scripted and co-produced a fifteen-minute TV pilot with the same title, the year before the collection

was published, starring Lucy Boynton as Bethany and also featuring another rising star, Jack Lowden. It's available to watch on YouTube but it didn't get further than that. Why not?

Bad luck, I think. I first pitched a Bethany series with a couple of production companies, and the comedy commissioners thought it was too dramatic, and the drama commissioners thought it was too comedic, and I thought, 'Does it have to be one or the other? Can't it be both?' Having failed with that, I teamed up with Hilary Bevan Jones and Endor Productions, who'd done *Restless*, and we decided to make this little pilot. We paid for it jointly, me 50 per cent and Endor 50 per cent, and we thought this would solve the problem of people saying, 'Is it comedy or is it drama?' Instead of trying to explain it to them, you just show it to them: 'This is it. We can do another ten or twenty episodes. They can be fifteen or thirty minutes long. Yes or no?' And the answer was, 'No.' We still couldn't get anybody to commission a series. Amazon were very interested, then they turned around and said, 'We've just bought *Fleabag*, and we can't have two shows about an English girl in London.' Of course, they're entirely different beasts.

So the experience of trying to dramatize Bethany was a bit like the experience of actually being Bethany: 'Everything she dreamed of appeared to stall . . . or else other people messed it up.'

Exactly. Life was imitating art. That applies to lots of things I pitch, though. I say to people that I have a professional disappointment once a week and they don't believe me, but it's true. However successful your working life may seem to be on the surface, it's also a collection of frustrations because things don't happen or – my old mantra – things go wrong. But making the pilot was a great experience, and we were all thrilled with the way it turned out. The music was fantastic. The director, Stefan Georgiou, did a brilliant job on a small budget. And the great thing is that because Hilary and I and her company paid for the pilot, it belongs to us and we can still pitch it. Lucy Boynton is a big star now and probably wouldn't want to be Bethany again, but maybe some new rising star will think, 'This is for me,' and Bethany's time will come. The stories are all there and the scripts don't take long to write, so you could very quickly put together a ten-episode season if required. *Seinfeld* was said to be 'a show about nothing', and if you wanted to you could do a fifteen-minute episode of Bethany being bored out of her skull, because even if nothing is going on in her life she can put some music on and take herself off anywhere she likes in her dreams.

The ability to show her dreams is one difference between page and screen. The other is that the drifting quality of the stories becomes more tangibly grounded in the pilot.

You're absolutely right: it's rooted in a time and a place. That's partly to do with the nature of shifting from fiction to film, but it's also what the people you work with bring to it: you get other sensibilities and other points of view.

We shot a lot of the film in the East End of London, which is like a foreign country to me, so it was something of an adventure to go there. We were shooting one scene in a sort of arts centre; it was a Saturday morning, I think, and the guy who was running this place said, 'You have to be out by four,' and we said, 'Why?' and he said, 'We're having a rave here this afternoon.' And as we wound up, the partygoers were arriving: they'd all been up since the previous night and just segued into Saturday afternoon, like a thirty-six-hour blitz. So it was anthropologically interesting as well to encounter the tribes of London and see how their weekend was radically different from mine.

The Bethany stories form Part Two of the collection. Part One comprises seven standalone stories, the first of which, 'The Man Who Liked Kissing Women', is also set on the lunatic fringes of the art world. Do the characteristics of its protagonist Ludo Abernathy – vain, selfish, deceitful, irresponsible – reflect your view of that world?

I find the art world fascinating because so many things swirl around it: pretension, aspiration, acquisition. It's a portrait of our times, even though it only applies to a wealthy elite. Somebody says to Ludo, 'The art world is more corrupt than the Mafia,' and Ludo says, 'That's probably putting it mildly,' and one of the things I wanted to do in that story was show how that corruption eats into the souls of the people who profit from it. I remember going to an auction house and meeting a friend who worked there, and I said, 'How are you?' and he said, 'I can't get the taste of shoe leather off my tongue.' It was the season of Russian and Indian and Singaporean billionaires coming in, and all he'd done was schmooze. It's a kind of pimping, really: very clever people who know about art wooing very stupid people who want to buy art, and however well you're doing out of it you begin to feel a bit sick because it's like taking candy from a baby. It's a totally unregulated, multibillion-dollar global business, and I'm thinking of writing a novel about it, I find it so interesting.

I noticed that Ludo used to work for the same art dealer that Henderson Dores is employed by in *Stars and Bars*. Similarly, the fictional African country of Douala from your first Morgan Leafy story pops up in 'Camp K101'. And in an echo between stories, the novel by Yves Hill which has been critically mauled in 'Humiliation' is called *Oblong*, and the unnamed film-maker in 'Unsent Letters' – who was introduced in *Fascination* – is trying unsuccessfully to make a film called *Oblong or Triangle*. There seem to be more references to your other work in this collection than in your previous ones.

All sorts of writers do that. Nabokov does it. Waugh does it. A lead character from one story recurs in a minor role in another, and so on. As your body of work builds up you can go back to the quarry and pick up a nugget or two, and regular readers may quietly acknowledge the echo. If you don't get the reference it doesn't have any effect at all, but if you do it adds that little extra frisson.

'The Road Not Taken' is a particularly economical story. It reminded me of the François Ozon film *5x2*, which tracks a relationship backwards in five sequences from final break-up to first meeting.

That was a commission for a short film. The film never got made, but I was intrigued by the concept, so I turned it into a short story. By going backwards rather than forwards in time, each scene informs the subsequent scene in a curious way, so by the time you arrive at the end you have a mass of information that irradiates that first encounter. It's a well-known device – Harold Pinter used it in *Betrayal*, Martin Amis used it in *Time's Arrow* – but it's a tricky one to pull off, so you have to construct it carefully.

'Humiliation', a story about the young Yves Hill, harks back to your Logan Mountstuart story, 'Hôtel des Voyageurs', in *The Destiny of Nathalie 'X'*: a writer travelling through France who becomes involved with a glamorous and mysterious woman.

Cyril Connolly lurks behind them both: he had a type of personality that works well in fiction. A short, pug-faced man who only seemed to go out with beautiful women. A very seductive writer about life's pleasures who complained constantly. A super-educated gourmet who was lazy and obese and a drunk. He wrote about driving through the Dordogne in the 1930s, and that's where our house in France is, so I know the landscape. I was also inspired by those old femme-fatale movies where a clever woman is hoodwinking all these besotted men, and I can see someone like Barbara Stanwyck or Jean Harlow playing that role. So all these things coalesced in the story. I enjoyed writing it, and I turned it into a spec film script – which was interesting, because like all scripts based on short stories you have to flesh it out more.

The final story in Part One, 'The Diarists', like 'Incandescence' in *Fascination*, is told from multiple points of view – although it's something of a conceit that five people involved in one event would all be writing diaries.

Yes, but it's amazing how many people do write things down. And it was also the *Rashomon* conceit: that everybody has a different take on this thing they've all experienced. I've been writing a diary for forty-odd years, and thank God I have because that record is often at odds with my memory. Memory is as creative as imagination – it's constantly being reshaped, usually to your benefit – and something that was written down at the time can confirm the reality of the situation. I'm a great reader of diaries, too, and it struck me how askew two people's accounts of the same meeting or incident can be, and I thought you could exploit that. It's a social comedy set amongst the leisured, wealthy, artistic class.

A lot of the characters in the various stories belong to that class. Were you aware of that as you put this collection together?

It was actually just happenstance, although I'm aware that I'm doing it more often. Having tried very hard at the beginning and in the middle of my career not to write about writers, for example, I've ended up writing about them more as I'm approaching the end of my career. Mind you, I have written a novel about a piano tuner recently, so I do stretch myself occasionally – and in the novel I'm writing now the central character has about fourteen different occupations. But as your experiences mount up and you get the opportunity to exploit them, it's easier and more authentic to write about worlds you know well. If I wanted to write a novel about a London cabbie, I'd have to go off and do a ton of research. Whereas if I wanted to write a novel about a London gallerist, I've met a lot of them so I don't need to do as much work. In a sense, it's the path of least resistance: 'What job shall I give this character? I'll give him a job that I'm familiar with and I can make seem real.'

Part Three is a long short story, again almost a novella: 'The Vanishing Game'. That was a rather unusual commission, wasn't it?

It's probably the most bizarre commission I've ever had. The last two Bethany stories were commissioned by the Mandarin Oriental hotel chain, which was a nice gig, but this commission was extraordinary. I was approached by Land Rover USA to write an adventure story, and all I had to do was mention Land Rover somewhere in there. So I came up with this man-on-the-run story, tapping into the page-turners of Buchan and Stevenson, and I decided to make a Land Rover integral to the story – an old, beat-up, long-wheelbase Defender – which they were pleased about. They then created a multimedia ad campaign based around this narrative. They cast it, shot it, scored it, added sound effects – rain dripping steadily, wind rushing through the trees – so when you went onto their website you could read the story silently, or with the score, or with the sound effects, or with clips of the action. It was an unbelievable reading experience, and they threw money at it. It's the only time I've been drawn into that commercial world, and it was very seductive. There are film directors who will probably never direct a film again, because they get paid millions of dollars and given the budget of a feature to make a two-minute commercial and they think, 'Why would I go to all the trouble of making a feature when I can do this?' Anyway, I licensed the story to Land Rover for a couple of years, then it was published in this collection, and now I've adapted it on spec as a TV series.

Which makes sense, since the lead character is a resting screen actor.

Exactly. Because this guy has only been in crap action movies, you could have wonderful fun parodying them: 'I know how to plant a bomb,' or, 'I know how to lure somebody to an ambush point,' and you flash back to the terrible films he's made. It's a caper, a bit of fun. More and more, my experience of film and TV is that it's the actor who triggers the commission rather than the director. The writer is still important, but unless the piece is squarely in a genre, like horror or fantasy, the question is often, 'Who's going to be in it?'

From your fourth short story collection to your fif-teenth novel, *Love is Blind*, which explores several of your abiding interests: Scotland, Russia and music. How did those elements come together?

Like all my novels, it became the sum of everything I was interested in at the time of writing. I'd just been to St Petersburg, which I thought was the most amazing city, so that went into the pot. I wanted to explore my Scottish-ness, and what Scottish literature shared with other literature and what was uniquely its own, so that went in too. The germ of the novel was this phenomenon I'd encountered, that certain pieces of music which had no sentimental or autobiographical link to my life seemed to provoke strong emotion in me. Whether it was Rachman-inoff's second piano concerto, or a song called 'Tomorrow Morning' by the Scottish group the Blue Nile, or Alison Krauss singing 'Away Down the River', I could identify the precise moment when this effect kicked in, and it wasn't to do with the instruments, it was to do with the notes. I could play the piece over and over and it would trigger the same response, a cause-and-effect link between certain sequences of notes and my tear ducts, and I won-dered whether there was a musicological reason for this. I went to a friend of mine, Patrick Doyle, the film composer – and his son, also called Patrick, who com-posed the music for my play *Longing* at Hampstead Theatre – and I said, 'Can I bring you seven pieces of music that all have this effect and could we analyse them?' So I went to their studio at Pinewood and played them this music; the two Patricks went to work at their pianos analysing these pieces; and I sat there taking notes and put it all into the novel virtually verbatim. Fundamentally, it's to do with the unexpected chord. We all listen to so much music that we expect a certain musical progression, and when it doesn't occur, or it occurs in a different way, it's surprising – and it's that surprise, to put it simply, that provokes this response. Anyway, that desire to try and pin down what was going on triggered the idea, 'What if you wrote a song that made people cry when they heard it, and somebody stole it?'

I then thought, because I'm a great music lover and listen to all types of music – classical, rock, bluegrass, folk – that I'd make my hero or heroine a musician, a virtuoso of some sort. But I realized that there are hardly any novels about musicians because it's incredibly hard to write about music in fiction: there's not much you can say about it that isn't banal. So I was sitting in the Chelsea Arts Club one day, and somebody was tuning the Steinway piano that they have in the big bar there, and I suddenly thought, 'Don't make the character a musician, make the character a piano tuner.' Once I had that idea, I realized I'd be able to write about music in a way that was almost like machinery: the mechanism that is a musical instrument, rather than how wonderful the music sounds. Bingo! Sorted. Through a friend of a friend of a friend I made contact with possibly the best piano tuner in the land, a man called Clive Ackroyd, who's the head piano technician at the Royal Academy of Music. He was thrilled to bits that somebody was going to write a novel featuring a piano tuner, so we met up on numerous occasions and he told me all his secrets. I'd say things like, 'If you wanted to sabotage a piano during a concert, could you do it?' and he said, 'I've been tempted many times.' I came up with a good way of doing it, but he came up with a better way, so it wouldn't look like sabotage. He tunes for famous pianists, but he told me that a lot of them haven't got the faintest idea how, when they strike the keyboard, that note is produced. He also said to me, 'I've been at big concerts where the piano has gone out of tune after twenty minutes. Nobody else can hear it, but I can.' It was a fascinating education; the scales fell from my eyes – no pun intended. So that provided the context for the story I was going to tell, which was about an impossible love affair, and then the novel just grew and grew until it took its final form.

The novel draws a direct comparison between Russia and Scotland, reflected in the two epigraphs, from Olga Knipper-Chekhova and Robert Louis Stevenson.

That's something that struck me a long time ago. When I was TV critic at the *New Statesman* in the early '80s, I reviewed a BBC adaptation of *The Cherry Orchard* directed by Richard Eyre, who I didn't know at the time but is now one of my closest friends. It was made in the studio but it was shot like a movie – with an amazing cast led by Judi Dench – and Richard had this brilliant idea of representing the different layers of Russian society by employing different types of Scottish accent. You had the terribly polite Scottish public schoolboy, and the slightly pretentious Morningside bourgeoisie, and the nasal twang of the Scottish football manager, and the demotic working-class

Glaswegian; and I suddenly realized that the little country of Scotland could be seen as a microcosm of the giant country of pre-revolutionary Russia. And that idea, all those years later, filtered into *Love is Blind*. To this day, in Scotland, there's a declining aristocracy, there's a thrusting middle class and there's almost a serf class. It has an establishment that's very English – aristocrats in their castles in the Highlands, judges and lawyers in their clubs in Edinburgh – but it also has a feudal tinge that's very Russian.

You've explored your Scottishness before in your novels, particularly in *The New Confessions* and *Sweet Caress*. What new ground did you want to cover here?

Looking back, there was an autobiographical and a literary impulse working in tandem in *Love is Blind*. The village where Brodie Moncur's family live is located precisely where we used to live in the Scottish Borders, and Lady Dalcastle's name was lifted from Hogg's *Private Memoirs and Confessions of a Justified Sinner*. I explored the Scottish class structure and the sway the Calvinist religion holds. I also took certain tropes of Scottish literature and threw them into the cauldron, like the demonic father and the suspicious brother and the figure that haunts you and pursues you throughout your life – so obviously Robert Louis Stevenson lurks behind the book as well.

The demonic father in question, Malcolm 'Malky' Moncur, made me think of Felix's father in *An*

Ice-Cream War and Todd's father in *The New Confessions*, who are both martinets in different ways. Even Talbot's father in *Trio*, who's only referred to, is clearly a rather severe character.

That's interesting. John James Todd's father is indifferent rather than a demon, and Felix's father is a bit like Evelyn Waugh's, Arthur, who doted on his eldest son, Alec, but didn't seem particularly interested in Evelyn. What kind of psychic wound does that produce? My father died when I was in my mid-twenties and I was sent to boarding school at the age of nine, so we didn't have a strong connection but he wasn't a martinet. His father, my grandfather, was, but maybe that's because he had seven sons and the only way he could rule that brood was with a rod of iron. I never knew my grandfather – who was also called William Boyd – but he was vivid to me growing up because my father and my uncles had strong memories of him and he was often talked about. In my case, I think this interest is more to do with the echoes of fathers you find in Scottish literature, particularly in Stevenson's *Master of Ballantrae*. The Moncur family was also loosely based on James Joyce's family, a huge, unruly brood dominated by this monstrous personality – although John Joyce was a drunk and a braggart, whereas Malky Moncur is a religious bigot who's feathering his own nest. Malky basically wants to terrorize his family but he can't terrorize Brodie and that makes him even more angry. So you get these ideas from your own reading and your own history and your own interpretation of people, and, again, it all trickles down into the novel.

Malky also made me think of Deacon Brodie, the eighteenth-century Edinburgh city councillor and cabinetmaker whose double life as a housebreaker and gambler partly inspired Stevenson's *Dr Jekyll and Mr Hyde*.

Stevenson actually wrote a play about Deacon Brodie; he's one of those Scottish archetypes. And *Jekyll and Hyde* is possibly the dominant Scottish myth. People bandy the term 'Jekyll and Hyde' around without even thinking about it, but it's extraordinary how, in this short novella, he unearthed something, pre-Freud, that's gained a permanent place in the global psyche.

Malky's disdain for his eldest son stems not just from the fact that Brodie stands up to his father, but also from the fact that Brodie has a darker complexion than his siblings. Did you imagine that his mother had an affair, or did you see it simply as a genetic anomaly?

I'd say it's genetic – and wishful thinking on Brodie's part – but it can happen. Thinking of my grandfather's seven sons, there's a distinct Boyd look – and now they've had children, I can see that look in my cousins. I've got a cousin who looks so much like me that once, when he came to our house unannounced, Susan opened the door and screamed. But I've got other uncles and cousins who don't look anything like the rest of us, and they're probably genetically more like my grandmother's side of the family. It's just an anomaly I've experienced and I thought it would feed Malky's paranoia and rudeness. Malky is highly suspicious of why Brodie doesn't look like the rest of the family, and Brodie would love not to be the son of Malky Moncur, so it's another part of that father–son relationship.

Malky is also another of your alcoholic characters, a trait apparently shared by Brodie's brother Callum.

That's a Chekhovian echo. Chekhov had two feckless brothers, one of whom died of tuberculosis and one of whom drank himself to death, so Brodie's relationship with Callum, who becomes a drunk and behaves badly, was drawing on that. Going back to the Scottish–Russian connection, there's a melding of Scottish and Russian literature as well as Scottish and Russian archetypes in the novel, which is even more evident when Brodie goes to St Petersburg and falls in love with a Russian woman – Lika Blum, who has the same name as the woman I think Chekhov was in love with, Lika Mizinova. Chekhov himself has a walk-on part as well: he pops up, unnamed, as the Russian doctor Brodie meets in Nice – and, indeed, the young Frenchwoman who asks if she can go with Brodie to Paris is based on a girl that Chekhov had an affair with in Biarritz. If you didn't know the details of Chekhov's biography you wouldn't pick that up, but the book is peppered with those sort of allusions and associations. That's probably true of all my novels if you unpack them, but a lot came together in this one, both personal and literary – and touristic: all the places that Brodie goes, apart from the Andaman Islands, are places I know well or have visited.

Given your Chekhov obsession, I'm surprised you hadn't visited Russia sooner.

The obsession was a literary one: an exploration of the work and the man. Having seen Richard's film of *The Cherry Orchard*, I started seeing the plays whenever I could and reading the short stories. Then, in the late '90s, I read Donald Rayfield's wonderful biography – which was a revelation, because the Soviet archives had opened up and so much information about Chekhov's life was suddenly available. He's revered as a saint in Russia but he wasn't saintly at all, he was a living, breathing, complex, difficult man. Then I wrote my own short story about him, 'The Pigeon'. Then, in something like 2008, I wrote the play *Longing*, which cherry-picked two of his stories to form a Chekhovian narrative but took about five years to reach the stage. And it wasn't until the play was put on in Tallinn, in Estonia, and that production transferred to St Petersburg, that I finally went to Russia. I only had four or five days there, but it all went into *Love is Blind*. St Petersburg is one of the great cities of the world. It's like Venice or New York – once seen, never forgotten – and it's remarkably unspoiled. Because the city is built on a marsh you can't put up skyscrapers, so the cityscape is fundamentally the one that Peter the Great envisaged. You can imagine Dostoevsky walking the streets of St Petersburg, the same way you can imagine Kafka walking the streets of Prague, and being there as an author rather than as a tourist made it even more wonderful. So all of that ultimately contributed to the novel.

It's your only novel, apart from your 'whole life' novels, with a subtitle: 'The Rapture of Brodie Moncur'. Which made me wonder whether it actually *is* a 'whole life' novel.

I never set out to write it like that – we pick it up when Brodie is already in his twenties – but because he dies so young, and because we flash back to his childhood, and because his entire biography is presented to the reader, maybe it does creep into that category. It doesn't start with his birth, though, which I think a 'whole life' novel has to do in order to be admitted to the pantheon. And, despite the accretion of detail, it's meant to be a powerful love story: from the moment Brodie meets Lika, right up to his death, he's obsessed with her, yet we're never entirely convinced that she loves him. She says that one day she'll come and knock on his door, and she does, but only when it's too late. The novel is about that sort of love which you think is reciprocated but you can't guarantee it, and I leave it up to the reader to make the final judgement. Was Lika true to Brodie? Or did she have her own agenda?

It's also the first time you've used an existing phrase as a title rather than coming up with something of your own.

It was one of my late titles rather than something I had early on, but it seemed very apt when I came up with it – and I was surprised that it had been used so little as a title, even though the phrase is in common parlance. It also translates very easily for foreign editions, which is a nice bonus. And, to be honest, the subtitle takes the curse off the title: it gives that common phrase another dimension – and emphasizes the Scottishness of the novel. Although, actually, 'rapture' was a more difficult word to translate into other languages. It has a precise meaning in English, and you can't quite get that religious obsession aspect in French and German, so it had to be an approximation. With *Trio*, on the other hand, I had the title before I started writing it, but unlike *Love is Blind* it had been used a lot. If you type the film title *Trio* into IMDb, there are a great range of variations on it.

One of those variations is a 1950 film called *Trio*, based on three short stories by Somerset Maugham. Was that an influence, or was it just a coincidence?

Just a coincidence, I think. In fact, the origins of *Trio* are quite unusual. Possibly my favourite novel ever is *Pale Fire* by Vladimir Nabokov, which I've always described as a unique novel, and I originally had this idea for my own unique novel, a novel that's never been done before. I was going to write three novellas that all covered the same time frame, but in each novella the story would be narrated by a different person, and in each story the narrator would have a different secret. My idea was that I would publish the three novellas in different colours in a slipcase, with the instruction that you could read them in any order you liked, and the narrative would hang together whichever order you chose. I played around with this concept for a long time, racking my brains as to how I could write this endlessly overlapping, subtly changing narrative, but I eventually abandoned it, because I felt it was a smart-arse gimmick rather than a super-clever idea. It probably would have worked, but I wonder how interested readers would be in that USP: 'Shall I read red first, or shall I read blue?' But the basic idea – three people with three secrets, and how those secrets impinge on each other – stayed with me. And having had this idea, I then thought, 'Where are they? Are they living in a village? Are they stranded somewhere?' Because I've spent so much time on film sets, I realized they could all be involved in making a movie, which would be the perfect glue to join the disparate stories together; and since the three slipcased novellas would have been called *Trio*, I kept that title, as it suggested a certain vivacity and intrigue.

The three people in the novel are a novelist, Elfrida Wing, a producer, Talbot Kydd, and an actress, Anny Viklund – and, as it happens, their secrets don't particularly impinge on each other and their stories are quite distinct.

The narratives are interconnected – and there are also connections between the principal characters and the minor characters that took a lot of plotting and pondering – but their individual journeys don't have much of an influence on each other. They're geographically in the same place for much of the novel, within the bubble of this ridiculous film, but their lives don't intersect in any meaningful way, apart from Talbot and Anny on the set. So there's a social and professional cement that binds them, but their secrets remain secret to themselves.

Hence the first epigraph – alongside the Camus quote you mentioned earlier – taken from Chekhov: 'Most people live their real, most interesting life under the cover of secrecy.'

That quote was what gave me the impetus for the novellas – the three narratives would be driven by the separate secrets that each narrative contained – and that's still fundamentally the structure of *Trio*. Elfrida's alcoholism is hidden from everybody except her husband, who's so selfish he barely notices she's pissed most of the time. Elfrida has no idea about Talbot's sexuality. Talbot has a glimmering about Anny's past but doesn't believe she's having an affair with her co-star, Troy. They're hermetically sealed off from each other, and as their secret lives spill over into their public lives they each have to work out their own solution to that.

I understand the title of the first part, 'Duplicity', and the last part, 'Escape', but why is the second part titled 'Surrender'?

'Recognition' would be another good word. It's to do with facing up – or fessing up – to the secrets you're keeping. Hence the Camus quote: if you feel your life isn't worth living, what do you do about it? Talbot realizes he's living a lie and finally manages to resolve it. Anny becomes more and more desperate until she runs away and kills herself. And Elfrida decides to follow Virginia Woolf into the River Ouse but is thwarted by the loathsome Maitland Bole and his ramblers, which prompts her to change direction and find serenity at the end. They're all overwhelmed to differing degrees, and all find a different way to escape the labyrinth.

Part One is one hundred and eighty pages, Part Two is eighty and Part Three is sixty. Was that to create a sense of tension, a feeling of events speeding up and closing in?

It was only when I finished it and looked at it that I realized the pace was picking up. All my novels are meant to be a compelling read, but people do seem to gallop through this novel in particular. It's also meant to be funny, and in the same way that no comedy film should be more than ninety minutes long, if a novel is ostensibly a comic novel, albeit a serious comic novel, I don't think it should be a five-hundred-pager.

Were you concerned about achieving a balance between the characters?

If you asked me, 'How many chapters feature Elfrida, how many chapters feature Talbot and how many chapters feature Anny?' I'd actually have to count them. I deliberately didn't tot them up to see if each character had their fair share, because I didn't want to know. I might have felt compelled to write another chapter about one or the other of them, and that might have been a mistake. The narrative seemed to me perfectly proportioned – and apportioned – already.

The basic concept – three people with three secrets – could have been set anywhere at any time. Why did you set it in Brighton in 1968?

I'd been doing a lot of work set in the 1960s. *Solo* was set in 1969. The TV series *Spy City* was set in 1961 – and the second series, which I've developed but hasn't been commissioned, is set in 1963. I was also developing another series set in the '60s, about CIA destabilization of Central America. So I'd been very focused on this decade, which was one of those watershed decades – a time when society and sensibilities changed – and the more I researched it, the more I realized that 1968 was a fascinating year. I started writing the novel before the pandemic but finished it as the pandemic arrived, and the mood in 1968 was very similar to the mood in 2020: widespread unhappiness and apprehension and fear, and a sense of the world being in crisis. In 1968 you had the Tet Offensive in Vietnam, the Soviet invasion of Czechoslovakia, the assassinations of Martin Luther King and Robert Kennedy, and riots in America, Germany, Italy and Paris. It looked like the world was falling apart – except in Britain, where the pressing question was, 'Will the Beatles split up or stay together?' There was an article in the *New York Times* when Swinging London was at its height, and the journalist said he'd never seen such a disconnect between the mood of a country and the mood of the world as he'd witnessed in England in 1968. So I thought that was a very good year to set the novel. Just as our characters' secret lives begin to intrude on their public lives, so the real world begins to invade the world of the movie. It's subtle, but the signs are everywhere: Talbot goes to Paris after the riots, Anny's brother is in Vietnam, urban terrorism is stirring in the shape of her ex-husband. That's the context in which this comedy is happening. Also, as I've said, I'm more and more inclined to go back to the past to avoid obsolescence. There's something reassuring about setting a novel in the past, although there's not a lot of '60s stuff in *Trio* apart from 'MacArthur Park' and the odd reference to miniskirts. It feels steeped in its era but not overloaded with detail.

And, presumably, if London felt disconnected from the world, then Brighton was even more so.

Precisely. Having written two novels set in London, I wanted to move away from there; and with its slightly louche, racy reputation, Brighton seemed to fit the nature of the film the characters are making. It was quite a theatrical place at the time as well: Laurence Olivier was living there, John Osborne was living there. And you could get up to London easily enough. So it fitted the bill in a number of respects.

Was Laurence Olivier the model for the character of Dorian Villiers?

He's sort of a cross between Laurence Olivier and Donald Wolfit. There are echoes of real people in the novel, but apart from various thespians at Dorian's party they're not precisely identified. Elfrida is loosely based on an author called Rosemary Tonks, who was a presence on the '60s scene as a poet and a novelist but then just disappeared – and was unearthed forty years later, living in Bournemouth, having found religion. Disappearing was something you could do in those days, and Rosemary Tonks managed to pull it off – a bit like J. D. Salinger, although everybody knew where Salinger lived. A book of her poems was published recently, *Bedouin of the London Evening*, with an essay explaining the strange life she led, and it's an extraordinary story. So she lurks behind Elfrida the way that Gerhardie lurks behind Logan.

The same way that Jean Seberg lurks behind Anny Viklund.

Anny is based quite closely on Jean Seberg, who died in very similar circumstances. She was discovered by Otto Preminger when she was seventeen, plucked from the Midwest and put in his film *Saint Joan*, and in a way it completely fucked up her life. Marilyn Monroe also lurks behind Anny to a certain extent: it's about what happens to you when you're young and vulnerable and you suddenly achieve enormous fame and wealth. The film industry is full of examples of people going off the rails, and like a lot of these actresses Jean Seberg was drunk a lot of the time and taking tons of pills, but her self-destructive path also took her in the direction of radical politics. She married the French novelist Romain Gary and moved to Paris – her most famous film is probably Godard's *Breathless*, and she's incandescent in it – but she was targeted by the FBI because of her left-wing ties and was found dead in her car in Paris in 1979. It's one of those conspiracy theories: did she kill herself or was she killed because of her involvement in politics? The jury is still out, but she was at a very rackety stage of her life – and older than Anny; at least forty by then.

Anny clearly does kill herself, and in an unshowy way; whereas there's something performative about Elfrida's attempt, recreating how Virginia Woolf did it.

Of course, Elfrida is drink-crazed at that point: she's reached the stage of delirium tremens and thinks parasites have infested her body, a level of alcoholism that I've unfortunately witnessed a couple of times with friends of mine. Your grip on reality begins to go. The fur coat and the gumboots and the stone in her pocket is a deranged attempt to curate her end.

It occurs to me that Anny doesn't have a significant connection with another woman in the course of the story: she's simply bounced from pillar to post by men who want things from her.

That's very like Marilyn Monroe: all these powerful older men homed in on her – and one of the things Anny loves about Troy is not just his naivety but the fact that he's younger than she is, because she's only gone out with older men. But you're right, there isn't really another woman friend in her life. She has a female assistant who fetches and carries for her, but her mother is dead, she's making a movie in Brighton rather than being home in America, and it's only when she goes to Troy's house and meets his family that she actually finds herself in a normal domestic situation. So yes, she's a lost soul.

All three of the principal characters are lost souls, I'd say.

They're all loners, really. Talbot has his producing partner, but his partner is ripping him off. He's also distanced from his son. When he goes to see his son playing in a concert, what should be a bonding moment sees the wedge being driven ever deeper between the two because of the awkwardness inherent in both their natures. So they're very much fighting a lonely battle.

The movie they're making, *Emily Bracegirdle's Extremely Useful Ladder to the Moon*, made me think of a film I once read about in *Halliwell's Film Guide* but have never seen: Anthony Newley's 1969 musical comedy *Can Heironymus Merkin Ever Forget Mercy Humppe and Find True Happiness?*

Well, you'll have noticed that I mention Dame Joan Collins in the acknowledgements at the end of the novel; she's an old friend of ours and was in that film – which, as she says herself, brought an end to her complicated, difficult marriage to Anthony Newley. It's possibly the stupidest film title ever, but there were a whole bunch of British films like that at the time: zany, sexy, larky, contemporary and, when you look back at them, very dated. The period starts in 1964, with Richard Lester's Beatles film *A Hard Day's Night*, and ends with *If. . . .* and *Performance*, because the mood changes to something much darker as the '70s arrive. The kitchen sink gave way to the Swinging Sixties, then we got all political and druggy and violent. But yes, Newley's film was the model; he'd been watching his Godard and his Buñuel and was determined to allude to them, in the same way that the pretentious director, Rodrigo Tipton, does in the novel. It's very hard to find the film now. I remember seeing it when it came out, and you can sort of reconstitute it by reading about it, but I couldn't track down a DVD anywhere.

Your recurring fictional film-maker, Mavrocordato, is namechecked again in *Trio* – although when he last popped up, in the story 'Visions Fugitives', his first name was Jean-Didier rather than Gianluca.

I think you're the only person in the world who's spotted that. He goes back a long way. I remember entering a talent competition when I was very young, and one of the things you had to do was a short interview with a famous person. I didn't know any famous people and had no idea how to get hold of one, so I invented this film-maker and wrote a fake interview with him – shades of *Nat Tate* – and over the years when I've needed a name I've reached into my name kitty and plucked him out.

You've referred to it as a comic novel and it certainly starts in that vein, in keeping with the lightness of the movie, but it feels like it becomes darker and more serious during the course of the story.

When the novel was published in Spain, a radio journalist said, 'Tell me in one or two sentences what sensations you want the reader to leave this novel with,' and the answer I came up with chimes with what you're saying. I said, 'The last page contains all the clues you need.' Elfrida remembers watching a flock of swifts swooping down to drink from a swimming pool and then disappearing up into the blue sky, and that shows you the trajectory of the novel. It's a magical, almost transcendental moment, and I took a lot of trouble over those final sentences; I rewrote them and rewrote them to get the tone and the rhythms and the word order absolutely correct. It does slow down and become more serious on that last page, and the reader is meant to think about this image and make of it what they will. Is it about the transitory nature of life? Or is it about the fleeting pleasures to be taken from life? It's not spelled out, but how the novel draws to its end does ultimately set the tone for it.

And mirrors the way it begins, when Elfrida wakes up in bed.

Yes, exactly. The indistinguishable birds on the wallpaper become the very real swifts drinking from the swimming pool.

Have you ever planned out a novel and found that the characters want to take it in a different direction to the one you envisaged?

Absolutely not. I think it's a romantic notion anyway, that somehow you become a conduit for the muse, and I spend too long planning a novel for that to be the case. I always quote Vladimir Nabokov's answer to this very question: 'My characters are galley slaves, and I am the man on the deck with a whip.' That's exactly how I feel. The characters are pawns on my chessboard and I move them around as I see fit. Of course there's room for improvisation on the day, and I get ideas as I'm writing that I hadn't planned; I've made enormous changes when I've had a good idea, and the domino effect has carried on through the novel. But I always start with a very clear idea of the whole novel, and more to the point a very clear idea of how it's going to end, to the extent that I could write the last page if I wanted to. This is true of my new novel: I know what happens to the central character and how his story ends, so I'm writing towards that destination.

Eight

Stage Plays

Six Parties (2009) – *Longing* (2013)
The Argument (2016)

Your first produced stage play, *Six Parties*, was commissioned by the National Theatre for its annual New Connections youth theatre festival. Was it, in fact, the first play you'd written since the one you entered for a competition at the Citizens Theatre in Glasgow when you were still at university?

I think it was, actually, and it coincided with a sudden urge I felt to write plays and work in the theatre. And now that I am writing plays myself, I realize that the theatrical education I had in my late teens and early twenties couldn't have been better. The Citizens Theatre in Glasgow in the early 1970s – the 'Citz', as it was known – was one of the most dynamic theatres in Britain, and every production was vibrant and visually stunning. I remember seeing an all-male *King Lear*, and a production of *Macbeth* where the three witches were dressed like the Supremes – and the first time I saw full-frontal nudity on stage, male and female, was at the Citz. It was compelling and controversial, and they deliberately set out to shock and be provocative. They had two theatres, the main theatre and the Close Theatre – which was a small theatre club where they put on even more daring stuff – and you could go to the bar after the show and mingle with the actors, which was really exciting. I'd obviously gone to the theatre before then, but it wasn't until I went to the Citz that I became stage struck, and I've been an avid theatregoer ever since. So then the obvious question is, why didn't I write more plays at the time?

To which the answer would be . . . ?

I was drawn to film instead, which satisfied that dramaturgical ambition. I was very much in that world, I just wasn't participating in it. I knew every artistic director of the National Theatre for twenty-odd years and never sent them a single play, fool that I was. Then I got this commission from the National to write a one-act play, which would be workshopped by the youth theatre groups they worked with and staged in the Cottesloe Theatre. So I responded very warmly to the invitation, I wrote this play about my youth in Africa and stitched it together with the music of that era, and it was put on in the Cottesloe for two or three nights – with a cast that included a young actor called John Boyega. I was called up on stage after the first performance, which was a great moment, and it was reviewed in the *Financial Times* and published in an anthology with the other New Connections plays for that year. It was really a perfect introduction to the world of theatre, and I thought, 'Off we go!' But not a bit of it.

Did you encounter any challenges in changing dramatic forms?

I don't think so. I've never had any problem with the concept or the structure of my plays. Because I love going to the theatre, I think I understand how it works and what you can do. It's almost as free a form as the novel – and much freer than film. The difference is that with theatre everything is slightly heightened. I'm a great believer in naturalistic acting, so I write dialogue that's as naturalistic as possible. But the dialogue you'd write for film, which could be whispered or grunted, won't work in the theatre, because the people sitting at the back won't hear you. It's like any art form: once you understand the grammar, and the demands and needs of the format, you tailor your writing to fit it.

And did *Six Parties* change much during the workshop process?

Not a great deal. What a workshop shows you is technical things like exits and entrances which often aren't apparent in the writing, particularly when you've got a large-ish cast: this character has been on stage for five minutes and hasn't said a word, so what are they doing? Do they listen in, or do they roam around, or do they go and get a drink? *Six Parties* doesn't have a particularly large cast, but in *Longing* there were sometimes lots of people on stage, so you had to think carefully about how you focused attention on what was important. You don't have that problem in film because you can just cut to a close-up, but on stage, where everything is effectively a wide shot, you have to think how that looks and what it delivers. Do you need all these people on stage, and if you don't, how do you get them off gracefully? So the workshop was real nuts-and-bolts stuff, but a learning curve as well.

The six principal characters are all between seventeen and nineteen, three African, two British and one American, and perhaps because of their age, and the setting, the play has quite an edgy feel to it. How much of it was based on your own experience, given that the country in which it takes place is unspecified?

It reflects my own biography in the usual vague way; in other words, the story is very much made up but the ambience is entirely authentic. When I was that age, I'd leave boarding school in Scotland and go home to Nigeria for the holidays, and because I'd been locked up for three months all I wanted to do was get drunk, take drugs and meet girls. A lot of kids would come back from Britain during the holiday months, and you could almost go to a party every night. Over one Christmas holiday, I went to about twenty-two parties, and because of the nature of those West African countries they were totally integrated. There was no sense of a party being whites-only or Blacks-only; you mingled in a completely egalitarian way with your Nigerian contemporaries as well as your expatriate contemporaries – which included Dutch, Canadians and Americans as well as Brits, because there was a big international community there. As the world has turned, the play probably does seem more extraordinary now than when it was first put on, but it reflects the Nigerian society I knew in the '60s and '70s.

There's also a political undertone, in that while these kids are busy having fun cataclysmic events are happening in the country around them.

That was very true of my own experience. I'd come back for the holidays wanting freedom and licence, but often the electricity or the water would only be on for an hour or two each day. I was late going back to school one year because there was a military coup. I remember standing outside our house and hearing gunshots coming from the centre of the university and seeing tear gas drifting through our garden as the riot got out of control, and then my father was called to his clinic to treat people with gunshot wounds. It's also very like the end of *A Good Man in Africa*, where a military coup is happening as Morgan Leafy's love life unravels. So you're right, the background to this hedonism was quite serious political mayhem. But when you're seventeen or eighteen or nineteen you're not thinking about these things – or *I* wasn't thinking about them. I wasn't unperturbed but I wasn't fearful, because it was normal – and even oddly exciting.

If you had to pinpoint the theme of the play, what would it be?

It's about the dynamics between the young people and how rich or privileged people have an easier ride than the poor and underprivileged. What interested me was the poor kid who acted as a gopher, who was very useful when the rich kids wanted their illicit gin but was just discarded when things became complex. You could set it in Thailand or Mexico and it would have the same dynamics between the privileged rich and the kids that did their bidding.

It was another four years before your next play, *Longing*, appeared. Why was there such a gap?

Somebody once told me that there are two thousand plays looking for a home in London at any one time, and there are maybe a hundred theatres from the smallest to the largest, so it's a highly competitive world and interlopers aren't particularly welcome. If you haven't paid your dues as a playwright, I think you're in a slightly lower category in the eyes of the theatre establishment. But having got the bug late in the day – or been reinjected with the bug, since I'd always had it – I thought I'd write *Longing* anyway. I originally wrote it as a TV film for the BBC to mark the centenary of Chekhov's death in 2004, but the BBC passed on it, saying they had, quote unquote, done the Russians. I said, 'What do you mean?' and they said, 'We did *Crime and Punishment* a couple of years ago.' So that didn't happen. Nevertheless, I was very pleased with the script, which took three Chekhov short stories – 'A Visit to Friends', 'My Life' and 'Ionych' – and wove them together, so I thought, 'Maybe I can jettison one of the stories and rewrite it as a play.' I dropped 'Ionych', I expanded my borrowings from the other two, I sent the play to Richard Eyre, who was going to direct the original film, and Richard said, 'Let's have a rehearsed reading.' Because of the esteem in which he's held, he assembled an amazing cast – people like Iain Glen and Eve Best – and we rehearsed the play in the morning, then it was read to a small invited audience in the afternoon. It was one of the great experiences of my non-novel-writing life, because it seemed to me to work really well. But nothing happened. Nobody wanted to do it. You complacently think, 'I've written lots of novels. I've written lots of films. I know lots of actors and directors. Surely I can get a play put on?' And the answer was, 'No, you can't, mate.' It was a real eye-opener.

The play was eventually picked up because of somebody who mentored me on *Six Parties*. The National commissioned twelve plays by various writers and there was a mentoring weekend in Buxton, in Derbyshire, and luckily for me my assigned mentor was a woman called Roxana Silbert, who was an associate of the Royal Shakespeare Company. She read *Longing* and sent it to the head of the RSC, Michael Boyd – no relation – and he really liked it and said, 'We're having a Russian season, and this would be perfect for it.' He suggested giving it to a young director he knew, Nina Raine – who I'd met when she was two years old because I'm a friend of her father, Craig Raine – and Nina read it and loved it, and we had high hopes that it would be on one of the RSC stages. But they lost their funding for the Russian season and the whole thing collapsed. Then Nina, who's also a playwright, had a play on at Hampstead Theatre – *Tiger Country*, about the National Health Service, which was a big hit – and they said to her, 'We'd love you to do another play. Have you got any idea what you'd like to do?' So that's how my second play got produced, thanks to Roxana and Michael and Nina. And, by a strange and pure coincidence, around the time *Longing* went into the works at Hampstead, I was making the TV version of *Restless*, and the director was Edward Hall, who was then running Hampstead Theatre.

Of the many stories that Chekhov wrote, why did you pick 'My Life', 'A Visit to Friends' and 'Ionych' for the screenplay, and why did you drop 'Ionych' from the play?

I just picked the stories that would lend themselves to dramatization: is there enough tension between the characters to sustain a full-length drama? If you were only going to read one Chekhov story, 'My Life' would be the one, because it's his longest story by some distance and gives you everything that is quintessentially Chekhovian. I only used a bit of 'My Life' in the play; I used a lot more of 'A Visit to Friends', which is a very interesting story in Chekhov's canon. He never reproduced it in his collected stories, but it was also the foundation for *The Cherry Orchard* – and I'm actually writing a libretto for an opera, called *A Visit to Friends*, based on bits of *Longing* and bits of the Chekhov story. 'Ionych' is a very funny story and provided a comic element in the film, but film uses up more material so I didn't need it in the play. They're not necessarily my favourite Chekhov stories, but if you're going to take bits from three stories and join them together seamlessly you have to be quite pragmatic.

If 'A Visit to Friends' was the foundation for *The Cherry Orchard*, were you ever concerned that you might end up with a play too much like Chekhov's?

It's almost impossible to write a play based on Chekhov's short stories that doesn't remind you of his plays, because he did exactly the same thing. Towards the end of his life he found himself strapped for cash, so he quarried the plays from his stories to make some money. In the West he's famous as a playwright and his stories aren't nearly as well known. In Russia it's the inverse: he's regarded as a short story writer who happened to write a few plays. I think the stories are the true manifestation of his genius: the atmosphere that people are familiar with in the plays is replicated a hundredfold in the stories. Of course, there's a clichéd view of Chekhov, but like all clichés it wouldn't be a cliché unless there was some truth to it. Russian aristocrats, a country house, a servant bringing on a samovar; it's almost a parody, but that was the world he lived in. It's like writing a drawing room comedy: there are certain tropes that are instantly recognizable, and the reason they're popular is that people respond to them. Chekhov's plays are endlessly performed but he only wrote four of them, so in a modest way I hoped that by adapting this play from his stories I'd create a fifth, because everything in it came from him, not me. I deliberately called the play an adaptation, because the situation and the characters are completely Chekhovian, I've just reorganized the narrative and given certain relationships a different emphasis. The aristocratic family clashing with the pushy developer in *Longing* isn't an echo of *The Cherry Orchard*, it's something that's in 'My

Life'; and the daughter, Cleopatra, in 'My Life' isn't like a figure in any other Chekhov play that I can see. I was able to take stuff from the stories that wasn't familiar, but in a way it would always *feel* familiar, because of the setting and the implications of that.

I seem to remember reading somewhere that Chekhov felt his plays should be played for laughs more than they were. Do you think *Longing* is a comedy?

It's comic in the Chekhovian sense; in other words, it's bittersweet. A line I often quote is that comedy admits everything but tragedy only admits tragedy, and I think Chekhov saw that. There are big laughs in *Longing*, and in the Estonian production the comic element was played up; I remember my Russian translator saying to me, slightly disapprovingly, 'When we put this on in Moscow it'll be done much more seriously.' But actually that would have been wrong. Chekhov is a very funny writer and sees comedy in the darkest situations, so it's meant to be played for laughs. At the same time, it ends in a moving way with a classic Chekhovian ships-that-pass-in-the-night moment: a relationship that looks destined doesn't happen for spurious reasons to do with one or other of the characters. Kolia and Varia should be together, but they don't make it because Kolia is a commitment-phobe – which is a kind of portrait, or self-portrait, of Chekhov himself. There was a great moment at the end of the play, which I don't think is in the script, when Varia is alone on stage and looks back at the summer house, and as she exits a few leaves fall from the tree. Wordless, but telling – and very Chekhovian. That's what makes Chekov so great: he refuses to console, because life isn't like that. Life is cruel and absurd and preposterous, and he won't manipulate things so that true love triumphs at the end.

Having spent so long trying to get the play put on, were you pleased with the eventual production?

Again, it was a fantastically fulfilling experience for me; much more rewarding in terms of collaboration than writing films, in a way. You have a six-week rehearsal period and the writer is welcome every day if they want to turn up. Which I did: not for the whole day but usually for an hour or two, and a lot of my suggestions were incorporated. Donald Rayfield, my go-to source for every Chekhovian question, also came to the rehearsals and spoke to the actors. I had a close working relationship with Nina Raine and became very friendly with a lot of the cast. It was a great team effort, and that, for me, was the most rewarding aspect of it – although that's true of my film experiences as well; they've brought a social dividend. I must have seen the play twenty times during its run. It got good reviews, it did good box office, and the final bonus was when it was picked up and put on in Tallinn and St Petersburg. I went to see both productions, and they ran for about six years in repertory. There was also a touring production in Russia that ran for a couple of years, but I didn't see that because it was in the Urals, which was too far to go! Seeing the production in St

Petersburg was one of the most extraordinary experiences of my writing life: a play in English that I adapted from two Chekhov stories, translated back into Russian and put on in a fabulous old theatre, in a city that Chekhov had a similar success in. It was a real dream-come-true moment. There was a party after the performance and my translator said, 'They'd like you to make a speech.' I don't speak any Russian, so I said, 'What do I say? Thank you very much, you were wonderful?' and she said, 'Oh, no, it has to be a long speech. So in the green room of this theatre, eating cakes and drinking vodka with the cast and crew, I had to extemporize a long speech about the play and the production and how magical it was. That was the apotheosis of my Russian experience. It was fantastic, and I felt I was now a fully fledged man of the theatre and would have a parallel career writing plays in the same way as writing novels. As if!

Did you feel it was more or less effective as a play based on two short stories than as a screenplay based on three?

They're different animals, really. As I said, I was very pleased with the screenplay. It opened with this classic Russian image of railway tracks going through a pine forest, and then, in the far distance, a naked figure running towards the camera, catching flies and eating them – which is straight from 'My Life'. You couldn't put that on stage, but as the opening of a movie it was great. I was very disappointed that the BBC, having commissioned it, lost their nerve or were distracted by something else. Chekhov's anniversary, three of his stories, Richard Eyre directing; it seemed to me to have all the ingredients for a very good cake. Unfortunately it never got baked. But that early viewing of Richard's Scottish version of *The Cherry Orchard* was right there at the start of the whole process, so it's been a long and fruitful literary relationship.

Your third produced play was very much a change of pace, as its title suggests: *The Argument*.

That was also put on at Hampstead, in the studio theatre downstairs. By then I'd forged a very good relationship with the team there and was in full playwriting mode, and I had this idea of writing a play about the inherent human ability to argue. Every person on the planet has argued at one time or another. Some people are good at it, some people are bad at it, but nobody can say they've never had an argument, and it struck me that you could write a play that just consisted of arguments. I've often thought that the unique thrill of live theatre is that it's like eavesdropping – you're sitting in the dark listening to these conversations and it's as if something secret has been given away – and that feeling was particularly acute in this case, because you were given privileged access to arguments that you would never, ever hear. You can have a public argument with somebody about Brexit, but nobody knows about the arguments you have with your husband or wife, because that's extremely private. If you see a couple in the street arguing about something personal, the minute they sense they're being listened to they stop instantly, whereas in the play the arguments get worse and worse. Meredith and Pip's arguments are full-blooded relationship arguments; we've all had them but we wouldn't like to see them on stage. With this play you get them, and that gave it a real frisson.

What determined the number of arguments?

A lot of planning. There are six characters; the two principals each have six arguments and the others have at least two; and all the arguments are about ten minutes long; so it was very carefully worked out and everybody has their moment on stage – or their twenty minutes. I then finessed it and fine-tuned it in rehearsal with the actors and the director, Anna Ledwich. An actor's sensibilities are often very acute, because they're looking in detail at their role. It wasn't like, 'Give me an extra line.' It was more, 'Why am I laughing here? Shouldn't I be furious?' It was another great experience for me, and a great success for the studio theatre. Its six-week run sold out, and because it was so intimate, in the round, the audience almost became embroiled in the arguments. There's a scene where Pip says to his father-in-law, 'Fuck you, you drunken cunt,' and somebody in the stalls shouted out, 'That's going too far!' It became a kind of immersive experience. Then it was picked up by the Theatre Royal Bath and it had another lease of life. It wasn't as well received critically as the first production, but we had a wonderful cast and packed houses, and it was really interesting for me to revisit a play for the first time and think of it with different actors and a different setting, strengthening the relationships here or adding an extra dimension there.

You realize that a play is a malleable, amorphous thing: much more than a novel, certainly, but more than a film, too. There are some playwrights who won't change a word, but I know that Tom Stoppard likes revisiting his plays and thinking how he can change them, and I'm very much in that category.

In what way did you revise the play for its second production?

I wrote some new stuff, and I also took some stuff out. I wrote an extra argument between the mother and the daughter, Chloe and Meredith, but I tightened up the play as well. The director, Christopher Luscombe, thought we should make it lean rather than wordy, so I cut quite a lot as we blocked it out. We also had a much more elaborate set at Bath, which changes things. It was a real collaboration, and I learned a lot from the experience of putting on a play in a mainstream theatre, particularly a play like this which is intimate and naturalistic. Moving from a studio space in the round to a proscenium arch theatre where the audience was further away, I had a slight worry about whether the play would be as funny or as pointed, but it worked just as well in both places and got the same laughs and the same detonations.

We've touched on your play about Jean-Jacques Rousseau, *The Language of Love*; your adaptation of your own story, *The View from Yves Hill*; and your play about the John Dryden play, *Secret Love*. Have any of them come close to being put on?

I wrote *The Language of Love* after *Longing*, and it's never really found a home. It's based on a funny episode in Rousseau's life, this summer he spent on the estate of his patron outside Paris. She's the mistress of a rich man but she fancies Rousseau; Rousseau is married to a common-law wife, Thérèse, who has her mother in tow; he then falls madly in love with his patron's sister, Sophie, who's also the mistress of some count or baron; and they had this passionate affair that ended in tears and inspired his novel *Julie, ou la nouvelle Héloïse* – which was a Europe-wide bestseller and the first true romantic novel. The way we talk about love today is as a result of that novel, and that experience. Through his strange romantic nature, Rousseau effected an enormous change in the way people expressed their emotions. He would say things like, 'My heart is beating so fiercely I think it will burst out of my body.' Now it's a cliché, but until then nobody had said things like that. People declared their love in a rather formal, hand on heart way, then suddenly it was tongues hanging out, panting. It's a great moment in literature and not really recognized, and that's why I wrote the play, to mark that shift in sensibilities. But it's set in the eighteenth century and it's got a big cast, so it would be quite hard to produce in the current climate. *The View from Yves Hill* may be a better bet: a cast of three and one set. *Secret Love* also has a big cast – seventeen, or something – although thirteen of them are women, which was a big selling point when I wrote the play. But then the pandemic arrived and completely flattened the theatre world.

Watching *A Waste of Shame*, which you wrote in 2005, it was slightly startling to see Shakespeare and Burbage talking about the plague closing the playhouses until the following year.

Yes, and Shakespeare looking out of his window and seeing them collecting bodies from the houses. The crisis in the theatre world during the pandemic is very similar to Shakespeare's time – and to the Restoration period, because Cromwell closed the theatres during the Interregnum. When Charles II reopened them and allowed women to play women for the first time, it was a watershed moment in the history of theatre. That's why this play by John Dryden was so fascinating. It's not a good play – it hasn't been performed for almost two hundred years – but it's interesting because of what went on during its run: it was Samuel Pepys's favourite play, and it was the play that allowed Charles to meet Nell Gwyn. Some nights all the roles were played by women, and the male courtiers would get incredibly excited at the thought of seeing Nell Gwyn pretending to be a boy. So *Secret Love* is a play within a play, moving from what's happening backstage at the Theatre Royal Drury Lane, and all the shenanigans involving Charles II and Nell Gwyn, and then on to the stage on this particular night when all the parts are being played by women. It's bloody difficult trying to get new plays put on, though, even if you're a highly regarded playwright. Just because you've had fifteen plays done doesn't mean your sixteenth will get produced. But I won't give up. I'll keep on keeping on, because I enjoy it so much.

Nine

Fiction 5

The Romantic (2022)

I have to say, I was enthralled by *The Romantic*: I devoured it in four chunks over one weekend.

It's a long book, but people are reading it very quickly, which is a good sign. When they tell me that, I always think, 'Read it again, so you don't miss anything!' But I'm glad it's been so well received.

It's your fourth 'whole life' novel, and your first novel not set wholly or partly in the twentieth century. What was the inspiration for 'The Real Life of Cashel Greville Ross'?

I'm trying to think what triggered the idea of another 'whole life' novel, but set in the nineteenth century; it may just have been the stuff I was reading at the time, in particular Stendhal, who lurks behind the novel – and not just the epigraph. He wrote this book called *The Life of Henry Brulard*, which in fact is thinly disguised autobiography: his real name was Henri Beyle, and Stendhal was his pen name. It's a fantastic book, very modern in its spirit, and Stendhal was a funny little bloke who classified himself as a hopeless romantic. So I was reading a lot about him, and reading a lot of his non-fiction as well as his novels, and I had this idea for a romantic character cursed by his romanticism. Because I'd written – but failed to complete – my doctoral thesis on Shelley, I thought that all this knowledge I had about Shelley and his circle and the period could go into a novel about a man who lived for eighty years in the nineteenth century, and slowly but surely that idea took hold. The more I read, the more I realized that if you were born in 1799 and died in 1882 you'd have seen changes the likes of which we've witnessed in the twentieth and twenty-first centuries – from coach and horses to railways and telegrams, with powered flight and automobiles just around the corner – so this nineteenth-century panorama would have contemporary echoes. Also, with hindsight, I realized I'd used Cashel's life as a way of revisiting and exploring places and themes that had figured in my work in the past, like Africa and colonial wars. Maybe it was the big three score years and ten in my own life making me think about those things, but it became a kind of echo chamber of work I'd already done.

It's actually the furthest back in history you've gone: it starts nearly one hundred years earlier than any of your other novels.

It's definitely my most historical novel, but I'm conscious that I've been inching backwards into the nineteenth century, particularly with *Love is Blind* and *Longing*. For me, though, the turn of the twentieth century isn't really history. My grandparents were born during the reign of

Queen Victoria and went on their honeymoon in something like 1889, so I knew people who lived at the end of the nineteenth century. But I didn't know anybody who lived at the beginning of the century, and because I was writing about a romantic I decided to set it at the peak of Romanticism. And, of course, I like to have my fictional characters meet real people, and to demythologize those real people, so it was very enjoyable to imagine what great Romantic figures like Shelley and Byron were really like and what was going on in their lives; to show them not as icons of English literature but as irritating egomaniacs who you might have bumped into on a villa holiday. I did a tremendous amount of research on them and on the period, and travelling through the lands they travelled through makes the past vivid and real. I wanted to take familiar aspects of nineteenth-century life, whether it was the Marshalsea prison or a community of souls in the Americas, and present them in a way that I felt was unusual.

You mentioned the epigraph from Stendhal: 'A novel is a mirror, taking a walk down a big road.' There's also a second epigraph, from Keats: 'A man's life of any worth is a continual allegory – and very few eyes can see the mystery.'

I used to be critical of writers who have more than one epigraph, but it's quite useful having two, and Keats and Stendhal are both representative Romantics. I'm not sure where I stumbled on the Stendhal quote but it fits the novel brilliantly, and the Keats quote is essentially the story of Cashel's journey. That's why I chose the subtitle, as if I'm exploring the mystery of this person's inner life – although it's also a nod to Nabokov's book *The Real Life of Sebastian Knight*, which purports to be a biography of a writer by one of his dodgy narrators. So I had both quotes in my notebooks and knew I was going to use them long before I started writing. Keats's letters were also a good source for how people spoke to each other, particularly his letters to his family. I read some biographies of him as well, and reread Anthony Burgess's *ABBA ABBA*, a strange little book about Keats's last weeks in Rome when he was dying. I was trying to imagine what life would have been like then. What did people eat? How did they clean their teeth? Where did they go to the lavatory? There's a defecation theme, as you may have spotted; at the end, when Cashel is in this swish hotel in Baden-Baden in 1882, there are flushing toilets. That's the sort of thing I find fascinating about the past, and I had great fun getting the granular details right.

Why did you decide to structure the novel as a biography rather than an autobiography – which *The New Confessions*, *Any Human Heart* and *Sweet Caress* all are, in their different ways?

I was using the technique of *Nat Tate* and expanding it. People like Hilary Mantel or Colm Tóibín take a real life and write it up as a novel; this was taking a fictional life and writing it up as a biography. That isn't the technique of the other 'whole life' novels, although they all have an artifice, a framework on which the fiction rests. *The New*

Confessions is a straightforward fake autobiography. *Any Human Heart* is in the form of a journal with footnotes and editorial commentary and an index. *Sweet Caress* is also a fake autobiography but with photographs. But *The Romantic* is a biography of Cashel Ross: I'm the writer of that biography and its editor, and that's the lens through which his life is seen. 'Fictography' is my new coining, although it's an old conceit: Defoe pretending that *Moll Flanders* is a true account of an eighteenth-century prostitute, or Fielding purporting to be presenting Clarissa's letters to the reader.

The photographs in *Sweet Caress* are replaced by twelve drawings in *The Romantic*: rough sketches of key places in the narrative. What was the thinking behind those?

Again, I was copying Stendhal. *The Life of Henry Brulard* is full of the flimsiest sketches, some of which seem utterly pointless, and I wanted to get that echo in there. Given that I've used devices in the past, I thought, 'Here's one I haven't tried,' but I decided not to overuse it in the way he did. The footnotes are another device. I could take them out and the book would be pretty much the same, but they're part of the artifice, the sense of something that isn't quite a novel. In fact, *The Romantic* is a natural progression of the project I've been developing since *The New Confessions*: pushing fiction so far into the world of fact that you begin to doubt its fictive status. So all these thoughts were in my head as I was pondering how to write the novel, but when I started it I wasn't entirely sure if it would work.

What were you unsure about?

Because it was nineteenth-century, I was very concerned about getting the tone of voice right. People didn't speak like characters in Austen or Trollope, they spoke much more like you and me, so I spent a long time searching through diaries and letters of the period to find that authentic voice. I also reread *The French Lieutenant's Woman* to see how John Fowles had done it. In his diaries he talks about deliberately making the dialogue cod-Victorian because he wanted the reader to be aware of these pseudo-conventions: 'I did not' rather than 'I didn't'. The notion that the Victorians never contracted their words was a twentieth-century one; their spoken language was as broken up and inconsequential and unfinished as ours. The dialogue in *The Romantic* is the only bit that's authentically nineteenth-century, because all the expository prose is me writing today; but my editors here and in America have spotted that it has a contemporary lilt and gait without quite being a twenty-first-century novel, so it was a technical challenge working out that fine blend. There was a certain amount of head-scratching when I was thinking about setting off on the journey, but once I got going and got into my stride I had no problems at all about how to present it – and that's why I changed the prologue to an author's note, so it was clearly my voice from the outset.

How did you decide what to put in the footnotes and what to put in the main text?

Footnotes can be irritating if there are too many of them, so it's like the question of where to put the drawings.

Sometimes the footnote dictated itself: historical facts that had a relevance but might jar if they were in the main text. And sometimes it was there to draw the reader up short: to remind them of the conceit of this trunk full of fragments that I was interpreting. In *Lolita* there's an editorial intro and then off you go, and you forget about the editor until you come across a footnote.

The subjects of your other 'whole life' novels all follow artistic paths – film-making for John James Todd, writing for Logan Mountstuart, photography for Amory Clay – but Cashel doesn't have a single profession, which means each section of the novel feels separate and distinct.

They're like little novels: soldier, jailbird, farmer, traveller. It's something that was true of certain nineteenth-century lives: people like Richard Burton and William Cobbett were many things. Burton was an explorer, a writer, a diplomat. Cobbett was a journalist, a politician, a farmer. Multifaceted lives were quite common in that era, and make it distinct from the narrow specialization of our own time – and that picaresque element of Cashel's life took me to all the places I wanted to go.

What's your definition of a romantic – with a small 'r'?

I think it's the one we'd all use: somebody who doesn't listen to their head but listens to their heart. That explains the intensity with which Cashel lives and the disastrous mistakes he makes, particularly in the love story at the centre of the novel, because he doesn't stop and think. He takes umbrage very quickly, leaves Raphaella in Italy and goes to live in rural France, and by the time he realizes he's made a mistake a year has passed – and when he journeys back, which takes weeks, he finds she's gone and got married. So that's what I mean by the word 'romantic': that Cashel's emotions govern his life.

You could say the same about Todd and Logan.

And it may well be true of me, too. But yes, they are both impulsive, and that gets them into scrapes and causes them problems – although they gain a measure of wisdom along the way. When you invent a character you try to make them as multidimensional as a real person, but there's no doubt that Cashel, Logan and John James Todd are all a certain type, in a broad sense, and share common traits.

Amory, on the other hand, is not as impulsive.

You're absolutely right; Amory is more reflective. She still gets herself into difficult situations, but she knows why she's doing it. She weighs things up, does a cost-benefit analysis and decides that it's worth it. What none of those characters do, which Cashel believes he's done, is make a mistake that ruins their life. And he's right, in a way. If only he'd stayed in Italy, everything would have been different.

But if he'd stayed with Raphaella, he wouldn't have had the adventures he had, he wouldn't have had the children he had. Different isn't always better.

That's true. It's easy to see the forking paths with hindsight, but you can't rewind the reel of your life, you just have to take what comes down the pike – and Cashel realizes that. He's gone off and led a life, done things and achieved things, and then good fortune allows him to reunite with Raphaella. But he's always thinking about her and wondering about her, and that's echoed in the Dante references: the image of the two lovers in their circle of hell, seeing each other being whirled around but never being allowed to touch. The myth of Paolo and Francesca is only a few pages in the *Divine Comedy*, but it's inspired innumerable artists and has tremendous resonance, so I decided to use it as a metaphor for Cashel and Raphaella. The novel he writes, *Nihil*, is about characters called Paul and Frances, and the *Divine Comedy* is the book that's chucked into his grave at the end, because he sees his own life as a version of the hell that the lovers were condemned to.

Did you find any of the individual sections particularly tricky to write?

The trickiest thing with any 'whole life' novel is the passage of time. It's hard to do, and you have to be very deft. The American section was the longest period I had to deal with, and a vitally important one, because Cashel is a middle-aged man by the time he's back in London. I can't remember the exact number of years, but I had to allow time for him to woo his wife, get married and have two children; for the children to grow up, his wife to go mad and him to have an affair; and for him to meet Ignatz, his Sancho Panza figure, and become a successful brewer. That's almost a whole life in one chapter but you can't write three hundred pages to cover it, so you have to make the reader feel that all this is happening at a natural pace without fast-forwarding through it. I made it harder for myself because I wanted to include the Burton and Speke expedition, which was in 1856, so I had to fill in some time before I could get to all that excitement and mayhem. The other challenge was that Cashel lives a long life, and the narrative pace had to be maintained. That wasn't an issue with *Any Human Heart*, because I could use editorial sleight of hand and say that Logan didn't keep a journal for several years, but in this case stuff had to be happening all the time. The letters that Cashel sent and received were a fantastically useful way of punctuating time, and allowed me to fill in gaps quite seamlessly.

Presumably a further challenge – or at least something you had to take account of – was the amount of time it took to travel to places and contact people.

Transport and communication were the two things that changed phenomenally in the nineteenth century. You might notice that Cashel gets to Oxford a lot faster at the end of the novel than he did at the beginning. A feature of Victorian lives was how common it was for people to be abroad for years. When Darwin sailed off on the *Beagle* he was away for eight years, for example, and I discovered that one regiment in the British army served in India for thirty years before they returned to England. Everything moved more slowly, because it took so long for ships to get out there and for letters to come back. It's extraordinary how much letter writing went on, given the vagaries of the postal system. You wrote a letter and hoped the other person got it, and even if they did you might not get a reply for six months. But then it started getting better and better. Trollope worked for the Post Office for much of his life – and famously introduced the pillar box – and by the time he packed in his job the post was probably more efficient than it is today. The penny post was rather like email, with several deliveries every day in London. If you sent a letter in the morning, you'd probably have a reply in the afternoon. And then the railways came, and brought the telegraph with them, and it suddenly became a world very much like ours. The nineteenth century was, in some senses, incredibly efficient – although incredibly smelly and dirty as well.

Going back to the character of Ignatz, there's actually more than one Sancho Panza figure in the course of the novel: Raphaella's page in Italy, Timoteo, and the farmer's son in France, Jaufret, both ask Cashel whether they can come with him and become his servant.

I realized as I was putting the book together that this was a nice, oblique way of saying that Cashel is a decent bloke, because these guys offer their services to him, he just can't take them up on it. Then, when Ignatz turns up out of the blue, it almost becomes a parallel love affair. I deliberately introduced the occasional homoerotic note to indicate that Ignatz is in love with Cashel, but then Ignatz is having an affair with Cashel's daughter by the end. You find these curious partnerships in literature – Quixote and Sancho Panza, Crusoe and Friday – and I wanted to establish that. And it's very useful having a practical person around who can speak many languages and launder your clothes. In the nineteenth century the domestic servant was omnipresent. Dickens could say, 'Let's all go to Italy,' and somebody would deal with it. Shelley would moan about how poor he was on a thousand a year, but he always travelled with cooks and nursemaids and so on. So he's a classic figure, Ignatz, and in the second half of the novel he's Cashel's saviour and guardian angel.

Were there any other literary or historical influences behind the long American section?

Cashel's American home was taken from a book by Thoreau, *Walden*, about his life at Walden Pond near Concord, Massachusetts. Thoreau wasn't isolated in the same way as Cashel, he just lived in a cabin and communed with nature, but it was the same period. It's not a very well-known book in this country, but I think American readers will pick up the echo, and it enriches Cashel's story.

Why did you send Cashel off to war, first at Waterloo and then in Ceylon?

Well, that's sort of what I do. I've done the Third Battle of Ypres in *The New Confessions*, and I've done colonial wars in *An Ice-Cream War* and *Brazzaville Beach*, and I decided very early on to do Waterloo as a homage to Stendhal – and, of course, to Tolstoy. In *The Charterhouse of Parma*, the battle is totally incomprehensible to Stendhal's hero, the same way it is for Cashel. Waterloo also ticked a Romantic box in the sense that Lord Byron visited the battlefield, as did Walter Scott. It was a big moment in the mythology of Britain, and the battlefield became a tourist attraction very quickly: you could go there and wander around and pick up souvenirs off the ground. And the rebellion in Ceylon in 1818 was another of these forgotten wars that I seem to make a speciality of unearthing. I've never visited India or Sri Lanka, but one of my favourite novels is *The Siege of Krishnapur* by J. G. Farrell, which is set during the Indian Rebellion of 1857. The Empire and the East India Company and the British Indian Army were part of the texture of that time, so it was good to acknowledge them; and Cashel's refusal to obey an order and kill innocent men on the battlefield, because everything in his body tells him it's wrong, shows his impulsiveness and his romantic nature. Also, periods of military service were a feature of the era, and in the way you stitch these things together, the man Cashel shares his billet with before he's kicked out of the army funds the expedition to Africa many years later.

I imagine that Cashel's expedition to find the source of the Nile drew on your unproduced TV series about Victorian explorers, *African Fever*?

That's right. I've read a lot about all those explorers: Burton, Speke, Stanley, Livingstone. Burton is a fascinating character, a late Romantic figure, but there was a real ruthlessness to exploration: it was a way of making loads of money and becoming famous at the same time. Cashel's expedition was carefully manoeuvred in time so that Speke could pinch his discovery and claim it as his own; and the whole business of Speke's death is absolutely true, I've just put Cashel and his demonic brother Hogan in the middle of it. I wrote a big piece for the *TLS* about Speke and got into a correspondence about whether his death was an accident or suicide, but of course the novelist can blithely step in and say, 'Actually, this is what happened.' I also lifted some stuff from a Lawrence of Arabia series I wrote for the BBC, which never got made. Lawrence's father was an Anglo-Irish baronet who had an affair with his daughters' governess and lived a double life with her, as you could quite easily do when communication was poor and absences were normal. They called themselves Mr and Mrs Lawrence, had five sons and moved to Oxford, and he'd occasionally go back to see his other family; and when Lawrence discovered that he was illegitimate, wasn't called Lawrence and had half-sisters in Ireland, he ran away from home and joined the army. I appropriated that, moved it back in time and gave it to Cashel, except that Lawrence was only away from home for a few weeks and Cashel ends up being away for nearly three years. So certain bits of the novel are very much rooted in historical events.

Including the bits about Byron and Shelley, neither of whom come out of the novel very well?

Yes, that's all scrupulously exact. I wanted to strip away the veils that had been thrown over them and see them for the people they were. Shelley was an extraordinary person for the time, but he was going to be Sir Percy when he inherited his estate, and a lot of his behaviour is that of an entitled toff. He was also physically totally different from the myth of this beautiful blond with his unbuttoned shirt: the best description we have of him is that he was very tall with bad skin and uneven teeth but perfect manners. Byron was pretty extraordinary, too. He was a radical but lived like an oligarch. He was very generous but behaved appallingly badly towards his mistress and their daughter. He had homosexual relationships and incestuous relationships. He really did try out everything, did Byron. In my research I tried to step back and evaluate them as if I'd been there: what would it have been like to meet them and what would I have thought of them? Interestingly, Stendhal met Byron and couldn't stand him. He thought he was a terrible snob.

Cashel seems vaguely repulsed by them, too – but as you said, he is basically a decent bloke.

He's flawed, like all my heroes, but I think his value systems are quite secure. It's part of his nature to do the right thing as best he can. And at the end, when he goes to Baden-Baden, he realizes that he cares more about what happens to Raphaella than he does about what happens to himself, and he thinks that's probably a good definition of love. So his romantic nature gets him into terrible trouble, but it also makes him a better person. He listens to his heart and doesn't second-guess it, and if your heart is a good guide then maybe that's not a bad way of finding a route through this vale of tears.

Looking at the publication dates of your four 'whole life' novels – *The New Confessions* in 1987, *Any Human*

Heart in 2002, *Sweet Caress* in 2015, *The Romantic* in 2022 – you return to the form roughly every decade. Can we expect a fifth in another ten years or so?

It's more an unconscious rhythm than any deliberate strategy. I don't write one after the other because they're all four to five hundred pages long and there's a massive amount of research involved, but I do get these ideas and the ideas will challenge me and take me over. Maybe the novel I'll write after *The Romantic* will be short and bright and funny; we'll see. But without any grand plan, I have carved out a little niche in this sub-genre of literary fiction. I wouldn't say I've mastered the form, but I understand how to pull it together and the sleight of hand which is required to cover eighty years in five hundred pages. It's because they're successful not just in terms of sales or reviews, but in the way that readers engage with them, that makes me think I must keep doing them. I have an idea brewing for a different kind of 'whole life' novel, about three generations of one family; that might defeat me, but perhaps in my dotage I'll have a stab at it. Scott Fitzgerald once said – and I paraphrase – that, 'Mostly, we authors repeat ourselves . . . and we tell our two or three stories as long as people will listen.' Well, I feel I have many more stories still to tell – many more than two or three, that's for sure – and I fully intend to keep on telling them for as long as I possibly can.

Acknowledgements

My thanks to Harriet Bourton, Isabel Wall, Emma Brown, Chloe Davies and the entire team at Penguin; Gaia Banks and Lucy Fawcett at Sheil Land; Jonny Geller at Curtis Brown; and Mary Chamberlain. Also to Wendy Watts for the transcripts; Louise Halfpenny for the champagne; Rob Benton for the dinners; Perri Blakelock for the walks (and all four of them for the feedback on the two versions of the introduction); Nigel Adey for the cakes; Vanessa Bunn for the biscuits; other friends near and far for simply being there; my parents for their love and support; and anybody else in the past few years who has asked about my progress with, listened to me talk about, or expressed an eagerness to read 'The Boyd Book'. And, of course, to Will himself, for trusting me.

– AO

Credits

Fiction

A Good Man in Africa (Hamish Hamilton, 1981)
On the Yankee Station (Hamish Hamilton, 1981)
An Ice-Cream War (Hamish Hamilton, 1982)
Stars and Bars (Hamish Hamilton, 1984)
The New Confessions (Hamish Hamilton, 1987)
Brazzaville Beach (Sinclair-Stevenson, 1990)
The Blue Afternoon (Sinclair-Stevenson, 1993)
The Destiny of Nathalie 'X' (Sinclair-Stevenson, 1995)
Armadillo (Hamish Hamilton, 1998)
Nat Tate: An American Artist 1928–1960 (21 Publishing, 1998)
Any Human Heart (Hamish Hamilton, 2002)
Fascination (Hamish Hamilton, 2004)
Restless (Bloomsbury, 2006)
The Dream Lover (Bloomsbury, 2008)
Ordinary Thunderstorms (Bloomsbury, 2009)
Waiting for Sunrise (Bloomsbury, 2012)
Solo (Jonathan Cape, 2013)
Sweet Caress (Bloomsbury, 2015)
The Dreams of Bethany Mellmoth (Viking Penguin, 2017)
Love is Blind (Viking Penguin, 2018)
Trio (Viking Penguin, 2020)
The Romantic (Viking Penguin, 2022)

Non-fiction

Bamboo (Hamish Hamilton, 2005)

Produced Screenplays

Good and Bad at Games (Jack Gold, 1983, UK)

Dutch Girls (Giles Foster, 1985, UK)

Scoop, from the novel by Evelyn Waugh (Gavin Millar, 1987, UK)

Stars and Bars, from his own novel (Pat O'Connor, 1988, US)

Mister Johnson, from the novel by Joyce Cary (Bruce Beresford, 1990, US)

Aunt Julia and the Scriptwriter, from the novel by Mario Vargas Llosa (Jon Amiel, 1990, US)

Chaplin, from the books *My Life* by Charles Chaplin and *Chaplin: His Life and Art* by David Robinson (Richard Attenborough, 1992, UK/US)

A Good Man in Africa, from his own novel (Bruce Beresford, 1994, US)

The Trench (William Boyd, 1999, UK/France)

Sword of Honour, from the novels by Evelyn Waugh (Bill Anderson, 2001, UK)

Armadillo, from his own novel (Howard Davies, 2001, UK)

Man to Man (Régis Wargnier, 2005, France/South Africa/UK)

A Waste of Shame (John McKay, 2005, UK)

The Three Kings (Richard Eyre, 2009, UK)

Any Human Heart, from his own novel (Michael Samuels, 2010, UK)

Restless, from his own novel (Edward Hall, 2012, UK)

Patient 39, from his own short story 'The Ghost of a Bird' (Dan Clifton, 2014, UK) (source material only)

The Dreams of Bethany Mellmoth, from his own short stories (Stefan Georgiou, 2016, UK)

Spy City (Miguel Alexandre, 2020, Germany/US)

Stage Plays

Six Parties (National Theatre, 2009)

Longing, from the stories 'My Life' and 'A Visit to Friends' by Anton Chekhov (Hampstead Theatre, 2013)

The Argument (Hampstead Theatre, 2016)

Radio Plays

On the Yankee Station, from his own short story (BBC Radio 4, 1988)

Homage to AB (BBC Radio 4, 1994)

The Destiny of Nathalie 'X', from his own short story (BBC Radio 4, 1998)

A Haunting, from his own short story (BBC Radio 4, 2001)

The McFeggan Offensive, from his own short story (BBC Radio 4, 2020)

Published Screenplays & Stage Plays

School Ties (Hamish Hamilton, 1985), includes *Good and Bad at Games* and *Dutch Girls*

New Connections 2009: Plays for Young People (Faber), includes *Six Parties*

Longing (Methuen Drama, 2013)

The Argument (Methuen Drama, 2016)

Unproduced Screenplays

Thicker Than Water, for John Schlesinger (1984)

The Galapagos Affair, from the book by John Treherne (1986)

An Ice-Cream War, from his own novel (1988)

The Island, for Universal (1990)

The Gunpowder Plot, from the book by Antonia Fraser, for Universal (1996)

À l'aventure, for Régis Wargnier (1997)

The Care and Attention of Swimming Pools, from his own short story (1998)

The Destiny of Nathalie 'X', from his own short story (1998)

Cork, aka *Nobody's Heart*, from his own short story (1998)

The Blue Afternoon, from his own novel (1999)

Stone Free (2000)

Woman on the Beach with a Dog, from his own short story (2002)

Elephant Moon, from the book *Travels on My Elephant* by Mark Shand (2002)

Brazzaville Beach, from his own novel (2002)

Hitler: The Rise to Power, for BBC/F/X (2002)

Love and War in Shanghai, for Box TV (2004)

African Fever, for Fremantle (2005)

The Last Harvest (2005)

Humiliation, from his own short story (2007)

Lawrence of Arabia, for BBC (2007)

Ordinary Thunderstorms, from his own novel (2008)

The Rising (2009)

City of Lies, from the book *The Last Days of Hitler* by Hugh Trevor-Roper, for Daybreak Pictures (2015)

Young Titan, for Carnival Films (2016)

Sweet Caress, from his own novel (2017)

Radetzky March, from the novel by Joseph Roth, for Moonriver (2017)

Waiting for Sunrise, from his own novel (2018)

The Captain and the Enemy, from the novel by Graham Greene, for Infinity Hill (2018)

The Vanishing Game, from his own short story (2019)

Finzi's Game, for Ecosse Films (2020)

I Was a Stranger, from the book by General Sir John Hackett (2021)

Paris Interzone, for Blue Bear/Léonis (2021)

Literary Awards & Prizes

Whitbread First Novel Award – *A Good Man in Africa* (1981)

Somerset Maugham Award – *A Good Man in Africa* (1982)

John Llewellyn Rhys Prize – *An Ice-Cream War* (1982)

James Tait Black Memorial Prize for Fiction – *Brazzaville Beach* (1990)

McVitie's Prize for Scottish Writer of the Year – *Brazzaville Beach* (1991)

Sunday Express Book of the Year Award – *The Blue Afternoon* (1993)

Los Angeles Times Book Prize for Fiction – *The Blue Afternoon* (1995)

Prix Jean Monnet de Littérature Européenne – *Any Human Heart* (2003)

Grand prix des lectrices Elle – *Any Human Heart* (2003)

Costa Book Award, Novel of the Year – *Restless* (2006)

Prix Fitzgerald – *Love is Blind* (2019)

Television Awards

BAFTA Television Award for Best Drama Serial – *Any Human Heart* (2011)

Index

The Romantic

Born in 1799, Cashel Greville Ross experiences myriad lives: joyous and devastating, years of luck and unexpected loss. Moving from County Cork to London, from Waterloo to Zanzibar, Cashel seeks his fortune across continents in war and in peace. He faces a terrible moral choice in a village in Sri Lanka as part of the East Indian Army. He enters the world of the Romantic Poets in Pisa. In Ravenna he meets a woman who will live in his heart for the rest of his days. As he travels the world as a soldier, a farmer, a felon, a writer, a father, a lover, he experiences all the vicissitudes of life and, through the accelerating turbulence of the nineteenth century, he discovers who he truly is. This is the romance of life itself, and the beating heart of *The Romantic*.

From one of Britain's best-loved and bestselling writers comes an intimate yet panoramic novel set across the nineteenth century.

'Picaresque, big-hearted and moving, this is Boyd
at the top of his game'
Guardian

'There are few reading pleasures as great as giving
in to a William Boyd novel'
Sunday Times

'Simply the best realistic storyteller of his generation'
Sebastian Faulks

Order now!

Any Human Heart

Every life is both ordinary and extraordinary,
but Logan Mountstuart's – lived from the beginning to the end
of the twentieth century – contains more than its fair share of
both. As a writer who finds inspiration with Hemingway in
Paris and Virginia Woolf in London, as a spy recruited by Ian
Fleming and betrayed in the war, and as an art-dealer in '60s
New York, Logan mixes with the movers and shakers of his
times. But as a son, friend, lover and husband, he makes the
same mistakes we all do in our search for happiness. Here, then,
is the story of a life lived to the full – and a journey deep into a
very human heart.

'A brilliant evocation of a past era and an
immensely readable story'
Sunday Telegraph

'Superb, wonderful, enjoyable'
Guardian

'A terrific journey through the twentieth century.
Thoroughly entertaining and enjoyable'
Jeremy Paxman

Order now!

The Blue Afternoon

A quest for secrets in the blue afternoon . . .

Los Angeles, 1936. Kay Fischer, a young and ambitious architect, is being followed by an old man. When confronted, he explains that his name is Salvador Carriscant – and that he is her father.

In a matter of weeks Kay will join Salvador on an extraordinary journey as they delve back into his past to not only learn the truth behind her own birth, but also to discover the whereabouts of a woman long thought dead – and to uncover the identity of a killer.

Order now!

Trio

It is summer in 1968, the year of the assassinations of Martin Luther King and Robert Kennedy. There are riots in Paris and the Vietnam War is out of control. While the world is reeling our three characters are involved in making a Swingin' Sixties movie in sunny Brighton.

All are leading secret lives. Elfrida is drowning her writer's block in vodka; Talbot, coping with the daily dysfunction of making a film, is hiding something in a secret apartment; and the glamorous Anny is wondering why the CIA is suddenly so interested in her.

But the show must go on and, as it does, the trio's private worlds begin to take over their public ones. Pressures build inexorably – someone's going to crack. Or maybe they all will.

From one of Britain's best loved writers comes an exhilarating, tender novel that asks the vital questions: what makes life worth living? And what do you do if you find it isn't?

'The ultimate in immersive fiction . . . magnificent'
Sunday Times

'An absorbing novel about lives spiralling out of control'
Economist

'William Boyd has probably written more classic books than any of his contemporaries'
Daily Telegraph

Order now!

Ordinary Thunderstorms

Around the turn of the twentieth century young pianist Brodie Moncur quits Edinburgh's slate skies for the lights of Paris, his preacher father's words of denunciation ringing in his ears. There he joins forces with the fiery Irish virtuoso John Kilbarron and together the pair take Europe by storm.

But when he falls for Kilbarron's lover – the mesmerizing Russian soprano Lika Blum – Brodie quickly realizes that the tide has turned and he must flee across a continent, haunted by his love for Lika, and pursued by the vengeful wrath of his rival.

'A giddying read . . . his most immersive historical
novel to date'
Daily Telegraph

'Elegant and affecting. A racing fin-de-siècle romance'
The Times

'Boyd's talents as a rollicking storytelling [are]
fully on display in this historical blockbuster'
Metro

Order now!

The New Confessions

Meet John James Todd:
Scotsman, auteur, Rousseau-fanatic – and 'subversive element'.

Born in 1899, John James Todd is one of the great, failed
geniuses of the last century. His reminiscences, collected in
The New Confessions, take us from Edinburgh to the Western
Front, the Berlin film-world in the Twenties to Hollywood in
the Thirties, Forties and beyond.

Suffering imprisonment, shooting, marriage, fatherhood,
divorce and McCarthyism, Todd is a hostage to good fortune,
ill-judgement, bad luck, the vast sweep of history and the cruel,
cruel hand of fate . . .

'A magnificent feat of storytelling and
panoramic reconstruction'
Observer

'Paced and plotted with sinewy, unfailing skill . . .'
Sunday Times

'Simply the best realistic storyteller of his generation'
Independent

Order now!

Stars and Bars

Henderson Dores is an Englishman in New York –
and completely out of his depth.

He should be concentrating on his job as an art assessor,
but his complicated personal life keeps intruding. And that's
before we even get to his sense of alienation, of being a fish
out of water. For Henderson is a shy man lost in a country of
extraverts and weirdos. Subway poets, loony millionaires,
Bible-bashers and sharp-suited hoods stalk him wherever he
goes. But it is only when he's sent to America's deep South to
examine a rare collection of paintings that matters take a life-
threatening turn. Still, if it doesn't kill you, they say it can only
make you stronger . . .

'A giddying read . . . his most immersive historical
novel to date'
Daily Telegraph

'Elegant and affecting. A racing fin-de-siècle romance'
The Times

'Boyd's talents as a rollicking storytelling [are]
fully on display in this historical blockbuster'
Metro

Order now!

Brazzaville Beach

On Brazzaville Beach, on the edge of Africa, Hope Clearwater ponders the strange circumstances that led her to leave her husband John, and his mathematical obsessions, in England and venture to Africa to help world-renowned scientist Eugene Mallabar with his studies of wild chimps.

But the more Hope studies Mallabar, the more she comes to believe that something isn't right. That behind Mallabar, and his obsessive work, there lies another, more sinister truth: one that might also help explain Hope's reasons for leaving England . . .

'A most extraordinary parable about mankind.
Quite unlike anything else I have read'
Sunday Express

'Brilliant, daring. A gripping and compulsive story'
Herald

'Hilarious and edgy'
Sunday Times

Order now!

An Ice-cream War

'We will all melt like ice-cream in the sun!'
British soldier, East Africa, 1914

On the Western Front millions are being slaughtered. But in East Africa a ridiculous and utterly ignored campaign is being waged – one that continues after the Armistice because no one bothers to tell the participants to stop.

As the conflict sweeps up Africans and colonials, so those left at home and those fighting abroad find themselves unable to escape the tide of history bearing down on them.

'A towering achievement'
John Carey

'Compulsively readable'
Blake Morrison, *Observer*

'Funny, assured, a seriocomic romp. A study of people caught in the side pockets of calamity that dramatizes their plights with humour, detail and grit'
Harper's

Order now!

Nat Tate:
An American Artist 1928 – 1960

On January 8 1960, artist Nat Tate set out to burn his entire life's work. Four days later he jumped off a Staten Island ferry, killing himself. His body was never found.

When William Boyd published his biography of Abstract Expressionist Nat Tate, tributes poured in from a whole host of artists and critics in the New York art world. They toasted the troubled genius in a Manhattan launch party attended by David Bowie and Gore Vidal.

But Nat Tate never existed. The book was a hoax.

William Boyd's biography of a fake artist is a brilliant probe into the politics of authenticity and reputation in the modern art scene. It is a playful and intelligent insight into the fascinating, often cryptic world of modern art.

'William Boyd has probably written more classic books than any of his contemporaries'
Daily Telegraph

'A deft and resonant alchemy of fact and fiction'
Guardian on *Love is Blind*

'One of Britain's most celebrated contemporary novelists'
Sunday Times

Order now!

A Good Man in Africa

Overweight, oversexed and over there ...

Morgan Leafy is hardly the most respectable of Her Majesty's
representatives in the West African state of Kinjanja. For
starters, he probably shouldn't have involved himself in
wholesale bribery. Nor was it a good career move to go chasing
after his boss's daughter; especially when his doctor banned him
from horizontal pursuits.

But life is about to change for young Morgan Leafy. Every
betrayal and humiliation he has suffered at the hands of petty
persecutors is suddenly put into perspective. For Morgan has a
dead body on his hands – and somehow, some way he's going to
have to get rid of it ...

'If a widening grin is the test of a novel's entertainment
value ... *A Good Man in Africa* romps home'
Guardian

'Wickedly funny'
The Times

'A delight'
Washington Post

Order now!

Armadillo

One winter morning, Lorimer Black – young, good-looking, but with a somewhat troubled expression – goes to keep a perfectly routine business appointment and finds a hanged man. A bad start to the day, by anyone's standards, and an ominous portent.

For Lorimer works in the only-slightly corrupt business of financial adjusting, and he is about to learn that it is much uglier – and even more crooked – than he ever imagined. Suddenly, he's being unfairly blamed for all kinds of irregularities. Next, his life is threatened. And, lastly, he's coming to realize that the life he has led till now – the one someone wants to rub out – is one big fat lie . . .

'A joy to read: easy to get into, addictively plotted and beautifully written'
Daily Mail

'A novel that is truly comic, and, like all true comedy, also disturbing'
Scotsman

'A pleasure to read'
Independent on Sunday

Order now!